10.00

Martyn Rouse

Orientations in Special Education

Orientations in Special Education

edited by

K. WEDELL

University of Birmingham

JOHN WILEY & SONS
London · New York · Sydney · Toronto

Copyright © 1975, by John Wiley & Sons, Ltd.

Reprinted August 1978

Library of Congress Cataloging in Publication Data:

Wedell, K.
Orientations in special education.
Includes bibliographical references.
1. Handicapped children—Education—Addresses, essays, lectures. I. Title.

LC4019.W4   371.9′08   74–6660
ISBN 0 471 92443 1

Text set in 11/12 pt. Photon Times, printed by photolithography, and bound
in Great Britain at The Pitman Press, Bath.

Preface

In recent years there has been an increase in concern for children whose needs are not met in the ordinary school system, and this has resulted in an accelerated expansion of special educational provision. At the same time, a more critical approach to special education has developed. This has probably come about for at least four reasons. Firstly, the outcomes of special educational treatment have often been disappointing. Imposing programmes, often expensive in time, materials and manpower, have sometimes failed to achieve the outcomes claimed for them. Secondly, special education has ceased to be regarded as a charitable gesture made by the non-handicapped members of the community to the handicapped. The recipients of special educational provision, and particularly their families, have become more ready to express their misgivings about shortcomings in the services offered. Thirdly, the current period of economic stringency has made it necessary for administrators to find out whether special educational measures are producing results commensurate with the financial investment made in them. Lastly, along with many other educational principles, the relationship between 'special' and 'normal' education is being re-evaluated.

Those concerned in special education, as teachers, administrators, psychologists, doctors or whatever, are consequently having to face wider issues relating to their work and finding themselves forced to consider the topic from a broader perspective. For example, it is becoming apparent that a view of special education which divides children up by categories of handicap leads to a grossly oversimplified conception of their needs. Similarly, an approach to remediation based solely on one particular conceptualization of a problem will tend to lead to inadequate, if not inappropriate, action. It seems particularly necessary to consider a variety of orientations to special education, and thus it seemed a possibly useful project to bring together into one volume accounts of some of the main types of approach represented today. The adequacy of such a project is clearly limited if carried out on this small scale, but the juxtaposition of different viewpoints may make it easier to see their complementary as well as their contrary aspects.

The contributors to this volume are drawn from Canada, the United States and Great Britain. Most of them have worked on both sides of the Atlantic, as will be evident from their presentations. It has been interesting to note how the same issues arise in different countries, although the problems may have reached different stages.

A discussion of different orientations in special education presupposes certain assumptions about special education itself, and so the first two chapters are devoted to a consideration of these. Dr. Keogh examines the relationship of special education to societal expectations, and includes a discussion of some of the legal issues being raised currently in the United States. Dr. Yule considers special educational needs in an epidemiological context. The remaining chapters are devoted to accounts of specific special educational orientations. The compensatory educational approaches discussed by Dr. O'Bryan in the third chapter represent the preventive counterparts to special educational measures. He outlines several compensatory programmes, ranging from direct instructional methods to general developmental stimulation, and raises important queries about the purpose of compensation itself. The next three chapters deal with special educational approaches concerned, respectively, with individual differences among children, with the manipulation of learning, and with an analysis of what is taught. The concept of specific learning disabilities has brought the idea of deficits in limited areas of psychological functioning into special education. Dr. Wedell traces the assumptions behind these views and examines the special educational programmes based on them. Dr. Ward, in his chapter on Behaviour Modification, looks at the contribution of theories of learning and considers the control of motivational factors. Mr. Widlake considers how far the principles involved in task analysis and programmed learning can be applied to the objectives of special education.

Mr. Gulliford makes a plea that special education should not represent a narrowing of educational content and describes approaches which have attempted to bring in aspects of the 'normal' school curriculum. Miss Caspari, discussing the psychodynamic view-point, shows how this identifies the interpersonal features of the educational setting as an effective component.

A clear evaluation of the physical condition of the child is an obvious prerequisite for assessing intellectual and emotional handicaps. Dr. Griffiths describes some of the physical conditions which affect a child's need for special education, and discusses how the doctor can contribute at various stages of the handicapped child's development. Dr. Brown, in the final chapter, raises the essential question about how special education can be planned to maximize independence in adult life. Clearly this is a crucial point, since without an effective transition at this stage, the whole purpose of special education is put in question.

No attempt has been made to consider specific categories of handicapped children. Indeed, it is hoped that the accounts of the selection of special educational orientations presented will indicate that educational approaches should be directed at the pattern of special needs presented by the child, rather than at a stereotyped concept of a particular diagnostic category. It will be evident that the different special educational approaches are often more relevant to one type of special educational need than to another, and that this is one of the main ways in which contrasting approaches complement each other.

In the current climate of critical re-appraisal of the aims and objectives of special education, the range of views presented in this book will, hopefully, prove helpful to the reader in evaluating the particular issues with which he may be confronted.

K. WEDELL
University of Birmingham, 1974.

Contributors

DR. R. I. BROWN is Professor in the Department of Educational Psychology at the University of Calgary, Alberta, Canada. He is also Director of the Vocational and Rehabilitation Research Institute which is a demonstration centre for training developmentally handicapped adults.

MISS I. CASPARI is Principal Clinical Psychologist in the Department for Children and Parents at the Tavistock Clinic, London, and is responsible for the training of educational psychologists.

DR. M. I. GRIFFITHS is Consultant Paediatrician at Lea Castle Subnormality Hospital and co-ordinator of the Assessment Centre at the Birmingham Children's Hospital.

MR. R. GULLIFORD is Senior Lecturer in the School of Education, University of Birmingham, and Tutor to the Diploma in Special Education Course for teachers of Educationally Subnormal Children.

DR. B. KEOGH is Associate Professor of Special Education, Graduate School of Education, University of California, Los Angeles, where she is also Director of the Special Education Research Programme.

DR. K. O'BRYAN is Associate Professor at the Ontario Institute of Studies and Education in the Department of Applied Psychology. He is Co-Director of a research project on the early education of Canadian/Indian children and has also been involved in evaluation studies of other compensatory educational programmes.

DR. J. WARD is Senior Lecturer in the Department of Psychology, University of Southampton and is responsible for the training of Educational Psychologists. He was previously Associate Professor at the University of Victoria, British Columbia.

DR. K. WEDELL is Senior Lecturer in Educational Psychology at the School of Education, University of Birmingham, where he is responsible for the training of Educational Psychologists.

MR. P. WIDLAKE is a Principal Lecturer at Didsbury College of Education, Manchester and tutor to the course for teachers of disadvantaged children. He has been Advisor in Special Education to the Wolverhampton Education Committee and Senior Research Associate at the University of Birmingham.

DR. W. YULE is Senior Lecturer in Psychology at the Institute of Psychiatry, University of London. He is a member of the research team carrying out the prevalence study of educational handicaps among children in the Isle of Wight.

Contents

x

CHAPTER 1

Social and Ethical Assumptions About Special Education

B. K. KEOGH

This chapter is organized to provide a frame of reference for analysis of assumptions, issues and problems of concern in the definition and implementation of programmes of special education. Special Education is considered in terms of interactions with three major sources of influence: (i) the larger society, (ii) general education and (iii) other disciplines or professions. This organization allows focus on common issues and content from somewhat differing perspectives.

SPECIAL EDUCATION AND SOCIETY

Special Education as a distinct and formal part of school programming is a relatively new development; the product, in part at least, of changing social systems and social beliefs. Special Education has as its basis a focus on exceptional children. Yet the complexity and relativity of the construct 'exceptional' makes implementation of the underlying concern difficult, sometimes controversial and often uncertain. Exceptional children, and therefore Special Education, are a function of the prevailing societal views of 'normality' and what should be done for, and to, deviation from the norm. What constitutes normality varies, of course, by culture and historical period; norms also change relative to economic conditions. Is normal defined in terms of the ideal or optimum, as a condition of health, or as the statistical average? Is exceptional defined in terms of medical, legal, social, or educational parameters? The very definition of exceptionality, and therefore the incidence of handicapped persons, is determined in large part by the societal 'set,' the importance of certain deviations from the norm, and the attitudes which prevail as to what should be done for and/or about them.

Hewett and Forness (1973), in reviewing the history of Special Education, note that the contemporary practice of categorization by specific handicap is relatively recent, in that historically the groupings of importance were 'the *weak*, the *odd*, and the *poor*' (p. 15). They observe, too, that children and adults were treated similarly;

that handicapped children received few special considerations, little special help. Atypical adults and children were often viewed as threats to the economic, social, or moral well-being of the society, with relatively few surviving, either as a result of neglect or direct action. Societal practices aimed at elimination of the handicapped are well documented (Coleman, 1964; Doll, 1962; Hewett and Forness, 1973; Wallin, 1955). Concern for handicapped individuals, especially children, with major emphasis upon care or treatment, is a relatively new development which has led to finer differentiations as to kinds of handicapping conditions, and reliance on education as a major treatment procedure. There was no need for Special Education in a society where those who deviated from the norm were not allowed to survive. Special Education, in part, is an outgrowth or result of changed societal views toward children and handicapped.

Definitional considerations

Questions of who is exceptional or atypical have become increasingly complex as societies have become more urban and demands more complicated. Focusing on conditions within the United States, Coleman (1968) described historical changes in roles of children, families and communities, placing in perspective and contemporary issue of equality of educational opportunity. Coleman identified two elements of non-industrialized societies as especially important. First, the family was the unit responsible for the welfare and well-being of its members throughout their lives. Second, it was within the context of the family that the child learned the competencies he needed to be productive. Coleman noted in describing the pre-industrial family: 'It was a "welfare society", with each extended family serving as a welfare organization for its own members. Thus it was to the family's interest to see that its members became productive' (p. 8). In a contemporary urban society, by contrast, the child moves out of the family in order to master needed skills and competencies and the community or society, rather than the family, is responsible for many aspects of the individual's welfare and well-being. Further, rural living allowed handicapped individuals to make a number of significant, albeit limited, contributions to the family and local community. Few opportunities for real accomplishment or contribution are available to handicapped persons in societies where much of the business of living is conducted away from the home and where work is viewed as competitive and impersonal. It seems reasonable that the societal changes which Coleman proposed as influencing educational opportunity for ethnic minorities may also be important considerations in understanding, identification and education of exceptional children.

Rather than the general groupings of 'weak, odd, or poor,' contemporary views of handicap tend to be tied to a variety of specific non-health conditions, viz. deaf, blind, physically or orthopaedically impaired, profound mental retardation and overt emotional disturbance. The categories have a strong medical flavour, the major basis for homogeneity of category being patterns of physical symptoms which presumably dictate direction of treatment. However, current definitions of exceptional children also include less obvious and less medically based conditions such as, for example, mild mental retardation, behaviour or adjustment problems. In the United States, a new category, Learning Disabilities (LD), has been added to the list of already defined groups receiving support and recognition from Federal Government. Learning Disability children are defined in terms of specific problems or inabilities in school-related tasks, reading, arithmetic and the like, presumably linked to disturbance of some psychological or neurological process. LD children's exceptionality is thus strongly tied to the educational system. It is of interest to note that problems related to disadvantaged economic and social conditions are not usually viewed as being within the proper purview of Special Education. Deviation from legal norms, i.e. delinquency, is also not considered an exceptional condition which requires special educational accommodation, despite consistent findings as to the educational problems of juvenile offenders and to a possible conceptualization of delinquency as a social learning problem. Whereas special provisions for pupils of exceptionally high ability, i.e. 'gifted' children, have direct educational basis, programme development has been hampered by confusions and controversies over definitional criteria and procedures, and by inconsistencies of support and organization (Martinsen, 1966; Newland, 1961). Heterogeneity of gifted groups and somewhat unique goals and emphases may imply that 'giftedness' is outside the scope of traditional Special Education which is focused on handicapping conditions. It is possible that gifted pupils might be served more effectively through curricular and instructional modifications within regular education.

Definitional problems are also apparent within traditional categories of handicap. Conceptualization of mental retardation has been a major theoretical controversy. Luria (1963) rejects a psychometric definition and argues instead for a physiologically based definition of retardation, whereas Clausen (1967; 1972) stands squarely in the psychometric 'camp'. The American Association of Mental Deficiency definition of retardation (Heber, 1961) specifies an adaptive component. Leland (1972) views retardation as a 'social concept', a function, in part, of the requirements and characteristics of the community or society. Consistent with that point of view, Mercer (1971) has shown that somewhat different groups of children are identified as 'retarded' when biological, adaptive or psychometric criteria, either singly or in combination, are applied. In studying aspects of epidemiology of retardation, she observed that a number of school-age children identified as retarded by psychometric criteria showed no organic signs of deficiency, and performed adequately outside the school setting, appearing 'normal' in terms of adaptive criteria. These findings clearly implicate situational variables in the definition of retardation. Mercer suggests that some children are caught in the psychometric screen because of lack of specific experiences associated with cultural or socioeconomic conditions, rather than due to basic in-child deficit conditions.

From Clausen's (1967; 1972) point of view, however, the psychometric criterion is the single most important one in defining retardation. He notes:

'If mental deficiency is to be considered as a uniform field, it is necessary to find a common denominator for all individuals classified deficient. At the present stage of knowledge, it seems that in intellectual functioning alone has this common element been in any way approached . . . The measurement of mental ability, the unique contribution of psychology, may well be the most adequate instrument in defining mental deficiency.' (1967, p. 74.)

Even, or perhaps especially, in mental retardation, the screening or selection identifies somewhat different children. Further, the conceptualization or definition applied becomes the basis for determination of research and programme priorities (Albee, 1970). Issues of definition of exceptionality thus are not just matters of academic argument; they are the basis of Special Education at the operational level.

Given the complexities of the social setting, the variety of definitional criteria and the vagaries of techniques of identification, it is not surprising that incidence figures and estimates are sometimes inaccurate. It is likely, too, that definition of a new category, e.g. Learning Disabilities, results in fresh efforts to find children who 'fit'. The California category of Educationally Handicapped (EH) is a case in point. Formally approved in 1963 as a category for Special Educational programming, the category includes children with serious school achievement problems associated with emotional disturbances and/or neurological impairment, but excludes those with mental retardation, sensory handicap, and the like. In 1963 there were 2059 California children identified as EH, by 1968 35,244, and by 1972 58,000 (Keogh, Becker, Kukic and Kukic, 1972). These figures may be interpreted to suggest either that more children are being recognized and served or that children served in some other category (e.g. mentally retarded) are now classified EH, or even that an epidemic of major proportions has struck the State!

Treatment considerations

Questions of who is exceptional are tied closely to questions of what to do for, to, or about exceptional children. These, too, reflect the attitudes and values of the larger society. Is the family the primary unit responsible for care of the handicapped person? What are short- and long-term goals for handicapped individuals? Shall exceptional children and adults be integrated in, or segregated from, other streams of society? Shall priorities for financial support, research and programme development favour or penalize handicapped groups or persons? Whereas it is entirely possible that special treatment programmes based on categorization as exceptional may bring about major changes in status and improved functioning and adjustment, it is also possible that special treatment may be a mechanism for maintaining the status quo. That is, that selection, segregation, predetermination of goals and lowered expectations may serve to limit opportunities for full integration of the handicapped child into the normative society. In this sense, handicapped children are similar to other minority groups or individuals, reflecting common characteristics of minority membership.

Decisions as to care of exceptional children may be clearer in cases where the handicapping condition is extreme, physical and obvious, than in cases where the exceptionality is more adaptive or social in nature. The medical paradigm in which diagnosis dictates treatment allows application of appropriate remediation in many instances of physical disability. The same model is less powerful when applied to exceptionalities which are basically educational or social, partly because the handicapping conditions are less specific and more interactional in nature, and partly because the treatments or interventions are often uncertain. A case in point may be the current interest in implementation of Special Education programmes for preschool children identified as potential school learning problems. There is wide agreement, of course, that children with physical and sensory disabilities benefit from early and continuing treatment directed at improvement of, or compensation for, the specific handicapping condition. However, children with potential school problems may not have clear and specific in-child deficits or disabilities and, importantly, the handicapping condition (i.e. learning problems) is predicted as likely to develop, not already there. Keogh and Becker (1973) after review of techniques of early identification and programmes of intervention, concluded that 'It well may be that focus on effective educational programming *per se* is a more productive route ... (for prevention of learning problems) ... than is the search for precise measures for early identification of individual children.' Exclusive focus upon child characteristics as the basis for diagnosing social or educational exceptionality provides limited predictive data. Risk is also determined by the situation in which the child must function.

The complexity of treatment of handicapped individuals is clearly illustrated in the case of adolescents and adults, where treatment problems hinge around concerns for economic independence, interpersonal adequacy and the like, all having to do with long-term social outcomes. Examples of discrepancies in individual competencies and social and economic opportunities for handicapped adults abound. Josephson (1968) reported that only 36% of blind college graduates in the United States were regularly employed. When compared to the sighted population, the proportions of blind white collar workers was dramatically low for age and IQ equivalent groups. These findings support the interpretation that major areas of difficulty for blind individuals are in areas of social, vocational and emotional adjustments (Bauman, 1954; Bateman, 1967). Said differently, the critical problems for blind and other handicapped individuals may be more related to how other people view them than to the degree or kind of disability.

Special Education is but one aspect of the majority society's response to handicapped individuals. Whether the programmes are ones of separation or integration, of incarceration or cure, they are indicative of the majority attitudes, and feelings and attitudes are slow to change. Whereas the historical responsibility for care of the handicapped was primarily medical in basis, hopes are expressed that education may be a major avenue for change. It seems likely that success of educational services for exceptional children will be, in part at least, a function of the willingness and ability of the larger society to modify attitudes toward exceptionality. To focus Special Education exclusively on the exceptional is only a first and limited step. The real efforts in 'Special' Education may well be directed toward education of the larger society.

SPECIAL EDUCATION AND GENERAL EDUCATION

The scope of educational services has expanded dramatically over the last decades. Children who formerly were not eligible for state supported programmes, e.g. trainable mentally retarded, severely emotionally disturbed, are now accommodated. Regular class pupils are offered a greater variety of subject matter or content in addition to traditional academics such as, for example, health education, driver training; a broader age range of children is served, many school programmes now offering services to children from the 'preschool' years through young adulthood. In a sense, the formal educational system has been a major avenue for implementing the larger society's views about the roles of children and about its responsibilities to them. It should be stressed that for the most part educational response to exceptional children has resulted in increased numbers of exclusionary programmes, that is, educational arrangements separate from the regular system but designed specifically for particular types of handicapping conditions.

A major effect of broadened programme availability has been the identification of more children eligible for specialized educational services. Incidence figures vary by country and area, sometimes ranging as high as 30% (Robers and Baird, 1972), although most estimates of school-age children requiring Special Education hover around ten per cent (Rossmiller, Hale and Frohreich, 1970). This estimate does not include children of exceptionally high ability, i.e. 'gifted' children, who may profit from specialized educational opportunities. It is of interest to note that not only are larger numbers of children identified as eligible, but also that the parameters of 'exceptional' have been broadened to take into account children whose problems are primarily school-based. The California programme for Educationally Handicapped, already mentioned, is a case in point. It is just one of a variety of special programmes for pupils with serious school achievement problems. Breakdown of incidence in the United States and funding estimates by categories, may be found in Table 1.1. Examination of figures in this table shows clearly that Special Education is both extensive and expensive.

In one sense Special Education might be viewed as optimal general education. Individual differences in pupils' ability, competence, aptitude and learning rates are recognized; appropriate and unique instructional responses are provided for individual children; expectancies and outcomes are determined in relation to pupils' abilities. On the other hand, Special Education might be viewed as epitomizing the ills and problems which plague general education. Goals and outcomes are poorly conceptualized and uncertain; instructional techniques are outmoded and ineffective; motivational environments are often stultifying; expectations for performance are low.

In order to accommodate the specific educational characteristics of various kinds of handicapped children, schools have necessarily modified programmes of general education. Changes may be considered in terms of three major dimensions: (i) goals or outcomes; (ii) programme organization or administration; (iii) instructional techniques. These are clearly neither independent nor mutually exclusive dimensions, but each involves different aspects of educational planning, and each

Table 1.1. Prevalence rates, cost index and estimated cost per pupil for major categories of exceptionality[1]

Category	Estimate of prevalence (%)	Cost index per pupil[2]	Special programme costs[3] $	Marginal cost[4] $
Educable retarded (EMR)	2·3	1·87	1225	570
Trainable retarded (TMR)	0·2	2·10	1376	721
Auditorily handicapped	0·5	2·99	1958	1303
Visually handicapped	0·1	2·97	1945	1290
Speech handicapped	3·5	1·18	773	118
Physically handicapped	0·5	3·64	2384	1729
Neurological and specific learning disorders	1·0	2·16	1415	760
Emotionally disturbed	2·0	2·83	1854	1199
Multiple handicapped	0·04	2·73	1788	1133
Total	10·14			

[1] Estimates derived from figures summarized by Rossmiller, Hale and Frohreich, 1970 (pp. 119–121).
[2] The cost index is the relationship of per pupil expenditure in regular programmes and per pupil expenditure in special programmes.
[3] Based on median figure of $655 for regular per pupil programme expenditure.
[4] Additional cost of special programme.

may be manipulated somewhat independently of the others. Unfortunately, in many special programmes the dimension modified is not clear, resulting in confounding of goals, administrative organization and instructional techniques.

Modification of goals

While it is reasonable that long-term goals for handicapped children are similar to those for normal children, such goals are usually stated in global, non-specific terms. They are difficult to translate directly into curriculum and instruction, and are often long-term in nature. Operational goals may also be unclear. Should the major focus of educational programmes for handicapped children be on social competence or academic achievement? Should programme goals for handicapped groups be primarily vocational in nature? Should exceptional children be expected to accomplish essentially the same academic goals as normal children, but more slowly and at a lesser degree of mastery? In the case of many exceptional children, vague, long-term goals and lack of clarity of more immediate operational goals have resulted in a kind of 'watered down' curriculum, taught more slowly than in the regular system, yet often taught with traditional inefficiency. Improved educational technology may allow more efficient educational instruction, if *what* is to be taught *to whom* is agreed upon.

Modification of programme organization

Examination of Special Education programmes suggests that the single most common modification from general education has been in administration or organization of programmes. More specifically, the exclusionary, segregated model has been widely implemented in both the United States and Great Britain, resulting in Special Education being defined in terms of separate schools or separate classes within regular schools. Segregated arrangements have been the focus of a continuing controversy as to programme efficacy (Dunn, 1968; Christopolos and Renz, 1969; MacMillan, 1973). Segregation of exceptional children into separate programmes may well work to the benefit of regular education in that it removes different, sometimes troublesome children from regular class instruction. Benefits of segregation for exceptional children are less clear, however. A major assumption underlying segregated programming is that the handicapping condition, e.g. deafness, blindness, mental retardation, provides some homogeneity of educational relevance. That is, that particular groups of children are more like each other than they are like regular class children in terms of instructional needs and learning abilities. There has been little clear evidence, however, that learning or educational characteristics of particular handicapping conditions have any necessary or direct tie to the physical conditions which define the exceptionality. Despite the assumption that homogeneity of grouping provides homogeneity of learning process, exceptional children within any category display marked variation in learning abilities and characteristics. With the possible exception of children with sensory deficits or severe physical conditions, where modification of curricular materials is required to enhance availability of information, there is little evidence that exceptional children learn differently from normal children, or that they require dramatically modified instructional techniques. It seems likely that organization of Special Education programmes is often related to other administrative considerations, not necessarily to educational methods (Keogh *et al.*, 1972).

Modifications of instructional methods

Closely tied to administrative organization of programmes are questions of modifications of instructional techniques. It is presumed that programme organization, e.g. self-contained, integrated or combinations of these, allows specific application of appropriate instructional methods for each child. Individualization thus has been the major focus and justification for special programming. Special Education programmes are clearly based on assumptions of an aptitude–treatment interaction. As noted by Glaser (1972) research on aptitude–treatment interaction is aimed at determining which instructional systems or programmes maximize success for pupils with particular aptitudes. Based on review of major work in this area, Glaser concluded:

'. . . our generally used aptitude constructs are not productive dimensions for measuring those individual differences that interact with different ways of learning. These measures derived from a psychometric, selection-oriented tradition do not appear to relate to the processes of learning and performance . . .' (p. 8).

In short, despite selection and grouping on psychometric and physical characteristics as a means for ensuring homogeneity of learning, there is only limited evidence that instructional techniques and methods actually allow or support these individual differences in aptitudes or instructional needs.

In the case of Special Education pupils, decisions as to instructional methods are compounded by differences of opinion with regard to expected outcomes, and as to assumed causal conditions. For example, argument between the two major camps of deaf educators continues to affect the instruction of deaf children; instructional decisions are seemingly made in terms of the educator's advocacy of one or the other system rather than in terms of a given child's aptitudes for either or both systems. In the case of learning disability children, instructional programmes are often chosen in terms of the educator's view of learning disabilities as primarily perceptual, motivational, emotional or organic. Arguments wage as to interventions based on weaknesses or strengths, or as to the need for remediation of underlying deficits or reliance on development of compensatory abilities. Despite strong philosophic belief in individualization according to children's aptitudes and abilities, instruction in many special programmes is determined on some other basis than child characteristics; the child must accommodate to the system. In Glaser's terms (1972), the programmes are selective, not necessarily adaptive.

Outcome effects

Although administrative arrangements, curricular content and instructional matters may be modified purposely, it is the programme outcomes or goals which are affected. Administrative arrangements based on tracking or streaming may provide children with content and instruction compatible with their abilities and aspirations, thus leading to realistic achievement and self-understanding. On the other hand, streaming may also result in achievement far below what a child can do, may isolate him from positive peer models and may limit opportunities for significant educational experiences.

A major effect of exclusionary streaming or grouping based on presumed child limitations may be lowered expectations for performance on the part of the child and the adults in his world. Despite criticism of the specifics of methodology used to demonstrate the phenomenon (Thorndike, 1968), the well-known 'self-fulfilling prophecy' (Rosenthal and Jacobsen, 1968) deserves consideration as an effect of importance in Special Education programmes. From another point of view, MacMillan and Keogh (1971) and Keogh, Cahill and MacMillan (1972) have shown that children with long histories of school failure, e.g. retarded or educationally handicapped pupils, bring a generalized expectancy for failure to new problem-solving tasks. Self-perceived inadequacy and a 'set' for failure may explain at least part of their school problems. Labelling as exceptional, through special class placement, may serve as objective confirmation of this self-perception, leading to further disturbance of motivation. Alternatively, special placement may provide opportunity for supportive instruction which allows exceptional children to achieve at a mastery level.

In his report on equality of educational opportunity Coleman (1968) noted that it is outcomes rather than instructional techniques which were most affected by differentiated educational programming. Pupils are grouped or streamed in terms of expected achievement and the programme content is geared to those expected outcomes. The problem lies in the assumption that the outcome goals are certain, that the expectations have firm basis in pupil abilities. 'The distinguishing characteristic of this concept of equality of educational opportunity is that it accepts as given the child's expected future . . . this concept of differentiated curricula uses the expected future to match child and curriculum' (pp. 13–14). Too often with exceptional children the 'expected future' is viewed by others as limited, and pupils are exposed to correspondingly restricted programmes. In effect, it is outcomes or goals, rather than organization and instructional techniques, which have been modified. The special educator is thus faced with an interesting problem. Programme outcomes for any given child or group of exceptional children, determined *a priori* in terms of limitations thought to be related to their handicapping condition, are likely to be achieved by careful educational programming; pupil failure, with its compounding effects, is likely to be reduced. At the same time, programmes based on limited goals almost preclude achievement beyond or in addition to these goals, because the exceptional pupil is neither exposed to nor allowed opportunity to learn things provided in regular school programming for other children. The dilemma is that school programmes based on specific, limited goals have a high probability of pupil mastery of those goals. Such programmes also tend to reinforce and confirm the preconceptions about exceptional children placed in those programmes. MacMillan (1971) has emphasized the importance of alternative models of Special Education programming, suggesting that it is not a question of regular class versus segregated class, but rather 'To what extent, and under what circumstances, can a wider range of individual differences be accommodated in the regular class . . .?' The question is applicable to programmes of general education as well as of Special Education. Answers may benefit pupils in both educational programmes and serve to bridge the gap between 'special' and general education.

SPECIAL EDUCATION AND RELATED DISCIPLINES

Special Education may be viewed as a major consumer of the content and expertise of other disciplines or professions. Developmentalists and physicians describe normal growth patterns and delineate conditions of health or non-health. Psychologists provide a variety of possible theories of learning. Sociologists and social psychologists propose interpretations of the workings of societal groups. Engineers develop sophisticated technical instruments. Yet, the educational integration, organization, implementation and application of the contributions of these professions have been the responsibility of the special educator, very often the responsibility of the isolated special class teacher. Given a condition in which specializations are so narrow within any one profession that members of the same profession have difficulty in communicating, it is not surprising that special educators have difficulty in understanding and applying the volume of information available from other professional groups. This is not to deny that at least some of this information is useful; usefulness, however, depends on presentation in a form usable by the consumer.

Relationships between Special Education and other professions or disciplines may be summarized within two major areas: clinical or educational applications and research.

Clinical applications

By definition, the special educator is concerned with educational aspects of exceptional children's development. Yet adequacy of educational programming depends, in part at least, upon the child's physical, intellectual, emotional and social skills or, conversely, upon ways in which physical, intellectual, emotional or social handicaps require educational accommodation. Many aspects of the exceptional child's development and functioning are beyond the training and expertise of the special educator. The special educator thus depends upon members of other professions to alert him to child characteristics of importance in planning and implementing educational programmes. Unfortunately, this exchange of information is often unsuccessful, at least from the educator's point of view.

In the traditional pattern of diagnosis and referral for special educational services, a 'multidisciplinary team' meets, ponders, refers and leaves. A member of each discipline represented on the team provides information in the area of his expertise. Much of this information may be educationally irrelevant and obtuse, seldom leading directly to programme implementation or instructional techniques, tasks faced by the teacher. Part of the problem may be that the expert from other disciplines provides information of interest to those in his discipline, but not necessarily relevant to or translatable into educational practice. Diagnostic categories of minimal cerebral dysfunction, the hyperkinetic syndrome, developmental lag, are all examples of descriptive, non-specific and non-explanatory labels proposed by other professions. None of these is a category which dictates a specific educational response, although each category includes behaviours or child characteristics of possible importance in educational planning.

The special educator's growing disenchantment with the contributions of other professionals is in part a recognition of the lack of educational usefulness of much of this information. Psychometric preoccupation of psychologists is a case in point. Intelligence testing, a major stock in trade of the educational psychologist, may provide for legal categorization of children for programme placement, but provides little insight into instructional approaches. Data gathered from interviews with a large number of Special Education teachers (Keogh *et al.*, 1972) revealed that classroom teachers view school psychologists as testers who make only limited contribution to classroom management or instruction. Teachers also viewed traditional diagnostic categories provided by physicians as lacking implication for remediation. In Glaser's (1972) terms, medical and psychological analyses support selective, not adaptive, programmes. That is, children are identified to fit existing programmes, programmes are not necessarily adapted to them. If the contributions of other professions are to be utilized to maximize effectiveness of educational programming, information must be presented in ways which have meaning to the educator. The delineation and communication of educationally relevant information is the responsibility of professionals who work with exceptional children. It is neither reasonable nor possible to expect the special teacher to assume the burden of translation of data from other disciplines. Related professionals are obligated to provide the educator with meaningful and useful data. Educators are obligated to apply these data to educational programming and instruction.

Research

Legitimate research questions generated in fields of study related to Special Education are many and complex. The scope and diversity of research activities of possible relevance to exceptional children are so great as to make monitoring of research results, to say nothing of in-depth understanding, nearly impossible for the professional special educator. Research activities by special educators have also expanded, and often deal with topics viewed as being within the traditional parameters of other fields, e.g. Psychology, Sociology, Medicine. A real issue may have to do with the definition of research questions which are legitimately and perhaps uniquely asked by special educators. It seems reasonable that, because Special Education is an applied field, the critical research questions for special educators are essentially applied ones. In contrast, the researcher in other related fields is more likely to pursue questions which form the basis for application. The distinction is, of course, a fine one and is not intended to be either restricting or exclusionary; rather it is proposed as a focus for productive research efforts.

In a general sense research in Special Education might most appropriately be described as directed at identification of educationally significant variables associated with the development and learning of exceptional children; more precisely at the specification of educational variables and conditions which affect the behaviour and learning of these children. Examples of generalized questions might be: What are educationally relevant abilities and disabilities of differing populations of exceptional children? What instructional techniques and materials are most effective with particular kinds of exceptional children? What are the effects of differing classroom environments on the motivation and behaviour of exceptional children? In essence, the critical questions relate to ways in which schools can provide optimal, efficient and effective programmes for exceptional children. It should be emphasized that *research* in Special Education and *evaluation* of particular special programmes are not the same thing, programme evaluation representing a more circumscribed concern usually relating to immediate administrative decisions.

Many questions of research value to Special Education are derived from basic work done in other fields. For example, research on perceptual impairment of learning in disordered children had its basis in the extensive work on perceptual development conducted by developmental psychologists with normal children. Consideration of motivational characteristics of exceptional children came from constructs developed and investigated by personality theorists. It seems likely that researchers in Special Education may maximize benefits for exceptional children by using substantive work in related fields, rather than by attempting that more basic work themselves. Research in Special Education is not basic research in Psychology, Sociology, Medicine or other fields, nor is it replication of research in these fields. Rather, it is the extension and application of work in those fields to exceptional children.

Investigative techniques as well as research content need to be considered in the light of the kind of questions asked by special educators. The experimental paradigm, the mainstay of psychological research, may sometimes be inappropriate for studies in Special Education. In the experimental paradigm, it is assumed that the significant variables for study have been identified, that they can be manipulated or modified independently of other variables, or that other sources of variation (error) can be minimized or held constant. In research with exceptional children, however, there is real uncertainty as to what the significant variables are; variance from other sources may not be controlled and the confounding influences of child and setting have not been clarified. In short, much research in Special Education is still directed at determining the critical variables themselves. Further, research conducted in the classroom is subject to many extraneous sources of influence. The complexities of research in Special Education present such a challenge that many investigators may well choose to retreat to the experimental laboratory. Yet questions of real importance must be answered, in part at least, in classrooms where exceptional children receive instruction. Descriptive studies of children in educational programmes may provide data which lead to experimental investigation.

A broadened approach to research in Special Education in no sense argues against rigour or sophistication of research methodology. It does argue for a broad base of research techniques as legitimate for the study of exceptional children. Hilgard (1972), in an article titled 'The Translation of Educational Research and Development into Action', delineated three types of research: basic science research in learning, technological research and development bearing upon instruction and policy research bearing upon innovative curriculum and practices. It is logical that the bulk of research effort in Special Education should be directed to the latter two categories. The field of Special Education is sorely in need of careful, systematic and comprehensive research efforts. It is important that such efforts be directed toward questions of importance to exceptional children, and that the research methodology employed be compatible with the questions asked.

CHANGE IN SPECIAL EDUCATION

Prediction is, at best, a risky business. Yet it seems a reasonable guess, based on current status, that the single most powerful agent for change in the next few years will be the courts of law. The fields of Special Education has been slow to move and to change, has occupied a somewhat isolated position in terms of regular education and the society at large. Within the past few years, however, Special Education has become the centre of a number of critical issues within society. Change has resulted from legal, not educational, decisions. Court decisions in the United States have dramatically modified the conduct of Special Education. Legal action has drawn sharp attention to inequities of procedures involving ethnic minorities and has pin-pointed the confounding of ethnic or social class conditions and educational problems. Legal action has forced schools to take steps to change existing conditions and to prevent such conditions from occurring in the future. In short, legal action has been the spur to move a notably lethargic educational establishment. Comprehensive discussion of legal actions affecting Special Education may be found in reviews by Collings (1973), Cohen and De Young (1973), Ross, De Young and Cohen (1971) and Vaughn (1973).

Court decisions have resulted in changes in practices directed specifically at ethnic minorities, but have also brought about redefinition of eligibility for free, public education. Considering first the changes having to do with ethnic minorities, legal action has forced changes in identification and placement procedures for special programming. In particular, legal decision has forced modification to tests or assessment procedures used to identify and certify pupils for special placement, making clear the differential effects of standard English-based tests on children from varying language backgrounds. For example, six mandates were issued by the court in the case of *Diana vs. The State of California* (1970). In essence, the Court ruled that the child must be tested in her native language, and should be retested with a non-verbal test of intelligence; the State was required to develop norms for tests which were specific to ethnic groups, and school districts were directed to develop plans for revised testing programmes; further, districts were required to provide an explanation for any disproportionate representation of ethnic minorities in special education classes and, finally, districts were directed to develop programmes which would provide transition help for pupils decertified as retarded and placed back in regular educational programmes. As noted by MacMillan (1973), only the last mandate of the court was educational in nature, the first four specifically focused on the issue of use of verbal intelligence tests as the primary tool for identification of children as retarded.

Although primary targets of legal attack have been the psychometric or screening instruments employed, there has also been question and legal action in terms of placement procedures and representation of ethnic minorities in special programmes, especially segregated programmes. As noted by Ross, De Young and Cohen (1971), legal action has drawn attention to 'institutional racism' inadvertently fostered by some special educational programming. Patterns of ethnic representation in special classes, limited selection criteria, and the like, were shown to result in racial imbalance of faculties and student bodies in a large California school district (*Spangler vs. Board of Education, 1970*). In a separate action (*Arreola vs. Board of Education, 1968*) at issue were the due process guarantees in placement procedures; a specific result of the last case was more direct parental input into placement decisions.

A programmatic outgrowth of legal action in California has been a formalized programme for reclassification or decertification of over 19,000 pupils previously classified as Educable Mentally Retarded. Permissive 'transition' programmes developed rapidly under special provisions of the State Education Code. School districts were allowed to adopt differing administrative or organizational schemes to accommodate decertified pupils. Significantly, decertification, or at least re-evaluation, was mandated by law, change coming as a response to judicial decision.

Although California was an early 'battleground' (Ross *et al.*, 1971), litigation has by no means been limited to one geographic area or particular ethnic group. Actions in Boston (*Stewart vs. Phillips, 1970*) and in Washington, D.C. (*Hobson vs. Hansen, 1967*) were major influences on programme practices, the latter decision getting at one of the most widely implemented aspects of programme organization, namely 'tracking' or 'streaming'.

Major legal action has affected another aspect of Special Education, that is, the nature of the exceptional populations to be served. Specifically at issue is the right to free public education for all exceptional children. The question was tested in a class action suit in Pennsylvania (*Pennsylvania Association for Retarded Children vs. Commonwealth of Pennsylvania, 1971*). As in many areas, Special Education programmes in that State were exclusionary on the basis of severity of condition or because of age. In this case, the court guaranteed the 'right of access to education' to all retarded children between the ages of 6 and 21 (the age range of eligibility for free public education for all children in the State). There was an additional action dealing with parents' rights regarding the opportunity to be heard in matters of educational placement of their children. Effects of the Pennsylvania decision may well be public educational responsibility for more severely affected children. This issue of degree of public school responsibility for severely atypical pupils was tested in the case of *Lori vs. The State of California (1972–73)*, in which the decision of the court supported the State's contention of rights to limiting programmes. The question of scope of responsibility of the public educational system is not clear, and it seems likely that questions of eligibility, public school responsibility and the like, will continue to be tested over the next years. Gilhool (1973), in summarizing the directions and effects of legal action on education, noted eloquently: '. . . it is a new language, a language that suggests a new conception of the handicapped citizen . . . a conception that suggests that handicapped citizens no longer have what they may have by the grace or by the good will of any other person but that they have what they must have by right. It is now a matter of justice' (p. 609).

CONCLUSIONS

Special Education has been viewed in terms of its relationships to the larger society, to general education and to related disciplines. While it is clear that major growth has occurred in the development of services for exceptional children, it is also clear that there are many areas of confusion and concern. As suggested, the educational situation for exceptional children is not unlike that for the ethnic minority pupil. Questions relating to equality of educational opportunity are pertinent for the exceptional minority as well as the ethnic minority. It seems likely that many of the issues will be settled by the courts, not in classrooms. Coleman (1968) made very clear the change in a concept of equality of educational opportunity based on effects or outcomes of educational experience: 'The implication . . . is that the responsibility to create achievement lies with the educational institution, not the child . . . This shift in responsibility follows logically from the change in the concept of equality of educational opportunity from school resource inputs to effects of schooling. When that change occurred, as it has in the past few years, the school's responsibility shifted from increasing and distributing equally *its* "quality" to increasing the quality of its *students'* achievements. This is a notable shift, and one which should have strong consequences for the practice of education in future years.'

CHAPTER 2

Psychological and Medical Concepts

W. YULE

In many countries the provision of 'special' education is tied to the needs of children presenting with *medically* recognized conditions such as cerebral palsy, deafness, blindness and the like. The wisdom of educating children in groups according to the type of medical condition is now being questioned openly, and the provision of education to meet a child's *educational* needs is being discussed. This chapter will examine the various concepts of what constitutes a 'disorder' of educational concern; it will also attempt to bring together what is known from epidemiological studies about the nature and extent of handicapping conditions during preschool and school years.

THE NEED FOR EPIDEMIOLOGICAL STUDIES

Whilst all teachers would agree that, in an ideal world, education should be geared to the unique needs of each individual child, this ideal can seldom be realized. Crude economics force us to educate children in groups, so that inevitably some children receive less than optimal education. Further, some children arrive at school with physical, emotional or social problems which make it more difficult for them to profit from the ordinary teaching in the classroom. Thus, for a variety of reasons, many children will require some form of 'special' education: 'special' in the sense of being different from that which is more generally available.

In seeking to plan the special education services needed within a community (in a rational manner), educational administrators need to have some idea of the numbers of school children requiring special education—what problems will the children have, and what measures are needed to alleviate these difficulties? To answer these questions, one must turn to the literature on the *epidemiology* of children's disorders.

Epidemiology is originally a medical strategy for studying the spread of diseases. By tracing all people within a specified population who show the symptoms of a particular disease, the epidemiologist can obtain information about the mechanism of the transmission of the disease, the subgroups within the population who succumb most readily, and the like. Gruenberg (1964) has said that

'. . . epidemiology makes a contribution to what can be called "community diagnosis". The purpose of such studies of the cases of disorder in a community is to provide quantitative information to (i) estimate the size, nature and location of the community's problems, (ii) identify the component parts of the problem, (iii) locate populations at special risk of being affected, and (iv) identify opportunities for preventative work and needs for treatment and special services. Thus, epidemiology serves as the diagnostician for the official or community leader who is practising community medicine, social medicine, public health or public welfare. The nature of the community's health problems is approached diagnostically with epidemiological methods."

Strangely, despite the pioneering work of Burt (1925, 1937), the epidemiological approach has rarely been applied in the area of educational disorders, at least not until recently. In part, this is probably because of the greater difficulty in defining what constitutes an educational disorder as opposed to a medical disorder. It is relatively easy to get two medical doctors to agree that a child has German measles, a squint, or a limp, but it is difficult to get two educators to agree at what level of, say, spelling a child could be counted as having a spelling problem. This difficulty in agreement over definition occurs despite the availability of standardized attainment tests. When it comes to deciding whether a child is showing a behavioural or emotional difficulty, the problems are even greater. And yet one must agree on definitions in all these areas before one can begin to count the numbers of children falling in to each category of disorder.

One of the reasons for this difficulty in agreeing on definitions of particular disorders is that the concept of 'disorder' itself is less than clear. For example, difficulty in reading may constitute a handicap in a society which aims at universal literacy, but not in a society where reading is restricted to a privileged few. On the other hand, blindness brings its own problems, irrespective of the community into which the child is born. Blindness is an absolute, whereas reading difficulty is relative to all sorts of cultural and educational expectations as to what is 'normal' for a particular setting.

With some clear-cut cases of physical disorders, there may be no educational sequelae, but with other physical disorders, such as asthma or epilepsy, there can be educational consequences of varying degree. In planning for special education, it is necessary to define both the condition of concern and its effect on the child's life. To this end, it has become customary to distinguish among 'defect', 'disability' and 'handicap' (Gulliford, 1971; Oppé, 1972).

In a Working Paper on Risk Registers (Oppé, 1972) defined these terms as follows:

'Defect: a structural or biochemical abnormality
Disability: a loss or impairment of function
Handicap: an interference with normal growth or development, or capacity to learn, caused by a continuing disability of body, intellect or personality to such a degree as to need extra care or treatment from the medical, nursing, social or educational services.'

Thus, a congenital cataract would constitute a defect and a child born with such a defect would suffer a disability of vision which would handicap him in a great many areas of normal development. The poor reader, on the other hand, might not be suffering from any identifiable defect, but is disabled in his reading. This disability is known to interfere with both academic and emotional development, and so constitutes a handicap.

Oppé (1972) went on to state some of the difficulties involved in interpreting epidemiological data:

'Information regarding the prevalence of handicapping disorders in childhood must always be considered in relation to (a) the definitions used for the characterization of (i) specific defects or disabilities and (ii) handicaps (generally a much vaguer concept), (b) the completeness of ascertainment within a population, (c) the age distribution of the population and (d) the manner with which multiple handicaps are dealt with; the number of defects and disabilities enumerated exceed the number of affected individuals' (Oppé, 1972).

The importance of careful definition has already been touched on. To illustrate this, consider the question of reading disability. Vernon (1957) concluded that '. . . although the number of children who can scarcely read may be relatively small, there are many more who never learn to read fluently and effectively'. She goes on to quote estimates of 'reading backwardness' that vary from 1% to 16% of children aged 7 to 8 years. As will be seen later, one of the reasons for this disparity in the estimates of children with 'reading backwardness' lies in the different definitions employed in the various surveys: a variety of tests and a variety of cut-off points lead to vastly different findings.

The second caveat raised in the Risk Register report concerns the methodology followed in epidemiological studies. Ideally, all children in a given population should be examined when the investigators are trying to count the number with a clearly defined disability or handicap. But this is a costly procedure, so usually only samples of the population are studied. Samples can either be drawn at random or they can be carefully selected to be representative of the total population. Whilst this cuts down the work-load of the survey it increases the likelihood of error in the prevalence figures. As in all sampling procedures, the smaller the sample, the higher the error of estimate.

Alternatively, the work can be cut down by employing a two-stage examination procedure. The total population can be 'screened' by an appropriate test, questionnaire or brief examination during the first stage and then, during the second stage, small selected groups of children who are suspected of having the disability can be examined in greater detail. The disadvantage of this method is that it depends a great deal on the validity of the intermediate screening instruments. The less sensitive they are, the more children will be missed. This procedure was followed in the epidemiological studies carried out on the Isle of Wight (Rutter, Tizard and Whitmore, 1970), and will be discussed in greater detail below.

The age of the population studied is clearly an important factor when considering childrens' handicaps. To take one example, some fear of the dark is reported by parents to occur in just over 50% of five-year-olds, about 40% of eleven-year olds, and in less than 20% of fourteen-year olds (Shepherd, Oppenheim and Mitchell, 1971). There are many other childhood disorders which are age-related, so that it is important to take this into account when interpreting the results of any prevalence study. In a statistical sense, it is 'normal' for a five-year old to show some fear of the dark, but it is statistically 'abnormal' for a fourteen-year-old even to need a night-light.

Thus, it can be seen that estimating the numbers of children who require special education is a complex process, but it is only by attempting to do this that rational planning of services is possible. Well-executed epidemiological studies can identify the children requiring special help. They cannot specify what form such help should take. The principles underlying the practice of special education are discussed in other chapters in this volume.

WHAT IS 'ABNORMAL'?

Before defining the defects and disabilities which necessitate that a handicapped child should receive special education, it must be recognized that there are at least two different concepts of 'abnormality'. Since, as Eysenck (1953) points out, 'normality' can mean all things to all men, it is necessary to distinguish between the two usages.

(a) *Statistical normality.* Whatever characterizes the majority of the population is considered to be normal. Thus, the normal height of ten-year-olds is 146 cm for boys and 140 cm for girls (Rutter, Tizard and Whitmore, 1970). Children who are in the top or bottom 3 per cent of the distribution are usually considered to be abnormally tall or abnormally small, respectively. And yet the very small children are usually thought of as more abnormal than the very tall children. This is where the second concept of normality comes in.

(b) *Ideal normality.* 'We call a person normal the more he approaches the ideal, whether it be ideally high intelligence, good looks, or uninterrupted health. But the ideal norm may be one which is statistically very infrequent, or which in actual fact is not found at all in the population examined' (Eysenck, 1953). Thus, the person who 'never has a day's illness in his life' is statistically abnormal but normal in the ideal sense.

However, this second sense of the concept of normality is the one which causes most difficulty for the epidemiologist, for who is to decide what is ideal? Clearly, this is related to the society in which the study is carried out and, even within one society, what is considered to be normal behaviour can alter considerably from time to time. For example, it is no longer considered abnormal for a child to write with his left hand. Likewise, the changing mathematics curriculum means that children are no longer taught their multiplication tables in a rote fashion. This means that they would score abnormally low on older tests geared to the old curriculum, but few modern educationists would doubt the value of the newer, concept-orientated teaching approach.

Educational standards vary from time to time according to the prevailing values of society. This fact alone makes it difficult to give absolute definitions of abnormality in educational attainment. Indeed, the main point of the present discussion is to emphasize the relative nature of all definitions of abnormality.

Whilst the problem of definition is difficult enough in the educational field, when it comes to the area of children's behaviour and adjustment there are even greater difficulties. Epidemiological surveys can readily establish the frequency of occurrence of any particular pattern of behaviour, but who is to say which pattern is abnormal? In some schools, children are encouraged to remain seated for most of the day, to work quietly, and to raise their hands before answering a question. 'Talking out of turn' would be regarded as a deviant act. In other classes, the child who sits quietly and does not express himself freely and verbally, would be regarded as deviant. Even within a reasonably homogeneous community, such different standards of behaviour will exist, and who is to be the arbiter of normality in these circumstances? There can be no easy answer to this important question. An approach to the problem is discussed below.

CLASSIFICATION OF DISORDERS

There are four broad groups of disorders, the presence of which may give rise to educational concern. These are (a) intellectual retardation; (b) educational difficulties; (c) behavioural-emotional disorders and (d) physical defects and disabilities. Merely cataloguing all these would be both tedious and uninformative. Instead, the principles underlying the classification of disorders will be discussed. The major disorders will be described and, once the definitions have been clarified, the results of prevalence studies will be discussed.

Notice that this section is headed 'classification of disorders' and *not* 'classification of children'. A child can have measles at one time and chicken-pox at another. He may suffer a handicapping fear of animals at age nine, but be training as a veterinary surgeon at age twenty. In other words, it is possible for a child to have one kind of handicap at one age and another at a later age.

In a paper discussing the classification of psychiatric disorders, Rutter (1965) states two other principles of classification. Firstly, the system of classification must be based on facts and be defined in operational terms. Thus, if one is to categorize a disorder as 'neurotic', this decision must be based on an objective description of the child's behaviour—what does he do, how frequently, under what circumstances—rather than on interpretations based on some theoretical system such as 'is ambivalent', 'introverted', 'frightened', without saying how these states are shown.

Secondly, Rutter says the category must convey relevant information and have predictive value before it is useful. Although these were put forward in relation to psychiatric disorders, they also apply to the other main categories. Thus, classifying a particular level of reading attainment as 'backward' should carry an implication of what this means for the future.

The main purpose of any classificatory scheme is to aid communication between people concerned with the welfare of children. The lack of agreed definitions hampers communication and impedes planning of educational services. On the other hand, once a disorder has been identified and described, it can be studied and, if necessary, provisions made to help children afflicted with the disorder.

Information from a variety of sources can be utilized in compiling any classification system. Rutter's (1965) classificatory system draws on seven sorts of research evidence: (i) studies of symptom clusters: which sorts of behaviours tend to hang together to form distinct patterns? (ii) Response to treatment: some disorders are easier than others to alleviate. (iii) Long-term prognosis: some disabilities may become less handicapping as the child gets older, others get worse. Longitudinal studies help to sort out which disorders have the best prognosis and vice versa, a study of long-term outcome helps to make differential classification more meaningful. (iv) Aetiology: a knowledge of the cause of a defect or disability sometimes helps in differentiating among disorders. (v) Epidemiology: as discussed earlier, this provides information on the prevalence of individual behaviours and their relationship to more serious disorders. For example, reversals in writing individual letters are very common before age seven and, on their own, do not indicate any serious writing problem. Likewise, individual fears and temper tantrums on their own do not necessarily indicate a psychiatric disorder. (vi) Age and sex trends: inability to name and sound the letters of the alphabet is normal at age three but very deviant at age 14 in children of at least average intelligence. Bed-wetting is only considered a disorder if it persists beyond about six, and even then it usually exists as an isolated developmental disorder. (vii) Severity and duration of disorders: although cut-off points on the continuum of intelligence scores are necessarily somewhat arbitrary, the distinction between severe subnormality (below IQ 50) and subnormality (50 to 70) has proved useful in respect of suggesting aetiology, as well as in predicting response to training and education. Severity is harder to judge in other, less easily quantified disorders, but it is obviously important.

One way of judging the severity of a handicap is to consider how easily the defect or disability can be either circumvented or in other ways compensated for (Gulliford, 1971). This way of operationalizing the concept of severity helps to answer such questions as, 'Is blindness more handicapping than deafness?' or 'Is an anti-social disorder more handicapping than a neurotic one?'. These questions are not merely academic. The amount of money available for special education is far from unlimited and the answers to such questions, difficult as they are, will guide educational administrators in their financial budgeting.

Severity is, of course, only relative to the conditions pertaining at any one point in time. A child who is confined to a wheel-chair is less handicapped in a school with lifts and ramps, than in a school with only difficult staircases. The handicap of partial hearing can be alleviated by an effective hearing aid. Pharmacological control of epilepsy can reduce the frequency of seizures (although many anti-epileptic drugs may have equally serious side-effects; Yule, 1973b). Finally, as Gulliford (1971) makes clear, the severity of a handicap can be reduced by factors within the family and the child himself.

Any classificatory system worked out on the basis of this information will, of necessity, have to be flexible and subject to alteration. Advances in teaching techniques, in psychological and in medical practice will affect the handicapping sequelae of all sorts of disorders, and not always by reducing the numbers of children requiring special care. Advances in early surgical intervention have resulted in an increase in the numbers of surviving cases of spina bifida—a malformation of the spinal cord which, depending on the site of the lesion, can result in paralysis of the legs and incontinence. In contrast, if more effective techniques of remedial reading teaching became available, a disorder in reading attainment would have to be reclassified as less handicapping than it is at present.

Classification and prevalence

The principles and problems of classification of disorders outlined above should make it clear that no classificatory scheme will be entirely acceptable to everyone. Provisionally, this chapter chooses to look at disorders of childhood under the four main categories of intellectual retardation, educational disorders, behavioural-emotional disorders and physical disabilities. Whilst it is possible to discuss the disabilities in this discrete way, it must be remembered that children are often *multiply handicapped*. There are many more disorders than children, so that when it comes to planning services, these must be planned for the children rather than the separate disabilities, a distinction which it has taken the educational authorities a long time to recognize.

1. INTELLECTUAL RETARDATION

Intellectual retardation is a *psychological* concept which refers to a disability in intellectual functioning. Mental subnormality and mental deficiency, on the other hand, are administrative concepts which carry legal implications. As such, they are less clearly defined than the psychological concept which is usually expressed in psychometric terms: Intelligence Quotients of 70 or less on well-standardized individually administered tests of general intelligence are classified as intellectual retardation.

It is still the case that many individuals in institutions for the severely subnormal have IQ scores above 70 (Castell and Mittler, 1965) and equally that many individuals with IQ scores below 70 are well-adjusted in the general community (Rutter, Tizard and Whitmore, 1970). The former group have been institutionalized, presumably, because of handicaps such as behavioural disturbance or social problems; the latter group remain in the community because their intellectual disability is not seriously handicapping.

Admission to a subnormality hospital is a complex process which results in a very heterogeneous group of institutionalized individuals. Such as administrative definition is virtually useless for epidemiological purposes. Patients are referred as long as there are places available. Where there are long waiting lists, alternative placements or solutions are found. Thus, one cannot rely on administrative returns to get any precise information either on the prevalence of intellectual retardation or on its characteristics.

To give an example of how misleading administrative returns can be, consider the waiting lists for admission to special schools for 'Educationally subnormal children'. In 1946, 10,000 children awaited admission to ESN schools, while 20 years later, following the provision of 34,000 new places, the number awaiting admission was still 10,000 (Rigley, 1968). Even making allowances for the increase in population, it is clear that the 1946 waiting list seriously underestimated the need for special education in ESN schools.

There have been a number of well-planned epidemiological studies of the prevalence of intellectual retardation, and these have been well summarized in Gruenberg (1964), Kushlick (1966) and Rutter, Tizard and Whitmore (1970). Using psychometric criteria, 'severely subnormal' is defined as having an IQ below 50. This term covers the older terms of 'idiot' (IQ below 25) and 'imbecile' (IQ between 25 and 50). 'Mildly subnormal' is used to describe IQs in the range 50 to 70, the range previously called 'feebleminded'.

Theoretically, IQs are distributed normally throughout the population, so that there should be $2 \cdot 27\%$ of people with IQs below 70; $2 \cdot 23\%$ being in the 50 to 70 range and only $0 \cdot 04\%$ in the below 50 group. In fact, nearly all surveys are in agreement in finding an excess over the expected level, particularly in the severely subnormal range.

Kushlick (1966) concludes that below the age of 20 the prevalence of severe subnormality is $3 \cdot 7$ per 1000 in England and Wales. (Prevalence rates are usually expressed in rates per 1000.) This is nearly ten times the expected rate of $0 \cdot 04\%$. Recently, Rutter, Graham and Yule (1970), in a study of children aged 5 to 15 years on the Isle of Wight, found that 37 children out of 11,865 were not attending school by reason of severe subnormality. (This was prior to the change in legislation restoring the right of education to such children.) This gives a prevalence rate of $3 \cdot 1$ per 1000 in this age range. For once, the administrative prevalence is close to expectation from other studies.

Kushlick (1966) shows that the rates for severe subnormality are similar for urban and rural areas. Approximately one quarter to one third of all severely subnormal children have Down's Syndrome (Mongolism). The prevalence rate for mongolism is approximately 1 per 1000 (Carter, 1958), and only about 10 per cent of mongols have IQs over 50.

Figures for the prevalence rate of severe subnormality are surprisingly consistent across different countries, despite differences in survey methods, which make detailed comparisons difficult. In the USA, the Onondaga County (New York State, 1955) survey yielded rates of $3 \cdot 6$ per 1000 at ages 5–17, whilst a Baltimore survey (Lemkau et al., 1943) found $3 \cdot 3$ per 1000 at ages 10–14. Nowadays, differences in terminology and legal definitions at times obscure the consistencies which are present when psychometric definitions are employed.

When it comes to estimating the prevalence of mild subnormality, there are more difficulties. As Kushlick (1966) points out, the category of IQ 50 to 70 has not proved useful either clinically or administratively. In other words, whilst such a low IQ can be called a disability, it is not necessarily so handicapping as to bring the child to the attention of the services. In his earlier study in Salford (Kushlick, 1961), he found that the highest *administrative* prevalence rate for mild subnormality was 8·6 per 1000 in the 15 to 19 year age group. This is less than half the expected number of 22 per 1000. Looking at the population of schools for educationally subnormal children, the total number attending is less than half of the 2% expected, if all children of 50 to 70 attended. As was noted above, the number either actually attending a facility or on its waiting list is but a poor guide to the need for that facility in the total community.

However, schools for ESN children are not intended to cater solely for children in the IQ 50 to 70 range. They are intended, as their name implies, to cater for *educationally* subnormal children and not intellectually subnormal ones. Educationally subnormal children are defined as those who 'by reason of limited ability or other conditions resulting in educational retardation require some specialised form of education wholly or partly in substitution for the education normally given in ordinary schools' (Ministry of Education, 1959). In other words, in Britain, these facilities are provided to alleviate the *educational needs* of the children rather than to act as a sanctuary for children with a heterogeneous set of defects and disabilities. That these schools are catering for educational needs can be seen in the finding that about 34% of children in ESN schools have IQs over 70 (Ministry of Education, 1962).

In the more recent Isle of Wight surveys (Rutter, Tizard and Whitmore, 1970), out of 2334 children in the 10 and 11 year age groups, 59 (or 2·53%) were found to have IQs below 70 on the Wechsler Intelligence Scale for Children. Of these children, 9 were severely subnormal and not attending school, two attended a special unit for spastic children. Of the remaining 48 mildly subnormal children, 20 attended the local day school for ESN children whilst no less than 28 went to ordinary schools. About one quarter of the children of this age at the ESN school scored above 70 IQ on the WISC.

Pursuing this question further, the reading attainment of these children was examined. It was found that the reading attainment of the intellectually retarded in ordinary schools was considerably better than that of the intellectually retarded children in the ESN school. The seven children at the ESN school who had IQs above 70 were reading even more poorly than the remainder. Their educational retardation was more pronounced than that of the intellectually retarded children.

All of this shows that whilst in general there is a close relationship between intelligence and academic attainment, this correlation is far from perfect. Thus, placement in special schools should be in terms of the child's *educational needs*, not just in terms of IQ. In Britain, it is recognized that there are many *'slow-learning'* children who will require special educational help. Officially, the suggestion is that 10% of children will have minor defects and disabilities which will require extra help, mainly through special classes and remedial facilities within the ordinary school system. Over the country as a whole, ESN school places are available for only 1% of the school population.

Causes of intellectual retardation

The increase in prevalence over and above the expected frequency, particularly the increase in severe subnormality, has often been interpreted as indicating that there are two broad groups of mentally retarded. Firstly, there is the large group of mainly moderately subnormal children who are identified because someone is always at the low end of any distribution. Only about one quarter of children in ESN schools have clinical signs of brain damage (Stein and Susser, 1960). Kushlick (1966) argues that the causation of mild subnormality is more likely to be social and cultural in nature. The second, smaller group, mainly the severely subnormal, are as they are because something catastrophic has happened in their development: injury at birth, chromosomal abnormality or infectious disease.

Now, Gruenberg (1966) has shown that the statistical excess in itself does not argue for a differentiation between 'subcultural' and 'pathological' varieties of intellectual retardation. Nevertheless, there are very important differences between the mildly and the severely retarded. These have been summarized by Tizard (1966a):

'The severely retarded (with IQs in general less than 50) are biologically and socially distinguishable from the mildly retarded. Their subnormality is brought about by different causes as far as is known; they have quite a different expectation of life; the overwhelming majority are infertile (i.e. have no children) and are probably not fecund (i.e. not capable of having children); they are ineducable in the sense of not being able to learn how to usefully read and write; probably only one in ten is employable in the open market even in times of full employment and a shortage of labour; their dependence on adults is life-long. Eighty or ninety per cent of the mildly retarded, on the contrary are not like this. ... Although the mildly retarded are backward in school and many are socially immature and incompetent as adolescents, the majority eventually grow up, settle down, and disappear from sight (integrated into the general population).'

Further evidence to support this sort of distinction comes from studies of their distribution in the different social classes. Severely subnormal children are born to parents of all social classes; mildly subnormal children come predominantly from the lower social classes (Kushlick, 1966).

Beyond this, we are woefully ignorant of the causes of intellectual retardation. Evidence of brain damage is present in the vast majority of severely subnormal children (Crome, 1960), but the reasons for this are not clear. The largest single cause of severe subnormality is Down's Syndrome (Mongolism), a chromosomal abnormality in which each cell has one extra chromosome. Not only are the majority of these children intellectually retarded, they have many other physical defects and disabilities: heart lesions, defects of the lenses in the eyes, hearing defects and proneness to upper respiratory tract infections. The *incidence* of Down's syndrome is about one in 600 births. Many such children die before reaching school age, but improved medical care has resulted in more surviving to adulthood. Down's syndrome accounts for between a quarter and a third of known severely abnormal children.

About another third of cases are strongly suspected of being caused by a wide variety of other genetic, chromosomal, biochemical and physical abnormalities. (Berg and Kirman, 1959; Robinson and Robinson, 1970). In the remaining third, it is difficult to suggest even possible causal factors.

Multiple handicap and intellectual retardation

Intellectually retarded children are, as a group, amongst the most handicapped in the population. For example, in the Isle of Wight surveys (Rutter, Tizard and Whitmore, 1970), 90 per cent of children with IQs below 70 had at least one other handicapping condition. The lower the IQ, the more likely was the child to have multiple defects and disabilities. Physical handicaps, perceptual dysfunction, brain damage and epilepsy, to say nothing of social, emotional and education disorders, are all common among severely subnormal children. The extent of the overlap among handicaps will be discussed later.

Treatment and prognosis

There is no one cause of intellectual retardation, and there can certainly be no one 'treatment'. Mental retardation is not like some physical illness which can be cured by a special drug. In fact, the concept of 'cure' is out of place in this context. Likewise, society is moving away from the days when custodial care was all that was offered to the severely subnormal. Appropriate education (in the broadest sense of the word) and more child-orientated management practices can go far to improve the quality of life of the subnormal (Tizard, 1964; King, Raynes and Tizard, 1971).

Studies of intellectual development of the intellectually retarded show that, under appropriate conditions, more can be attained in the way of social and educational skills than was believed twenty or thirty years ago (Clarke and Clarke, 1973; Heber and Garber, 1971). Recent advances in behaviour modification techniques (Bricker, 1973; Gardner, 1971), hold out great hope for further improving the subnormal's quality of life. Even so, there will be a need for all forms of social, educational and medical help, including residential care, for a long time to come. However, as the Wessex experiment has shown, long-term residential care can be provided economically in small units within the community.

2. EDUCATIONAL DISORDERS

In considering the definition and prevalence of educational disorders, it is the educational handicap which is being studied rather than the defects or disabilities underlying the handicap. Children can have difficulties with any part of the school curriculum—from mastering the still basic subjects of reading, writing and mathematics, to having difficulty in any particular subject such as French and

History. However, it is difficult to reach agreement on what constitutes a handicap in, say, learning French. Children having difficulty in mastering a foreign language are usually persuaded to stop studying it, rather than be classified as 'retarded French learners'. Somehow, this latter sort of 'diagnosis' is rarely made, and the term 'educational disorder' is more commonly applied to difficulties in mastering reading, writing, spelling and mathematics.

Even within the basic subjects, most attention has been placed on learning reading skills. In an educational system where independent reading is the key to much independent learning, the reason for this emphasis on reading is obvious. As Burt (1950) puts it:

> 'A disability in reading operates in a more general way than a disability in arithmetic (or other subject). From the earliest years the child is heavily handicapped. If he cannot read a word he is not likely to spell it; and if he cannot spell, he is hopelessly at a loss in written composition. Further, the poor reader will eventually become backward in arithmetic as well, simply because he cannot make out the problems written on the board or printed in the text book. For a similar reason as the time goes on he will fall behind in all other studies that depend on book work—geography, history and even nature study and sciences—indeed wherever reading, note taking and essay writing are required.'

Where studies of reading difficulty can be numbered in their thousands, studies of spelling and writing problems can be counted only in their hundreds. Good studies of mathematical difficulties are notable by their rarity. Thus, this section must concentrate on reading disorders, but the fact that children have other sorts of educational difficulties will not be forgotten.

Terminology

Despite the multiplicity of studies of reading disorders, it is difficult to get good estimates of the prevalence rate, let alone any coherent view of the nature and extent of any associated handicaps. This can be accounted for in two ways: (i) hardly two studies have used the same definition of reading disorder; (ii) even where definitions have been carefully spelled out, the ensuing studies have been of highly selected groups. There have been very few well-planned epidemiological studies of reading difficulty.

In common-sense terms, a child can be deemed a poor reader if he is reading significantly below the level that is expected of him. The difficulties in agreeing on a definition come in attempting to operationalize 'significantly' and 'expected of him'. To deal with the latter, expectation can be based on the average level achieved on some standardized test of reading by all children of the same age (in Britain) or school grade (in America). In other words, one cuts off the lower end of the reading distribution at some arbitrary point and says that scores below this level indicate *reading backwardness*. However, to appeal to 'common sense' again, one normally expects dull children to attain reading scores more appropriate to younger normal children and, conversely, bright children should be reading a bit above the average. Discrepancies between obtained scores and those expected on the basis of ability give rise to the concept of *underachievement* and children who are 'significantly' underachieving in reading are said to be *reading retarded.*

Controversy has raged in the educational journals over how best to compare the actual and the expected reading levels. In the days when mental age (MA) was regarded as an index of the upper limit to scholastic attainment, it came as an embarrassment to find children whose Attainment Age exceeded their MA. In the 1920s, the ratio of Attainment Age to Mental Age was used as an 'Accomplishment Quotient' (Franzen, 1920), and AQs above 100 were regarded as rare exceptions. 'They occur sporadically in a few bookworms who show an extra zeal or talent in academic work, but less practical shrewdness and common sense. They occur rather more frequently in dull youngsters who have been assiduously coached by a good teacher . . .' (Burt, 1937). Somewhat uncharacteristically, Burt for once did not examine empirical data to seek support for this view.

Accomplishment Quotients, Attainment Quotients, Attainment Ratios and the like were severely criticized by Crane (1959). The most serious objections to their use are statistical, and the most important objection stems from the operation of the 'regression effect' (Crane, 1959; Thorndike, 1963). Wherever the correlation between measures (in this case between mental age and reading age) is less than perfect, the children who are well *above* average on one measure will be less superior on the other, and those who are well *below* average on the first measure will be less inferior on the second. For example, the average reading age of ten-year-olds with an average mental age of thirteen years will *not* be thirteen years, it will be more like twelve years. It was the opposite effect which Burt was interpreting as due to the effects of a good teacher.

Once Crane's (1959) objections to accomplishment quotients had been taken to heart, it was argued that it was better to compare attainment and ability by taking differences between standardized scores. This procedure is still very common in educational practice, but, as Thorndike (1963) points out, it does nothing to avoid the regression effects.

'If a simple difference between aptitude and achievement standard scores, or a ratio of achievement to aptitude measures, is computed, the high aptitude group will appear primarily to be "underachievers" and the low aptitude group to be "over-achievers". For this reason it is necessary to define "underachievement" as discrepancy of actual achievement from the *predicted* value, predicted upon the basis of the regression equation between aptitude and achievement. A failure to recognize this regression effect has rendered questionable, if not meaningless, much of the research on "under-achievement" ' (Thorndike, 1963).

The technique of regression analysis has long been available, but has been applied very rarely, and then mainly by British investigators. Ravenette (1961) predicted children's reading ages on Schonell's Graded Word Reading Test from their scores on a vocabulary test. Fransella and Gerver (1965) extended the technique to a multiple regression analysis predicting Schonell G.W.R.T. scores from WISC Verbal Scale IQ and Chronological Age. However, the equation was based on data gathered at a psychiatric clinic, and is therefore of limited applicability. Yule (1967) refined the procedure by using data from the epidemiological studies on the Isle of Wight.

Thus, following common practice, it is now possible to define both *reading backwardness* and *reading retardation* in statistically acceptable terms. If these definitions are also meaningful educationally, it becomes possible to estimate the prevalence of the two statistically separable types of reading disorder. Whether this distinction is educationally and psychologically meaningful is, of course, an empirical question open to experimental investigation.

Prevalence of reading disorders

Following Schonell (1942) and Burt (1950) it has become customary in Britain to consider a pupil as *backward* in reading if at age ten years he has a reading age of $8\frac{1}{2}$ years on a standardized test. Now, as Chall (1970) has noted, the same level of backwardness means different things at different ages; $1\frac{1}{2}$ years backwardness is more serious in an eight-year-old child than in a fourteen-year-old.

In a study of all 1544 children aged 7 years in Dumbartonshire, Clark (1970) found that 18% of boys and 12·5% of girls had reading quotients of 85 or less; i.e. they had not got beyond the earliest stages of learning to read. This sort of finding is repeated on a national scale in the National Child Development Study. Again reporting on the attainment of seven-year-olds, it was found that 10% of children had not made a start with reading and a further 38% had not mastered the mechanics of reading (Pringle *et al.*, 1966). Thus, although the school system expected the children to have mastered the mechanics of reading, almost 50% had failed to attain that goal.

Vernon (1957) and Morris (1966) both summarize the literature on the prevalence of reading backwardness, and all studies agree that the rate is uncomfortably high. For example, a Ministry of Education (1950) report estimated that 24% of eleven-year-olds had reading ages of 9 years or less. Since then, there is little hard evidence of any dramatic improvement in reading standards (Start and Wells, 1972).

A harsh definition of reading backwardness was used in the Isle of Wight studies (Rutter, Tizard and Whitmore, 1970): Reading backwardness was defined as an attainment in reading accuracy or reading comprehension on the Neale test (Neale, 1958) which was 28 months or more below chronological age. In the study of 9- and 10-year-old children, no fewer than 6·6% were found to be backward in reading. Boys outnumbered girls in a ratio of about two to one and, as a group, these children showed more neurological and developmental difficulties than the normal population.

Reading retardation was defined in the Isle of Wight studies as an attainment on either the reading accuracy or reading comprehension scales of the Neale test which was 28 months or more below the level predicted on the basis of each child's age and short WISC IQ (Yule, 1967). The cut-off point was chosen on the grounds that such a degree of retardation (which would be expected in about $2\frac{1}{2}$ per cent of school children) is likely to be a severe handicap at school. In the event, 3·7% of the children were identified as having such a severe level of reading retardation, and there were grounds for believing that even this underestimates the size of the problem.

The retarded readers differed both from the general population and from the generally backward readers in a number of interesting ways. The sex distribution was even more marked: more than three boys to every girl; they were, by definition, a more intelligent group; and there were differences on measures of language development, and neurological status (Rutter and Yule, 1973). More importantly, in a follow-up study, it was found that the prognosis for the retarded readers was significantly worse than that of the backward readers, although both groups made very little progress overall (Yule, 1973). This latter study gives some practical justification for making the statistical differentiation between the two types of poor reader.

More recently, in a study of all ten-year-old children in an inner London borough, Berger and Yule (1972), using the same procedures and definitions as used in the Isle of Wight studies, have found a greatly increased prevalence of reading retardation. Approximately 11% of 'indigenous' children (i.e. children both of whose parents were born in Britain, as opposed to the children of immigrant parents) were found to be retarded readers, a rate nearly three times greater than found on the Isle of Wight.

Clearly, there is no one prevalence rate for reading difficulties. There are different *types* of reading disorder with different distributions in the population and different prognoses. The prevalence rate varies according to geographical region and to social class. However, the rates quoted above make it clear that we cannot afford to be complacent about the reading attainment of junior school children. The handicap associated with a disability of reading is both pervasive and long-lasting.

'Dyslexia'

No account of severe reading retardation would be complete without a brief discussion of this concept. Various terms are used by different authors, word-blindness, strephosymbolia, specific dyslexia, developmental dyslexia and congenital alexia, to name but a few (Naidoo, 1972; Orton, 1937; Rabinovitch *et al.*, 1954). The World Federation of Neurologists defined Specific Developmental Dyslexia as: 'A disorder manifested by difficulty in learning to read despite conventional instruction, adequate intelligence, and socio-cultural opportunity. It is dependent upon fundamental cognitive disabilities which are frequently of constitutional origin.'

Thus, neurologists are in no doubt about the existence of a specific syndrome, and they go further in postulating a constitutional aetiology. Yet many educators remain to be convinced that this 'syndrome' is qualitatively different from what has been termed reading retardation in the discussion above. Rutter (1969) lists the characteristics which have usually been associated with dyslexia as: 'a family history of reading difficulties, disorders in speech and language; severe and bizarre spelling errors; arithmetic difficulties, clumsiness and incoordination; difficulties in the perception of space relationships; directional confusion; right-left confusion;

disordered temporal orientation; difficulties in naming colours and in reorganizing the meaning of pictures; and inadequate, inconsistent or mixed cerebral dominance'. He then notes that 'if you look hard enough and long enough any combination of features can be found in some child'. However, when he examined the data on the group of retarded readers in the Isle of Wight he found two things: (i) that taken one at a time, each of the above associated factors was indeed commoner in the retarded reader group than in the control group; but (ii) the factors did *not* cluster together to form either one or even a small number of distinct syndromes.

This latter conclusion was confirmed by Naidoo (1972) in her study of 98 'dyslexic' boys seen at the Word Blind Centre in London. At the end of a long investigation she concluded that, 'The evidence from this study does not support the existence of clearly defined sub-types of dyslexia'. It seems, then, that the concept of 'dyslexia' is of limited value in the educational setting.

Other educational problems

Reading is not the whole of education. Children can also be handicapped in mathematics, spelling, spoken language and any other area of the curriculum. However, good studies of the prevalence of handicap in these areas are sadly lacking. Although we know that backward and retarded readers also have considerable difficulties with spelling and arithmetic (Rutter, Tizard and Whitmore, 1970), it would be surprising if some good readers did not also have difficulties in these other areas. Thus, the prevalence rates quoted earlier for reading retardation and backwardness must be considered as very minimal estimates of the numbers of children having severe problems with academic work. (Speech and language disorders are considered separately later.)

Prognosis and treatment of reading difficulties

The outlook for poor readers is not good. Both reading retardation and reading backwardness have poor prognoses. In the Isle of Wight study, the average reading age of the retarded readers at $14\frac{1}{2}$ years of age was $8\frac{3}{4}$ years on Accuracy and $9\frac{1}{4}$ years on Comprehension (Yule, 1973). In fact, the progress of the retarded readers was slightly worse than that of the backward readers, although both groups were still very handicapped in their reading.

These findings agree with those of Morris (1966) who reports that more than half the poor readers whom she identified at age nine were still markedly backward at school-leaving age. Of Clark's (1970) 7-year-old backward readers (scoring reading quotients of 85 or less) half were still at least two years backward at age 10 years. The consensus of findings from these and other studies is that most disabled readers who are not given effective treatment continue to be severely handicapped in their reading throughout their school days.

The literature on remedial reading is not very encouraging. Remedial help provided on a small-group basis leads to some modest short-term gains, but unless help is continued the improvement is shortlived (Collins, 1961; Lovell *et al.*, 1962,

1963; Chazan, 1967; Shearer, 1967; Cashdan and Pumphrey, 1969). Individual remedial help may be of greater value. Programmed learning has its advocates (Winsberg, 1969), but it does not appear to be in widespread use. Of greater promise is the approach of Staats (Staats, 1970; Staats, Brewer and Gross, 1970) based on the principles of operant conditioning. Despite some impressive results (Wolf *et al.*, 1968) this approach needs further evaluation.

There are many other approaches to helping poor readers and the very multiplicity of the techniques bears grim witness to our ignorance of how to help children with reading difficulties.

3. PSYCHIATRIC DISORDERS

'Maladjustment' has been recognized as a problem for many years. The term was used in the 1920s, but was more widely adopted in Britain after the Second World War. However, it has proved difficult to get agreement as to what is 'maladjustment', 'psychiatric disorder', 'behavioural deviance' and the like.

The Underwood Report suggested that '. . . a child may be regarded as maladjusted who is developing in ways that have a bad effect on himself or his fellows and cannot without help be remedied by his parents, teachers and the other adults in ordinary contact with him'. However, it proved difficult to move from this broad formulation to more specific definitions and both the Underwood Committee and its Scottish counterpart (Scottish Education Department, 1964) failed to provide adequate estimates of the numbers of children who might require special educational treatment because of maladjustment. The position has improved only slightly since the publication of those reports.

Classification of psychiatric disorders

It will be recalled that one of the purposes of any classification system is to help communication between professionals so that in time better understanding of children's handicaps will emerge. There has been a great need for an acceptable system of classification in child psychiatry for years (Tizard, 1966b).

The Underwood Report (1955), following a medical model, had regarded children's difficulties as 'symptoms', and grouped them under six broad headings:
1. 'Nervous' disorders (i.e. disorders which are primarily emotional), such as fears, depression, anxiety, timidity.
2. Habit disorders: stammering, asthma, enuresis, nail biting.
3. Behaviour disorders: unmanageableness, jealous behaviour, stealing, aggression.
4. Organic disorders: conditions following head injuries, etc.
5. Psychotic behaviour: hallucinations, bizarre symptoms.
6. Educational and vocational difficulties, such as backwardness not accounted for by dullness.

Although widely used, this system is very limited. It calls for a great deal of interpretation in deciding, say, what is 'jealous behaviour', and also it does not take sufficient account of the age of the child (Gulliford, 1971). For example, as seen earlier, fears are commoner at some ages than others (Shepherd, Oppenheim and Mitchell, 1971), so that they do not necessarily indicate any gross deviation from normal development. But as an initial scheme, the Underwood classification spurred others on to improve it.

In a widely acclaimed article, Rutter (1965) put forward an eleven-fold scheme based on a wide review of the research literature. The two largest groups of problems are

1. *Neurotic disorders.*
2. *Antisocial or conduct disorders.*

Most children with difficulties present with a large neurotic or chiefly antisocial clinical picture. The neurotic disorders have a far better prognosis than the antisocial ones. However, in some children, the picture is not clear-cut so that a third category was called for:

3. *Mixed groups.*
4. *Developmental disorders:* enuresis or language disorders occurring in isolation would be placed in this heterogeneous category.
5. *The hyperkinetic syndrome:* this is a distinct type of severe overactivity.
6. *Child Psychosis:* this includes the rare condition, *early infantile autism*, and all disorders in this category are distinguished by their very poor prognoses.
7. *Psychoses developing at or after puberty* which are similar to adult-type schizophrenia.
8. *Mental subnormality.*
9. *Educational retardation as a primary problem.*
10. *Depression.*
11. *Adult-type neurotic disorders.*

Like the Underwood Committee before him, Rutter put this scheme forward in a tenative way in the hope that it would be refined as people noted difficulties in its use. And there will always be difficulties in using any scheme for, as Kanner (1968) pointed out, children do not read the text books and so do not present neatly to fit in with any scheme.

More recently, the World Health Organization have been preparing to alter the International Classification of Diseases. To this end, a 'tri-axial' classification of child psychiatric disorders has been proposed. Not only will the category of the disorder be noted, but the intellectual level of the child and associated or aetiological factors will also be recorded (Rutter *et al.*, 1969). The classification of clinical psychiatric syndromes proposed is:

0.0	Normal variation
1.0	Adaptation reaction
2	Specific developmental disorder
2.1	Hyperkinetic disorder
2.2	Speech and language disorder

2.3   Other specific learning disorder
2.4   Abnormal clumsiness ('developmental dyspraxia')
2.5   Enuresis (as isolated disorder)
2.6   Encopresis (as isolated disorder)
2.7   Tics
2.8   Stuttering
3.0   Conduct disorder
4.0   Neurotic disorder
5   Psychosis
5.1   Infantile
5.2   Disintegrative
5.3   Schizophrenia
5.4   Other
6.0   Personality disorder
7.0   'Psychosomatic' disorder
8   Other clinical syndrome
8.1   Acute confusional state
8.2   Dementia
8.3   Gilles de la Tourette Syndrome
8.4   Anorexia nervosa
8.5   Any other clinical syndrome
9.0   Manifestation of mental subnormality only (but *not* including any of the
        listed syndromes)

So it can be seen how classification schemes have developed over a fifteen-year period. They become both more elaborate and more precise. This is both inevitable and desirable as the schemes reflect the growth in knowledge and the richness of individual adjustment.

Prevalence of psychiatric disorder

In the Isle of Wight studies (Rutter, Tizard and Whitmore, 1970), a 'clinical-diagnostic' approach was used in defining psychiatric disorder which ... 'was judged to be present when there was an abnormality of behaviour, emotions, or relationships which was continuing up to the time of assessment and was sufficiently marked and sufficiently prolonged to cause handicap to the child himself and/or distress or disturbance in the family or community' (p. 148). The child's behaviour was assessed in relation to what was normal for his age, and it was found that two psychiatrists assessing the same children independently agreed in the vast majority of cases not only on whether any abnormality was present, but also on what form the abnormality took.

Out of 2199 ten- and eleven-year-old children whose homes were on the Isle of Wight, 126 (or 5·7%) were found to have a clinically significant psychiatric disorder. Despite the elaborate two-stage selection procedure for identifying cases, some cases were missed, and a corrected prevalence rate of 6·8% was estimated. Children with neurotic disorders accounted for 2·5% and those with antisocial and mixed disorders accounted for 4·0%. Eight children had monosymptomatic enuresis and only 5 children had other problems of sufficient severity to meet the study's criterion.

Somewhat surprisingly, no cases of persisting *school refusal* were identified. Clinic cases of school refusal are reported to be commonest at age 11 (Chazan, 1962), often following on a change of school (Hersov, 1960). It is possible that the Isle of Wight is atypical with regard to the frequency of school refusal.

Absence from school is very common. In 1954–64, the annual rate of absence from school was 10% (Tyerman, 1968), but it is largely accounted for by illness. Some 80 to 90% of all absences are of this legitimate type. Tyerman suggests a three-fold classification of 'illegal' absences, (i) withholding by parents for their own purposes—affecting about 12 children in a thousand; (ii) truancy: without parental connivance—estimated to affect 5 children in a thousand every now and again; (iii) school phobia, where the child is either afraid of school or afraid of separating from home, estimated to occur in about one child in a thousand. If Tyerman's (1968) estimates are correct, then it is less surprising that such a rare condition was missed on the Isle of Wight survey which, by its very nature, is more geared to estimating the prevalence of commonly occurring disorders.

To estimate the true prevalence of rare conditions, surveys of larger populations are required. For example, Lotter (1966) studied the prevalence of infantile autism in the county of Middlesex (population 78,000). He obtained a prevalence rate of 4·5 per 10,000, making this a very rare disorder. Even so, it is commoner than blindness and almost as common as deafness. This prevalence estimate has been confirmed in other studies both in Britain and America (Rutter, 1971).

Speech and language disorders have been classified under the heading psychiatric disorder, although they truly form part of a different group of developmental disorders. It has been estimated (MacKeith and Rutter, 1972) that at the age of 5 years, when children first start school, approximately 5% speak so poorly that strangers cannot understand them. About 1% of children at this age also have a handicapping language delay (Herbert and Wedell, 1970).

More serious language disorders are far less common. Severe language retardation, i.e. children of average intelligence who had only a few single words at age 3 and only limited connected language at age 5, occurs in about 0·75 per 1000 children (Ingram, 1963). Both severe and mild types of language disorder are associated with later difficulties in learning to read (Rutter, Tizard and Whitmore, 1970), and hence have important implications in planning educational services. A more detailed discussion of the classification of speech and language disorders in young children is to be found in Ingram (1972).

Prognosis and treatment

Prognosis varies markedly with different psychiatric syndromes. The thirty year follow-up studies of Robins (1966) have shown that children who had presented with neurotic disorders in childhood grew up to be very little more disturbed than a control group. In sharp contrast, the outcome of the antisocial children was very poor. Most had severe problems in adulthood, ranging from marital disharmony to criminal behaviour and psychiatric illness. Other follow-up studies reflect the same picture (Robins, 1970).

Traditionally, children with psychiatric problems have been treated mainly at child guidance clinics by some form of psychoanalytically derived psychotherapy. There is very little evidence that this has any beneficial effects (Levitt, 1971; Rachman, 1971). It is possible that such approaches are of benefit to children with some forms of interpersonal difficulties. Fortunately, there are other therapies now available. Enuresis can readily be treated by the 'bell-and-pad' technique, and the majority of cases are continent in a very short time (Lovibond, 1964; Turner, Young and Rachman, 1970). Behaviour modification techniques can be taught to parents (Patterson and Gullion, 1968) and to teachers (Berger, 1972; and Ward in Chapter 5 of this book), and through them children can be helped to learn new behavioural patterns.

4. PHYSICAL DEFECTS AND DISORDERS

The main problem in estimating the prevalence of physical disorders in the child population is one of deciding the *severity* of the disorder to be included. It has been estimated that nearly three-quarters of all children will be seen at least once by the general practitioner in the course of a year (Elder, 1962). Minor illnesses account for most absences from school. Chronic physical handicap is far less common.

The problem was faced in the Isle of Wight study (Rutter, Tizard and Whitmore, 1970) by including '... physical disorders which (a) were of a type which in childhood usually lasted at least one year (i.e. were chronic), (b) were associated with persisting or recurrent handicap of some kind and (c) were known to have been present during the twelve months preceding the survey (i.e. were currently present)' (p. 275). Cases were picked up from hospital records, a school register of physical handicap and lists compiled by head teachers, speech therapists and similar professional groups. During the intensive, second stage of the inquiry, further information was obtained from the parents, and all this resulted in 5·7% of ten- and eleven-year-old children being identified as having a physical disorder.

Asthma was found to be the commonest disorder, accounting for 2·3% of the total population. These children tended to be brighter than the average, but to have about double the expected rate of specific reading retardation.

Epilepsy was the next commonest condition, occurring in 8·9 per 1000 children. A rate of 8 per thousand is usually found and this means that there are about 60,000 school children in England and Wales with epilepsy (Gulliford, 1971). These children, as a group, have a high rate of reading difficulties, and there is some suggestion in the literature that they have even greater difficulties with arithmetic (Yule, 1973b). Most are educated in ordinary schools, where their special educational needs do not appear to be well understood.

Cerebral palsy, a disorder of motor functioning resulting from a permanent non-progressive defect of the immature brain, was found in 2·6 per 1000 in a study of five- to fifteen-year old Isle of Wight children (Rutter, Graham and Yule, 1970). This figure agrees well with those of other studies.

Other *brain disorders* occur in about 1·7 per thousand children.

Orthopaedic disorders, such as congenital malformation of the hip, were found in 3·4 per 1000.

Heart disease occurred in 2·4 per 1000.

Deafness of sufficient severity to require the wearing of a hearing aid or attendance at a special school was found in 1·8 per 1000 in the Isle of Wight study. However, this is only part of the total picture. Mild losses of 20 decibels at two or more frequencies occur in nearly 4% of school children (Anderson, 1967). It is well recognized that partial hearing losses, particularly affecting the higher tones, interfere with both language development and the acquisition of reading.

Diabetes mellitus was found in 1·2 per 1000.

Disorders of the Central Nervous System which did not involve the brain were also found in 1·2 per 1000.

There were many other conditions which occurred at rates less than one per thousand, whose prevalence could not be accurately estimated in the Isle of Wight study.

Blindness and partial sightedness were found in 1·3 per 1000 children in the whole age range in the Isle of Wight (Rutter, Graham and Yule, 1970). This is a conservative estimate, and other studies yield figures of 1·9 per 1000 (Oppé, 1972). Complete blindness, however, is very rare. These figures underestimate the proportion of children with minor visual defects. The National Child Development Study (Davie, Butler and Goldstein, 1972) reports that 3·5% of all 7-year-olds in their national sample have moderate or severe visual defects in their better eyes. Definite *squints* were reported in over 3 per cent of the children.

This is a formidable list of disorders, each of which has notable handicapping sequelae. It must also be remembered that these categories are *not* mutually exclusive. Many children are multiply handicapped. In particular, where the brain and central nervous system are involved, the child is likely to have more than one handicapping condition. The most handicapped of all, as a group, are children with severe subnormality.

THE OVERALL PREVALENCE OF HANDICAPPING CONDITIONS

In discussing the nature of epidemiological studies, it was noted that the total number of conditions was likely to exceed the number of handicapped children, because many children are multiply handicapped. For example, one third of retarded readers have a significant and recognizable psychiatric disorder (Rutter, Tizard and Whitmore, 1970). Most severely subnormal children have at least one accompanying physical defect.

The Isle of Wight surveys were designed to estimate the extent of handicapping conditions in the middle years of childhood. Looking at the overlap amongst the four groups of handicaps studied—intellectual retardation, educational retardation and backwardness, psychiatric disorder and physical disability—the following picture emerged.

One handicap only   120·8 per 1000
Two handicaps   30·5 per 1000
Three handicaps   7·8 per 1000
Four handicaps   2·3 per 1000

This means that 161·4 per thousand school children at the end of their junior schooling have at least one major handicap of educational concern. In other words 16 per cent, or *one child in six* in the 9 to 11 year age group, is handicapped to a significant extent.

As was noted earlier, higher rates of disorder are found in other geographical areas, particularly in socially deprived inner cities. Thus the figure of one in six with a handicap is likely to be a minimal estimate. This, then, is the extent of the problem facing society, and in particular the educational system, for teachers have to find ways of helping these children to overcome their handicaps and to capitalize on their assets. How this is done is discussed in the rest of this present volume.

CONCLUDING REMARKS

This chapter has concentrated on the British literature on epidemiological studies largely because this is the most comprehensive available. Living on a crowded island with national services for both health and education has led to a tradition of national surveys of childrens' growth, development and adjustment (Douglas, Ross and Simpson, 1968; Davie, Butler and Goldstein, 1972; Scottish Council for Research in Education, 1949). These national studies, which by their very size must look extensively rather than intensively, and must make great use of questionnaires, have been supplemented by intensive local studies such as those in Newcastle (Spence *et al.*, 1954; Nelligan and Prudham, 1969), Buckinghamshire (Shepherd, Oppenheim and Mitchell, 1971), Dumbartonshire (Clark, 1970), Aberdeen (Birch *et al.*, 1970), and the Isle of Wight (Rutter, Tizard and Whitmore, 1970; Rutter, Graham and Yule, 1970). It is unlikely that the picture represented by the results of all these studies will be grossly unrepresentative of the prevalence of handicapping conditions in most western industrialized societies.

The size of the problem facing society makes it clear that not all handicapped children could be educated in special schools, even if this were considered to be desirable. In fact, most handicapped children are educated in ordinary day schools, and so remain better integrated with their peers than would otherwise be the case. However, there is a great need for teachers to be given a better training to be able to meet the special needs, both educational and social, of handicapped children. Epileptic or maladjusted children are not only found in special schools segregated from the rest of their peers; they are to be found in every ordinary school and their needs must be recognized to avoid compounding their existing handicap.

This is not to say that there is no value in separate, special schools. Sometimes, the need for specialist facilities argues for these to be concentrated in one place on economic grounds. Sometimes, the particular needs of a specific group, say autistic children, can best be discovered if they are taught as a group. But it is clear from the earlier quoted prevalence figures that children do not present as neatly packaged with only one handicap. Moreover, different disabilities often result in the same sorts of educational handicaps. Thus, in Britain at least, there is a perceptible move towards providing a more comprehensive sort of special education facility. Wherever possible, children are educated at ordinary schools, or small units within ordinary schools. The minority who cannot be so accommodated are increasingly catered for in special schools which pay less attention to the disabling condition and more to the resulting educational handicap.

So far 'education' has been discussed as if it only occurred within schools. Increasingly, it is being recognized that parents have a major role to play, or rather, that fact has been recognized for centuries and now it is being acted upon. Amongst the most exciting developments are the various early intervention programmes in America where parents are actually taught specific techniques to aid the development of their handicapped children (Bricker, 1973; Klaus and Gray, 1968; Heber and Garber, 1971). With increasing emphasis being placed internationally on preschool education, one can look forward to an era of greater cooperation between home and school.

Finally, it is evident from all studies of handicapping conditions that many handicapped children can be identified from a very early age. There is a widespread assumption that early identification is obviously a good thing. It is assumed that early identification necessarily leads to effective treatment and thus to an alleviation of handicap. In some instances this is probably true: early language training for deaf children, training in self-help skills for severely subnormal children. But in many instances, 'treatment' is not so clear and there is always a danger that some children get labelled too early, thus lowering their levels of expectation. These comments are obviously speculative, but are put to challenge the cry for early identification. This well-intentioned aim led to the widespread inauguration of 'risk registers' which were intended to alert health and education authorities to the special needs of handicapped children. As Alberman and Goldstein (1970) demonstrated, such registers are not always effective in ensuring that the appropriate services are delivered to those who need them most. Sometimes, so many non-handicapped children were being periodically reassessed as to prejudice the effective working of the total services. For these, and other reasons, it is increasingly being recommended that Risk and Observation Registers as presently formulated should be abandoned and be replaced by periodic screening of all children, both before and during school. This, it is argued, is more likely to ensure that children who need special care will receive it.

This chapter has attempted to do two things. Firstly, it has tried to examine the main concepts used by the professions involved in deciding which children require some form of special education. Secondly, it has examined the results of epidemiological studies in an attempt to provide a picture of the prevalence of educationally handicapping conditions. Of necessity, the review has been selective.

However, the overall finding that at least one child in six has a handicap of educational concern is witness to the need to examine in detail the provision of special educational services within the school system. The techniques required to meet the needs of handicapped children are discussed in the rest of this book.

CHAPTER 3

Orientations in Compensatory Education

K. G. O'BRYAN

Orientations to compensatory education are at last beginning to descend from the heights of public enthusiasm to the hard ground of educational reality.

When the first *Head Start* programmes were undertaken in the United States in the mid-sixties they represented a reflection of a growing public awareness that learning was not easy for the child born outside the mainstream of middle-class America. But this reflection was cast in the pale, half-light of interparty politics and shadowed by the vexed questions of racial, social and cultural differences. Predicated upon a view that those children who were unable to cope with the standard elementary school curriculum and who came from groups outside the white middle class were the products of 'cultural deprivation', the original Head Start project attempted to compensate for supposed language inadequacies, perceptual problems, attitudinal and motivational deficiencies, low self-image and poor quality behaviour patterns by providing preschool, multifaceted programmes of intellectual and academic instruction.

Poorly planned, hurriedly implemented, expensively financed and subtly self-righteous, the first Head Start programmes produced quick, initial results in the performance of the children enrolled in them, but these gains were rarely sustained (McDill, McDill and Sprehe, 1969). Furthermore, even these initial gains began to become harder to achieve as the project began to lose political and moral support towards the end of the sixties (Fleming, 1971).

Apologists for Head Start have argued that the programme was producing disappointing results, partly because of the excessive haste that accompanied its introduction, partly because of a lack of properly trained teachers and adequate facilities, and partly because not enough was known about the programme's clients. They were, in fact, correct, but they might have also noted that most programmes arising out of a moral or social conviction that 'something ought to be done—and quickly' have a tendency to come to similar grief.

Quite clearly, a great need did, and does, exist for educational concern for children unable to profit from the standard school procedures and current curriculum. It is, however, an open question whether it is the children who are 'culturally deprived' or whether the curriculum is culturally irrelevant. Furthermore, it seems fair to demand of compensatory educators that the present range of knowledge about child development, learning and cognitive theory, psycho-social development, cultural integrity and individual differences be considered in the establishment of any programme aimed at educational intervention in the preschool years. When such questions are asked, programmes begin to harden and goals descend from the remote to the achievable. In addition, theoretical positions are developed and carefully conceived approaches embodying basic instructional principles are instituted.

In short, the global programme aimed at achieving a total solution is replaced by a variety of approaches arising out of differing views of the problem and the means by which it might be solved. Such is the contemporary situation in compensatory education in North America.

Currently, vigorous controversy exists between proponents of several theoretical positions on the optimal approaches to the preschool education of those children who would otherwise encounter serious problems in their efforts to cope with the standard elementary school curriculum. Essentially, two basic divisions of orientation towards compensatory education can be defined: the orientation towards direct instructional programmes and the orientation towards self-expansion and experimental programmes. Broadly speaking, these divisions reflect the differences that currently exist between two schools of educational psychology, the behaviourist position which invokes predetermined reinforcement schedules to differentially conditioned sequential response behaviour, and the cognitive or phenomenological approach which argues that the whole act performed by the whole child interacting with his environment is the key to his intellectual development.

Not surprisingly, compensatory programmes reflecting these divisions embody the range from extreme positions to those bordering on the eclectic. Indeed, not all programmes accept the *principle* of compensatory education, some are frankly preventative, others are combinations of prevention and compensation. Furthermore, not all the orientations are directed towards classroom intervention. Several, especially those that are preventative, involve parent/child interaction and are home centred. A number of other approaches reject entirely the notion of compensation for cultural deprivation and insist that the problem is one of *educational* deprivation.

It is obviously not possible in this brief chapter to describe all the variations on the theme of compensatory education currently in progress in the homes and preschools of North America and the United Kingdom. However, an overall view of contemporary approaches to the problem can be provided by reference to eight programmes in which the author has either been a participant or has had the opportunity of first-hand observation. Two of these approaches, The Behaviour Analysis Classroom, and the Bereiter/Englemann Direct Instruction Pedagogy, are examples of intervention through direct instruction. The Ypsilanti Early Education Programme, the Play School and the Open Plan Classroom are representative of the experimental, developmental orientation, while the Harvard Preschool Project is an example of a parent/child interaction programme aimed at prevention. O'Bryan and Silverman's Indian Education Project is also a prevention programme, but it is orientated towards the proposition that cultural deprivation is not the basis of early school failure. The eighth approach to be considered is that of a mass-media compensatory programme, Sesame Street, in which a wide range of theoretical and practical ideas are employed.

Perhaps one of the most aggressive programmes in all compensatory education is the *Behaviour Analysis Classroom*, which vigorously employs the basic principles of behaviour learning theory. In this approach the emphasis is placed on precise, contingent reinforcement in order to enable desired behaviour to be shaped with a high degree of certainty. In essence, the Behavioural Analysis method requires an absolute structuring of the learner's environment, the development of motivational systems through direct teaching, the use of positive and of mildly aversive reinforcement, and a carefully compiled, complete diagnosis of the learner's current performance. To be successful it demands the definition of specific instructional objectives and assumes that the responsibility for defining these objectives is solely within the province of the adults of the classroom.

Learning in a Behavioural Analysis programme is controlled by a coordinated group of specifically trained professionals, paraprofessionals and volunteers. At least four adults are required to be present in the classroom in which there are about thirty children. In most cases the adults are the 'lead' teacher, whose responsibilities include programme preparation and reading instruction, her full-time teaching aide and two parent volunteers. The full-time aide is usually in charge of the mathematics programme while the two parent volunteers instruct in handwriting and spelling.

No child in a behavioural analysis classroom ever 'fails', for failure is not possible, provided that an adequate reinforcer is available and that the programme is properly applied. Reinforcement is considered the key to appropriate performance and, in most systems using the method, the reinforcement is based upon the token economy plan. Under this plan the learner is introduced to tokens as a means to purchasing desired activities or material goods. As soon as these tokens become sought-after the teacher is immediately in a position to reinforce desired behaviour. Subsequently the tokens may be superseded as reinforcers by the approval of the adults or peers but, initially at least, they are heavily and immediately used as direct rewards for correct responses. They are, of course, withheld whenever a child does not provide an appropriate response. Aversive reinforcement is also regularly employed, especially in cases involving what Bushell (1973, p. 109) calls 'behavior which is potentially damaging or dangerous'. Should any child engage in such behaviour he is sent to a penalty chair where he sits in isolation for a fixed interval before being allowed to return to the teacher of the group. If he then displays the proper pattern of responses he is quickly and liberally rewarded for his correct behaviour.

While learning in the behavioural analysis classroom is certainly a social affair in that the approval, praise, warmth and token liberality of the adults is central to the conditioning of the learners, very careful consideration needs to be given to the nature of the socialization, especially in its direct application to four-year-old children. As Evans (1971) pointed out, the procedure bears a very close relationship to a particular ethic of thrift, work, accumulation of material goods and eventual salvation. Since the decision upon what constitutes salvation for the preschooler rests with the adults in the classroom, the Behaviour Analysis programme can be considered to be a closed-system procedure aimed at preparing the learner for entry to an educational process demanding a similar set of learning skills and promoting desires for approved reward structures. Effectively this places the learner in a position of *having* to comply with the expected behavioural aims if he is to earn the desired reinforcement to which he has been so thoroughly conditioned.

Questions might also be asked on such basic issues as the degree to which an as-yet-incomplete, scientific conception of the child should be made the sole basis of an instructional programme; the potential destructiveness of such an approach on the individuality of the child; the narrowness of the instructional objectives; the stress upon skill development (reading, mathematics, handwriting and spelling); and the general lack of concern for the child's own potential for structuring the learning experience.

Nevertheless, there is substantial evidence of success in the achievement of the prescribed objectives (Whitlock and Bushell, 1967; Haring and Hauck, 1969; and others) and it must be noted that the approach aims at using every available moment in the compensatory classroom to direct the learners into obtaining successful experience in the basic subjects of the curriculum. Clearly, the Behavioural Analysis Classroom is one in which no time is spent without accountability, in which any spontaneous activity engaged in by the children is carefully channelled by selective shaping into a mould preset by the adults.

Time is of the essence in another orientation to compensatory education, the Bereiter/Englemann direct instruction method. Bereiter and Englemann (1966) concluded that the cause of the failure of many compensatory programmes could be traced to an inadequate use of available time in the preschool programme. Essentially, they argued that if a child came to the process of formal schooling a year or more behind his peers in language and conceptual skills he would need to double his learning rate in order to at least break even. He could not, therefore, be allowed the luxury of free play, exploratory activities or general investigation of the world. His language and conceptual skills deficits would prevent him from achieving success when he entered formal schooling and unless these skills were given top priority for development in the preschool (Bereiter and Englemann argued) he would surely fail. Accordingly the direct instruction approach concentrates upon academic skill development and awards top priority to language training.

Essentially, the programme is founded upon the view that very rigorous teaching methods are not harmful to preschool children and that emphasis would be placed upon hard work, attention and improvement. In line with this, Bereiter and Englemann described the classes as proceeding in a business-like manner but added that the atmosphere in them was 'usually friendly and pleasant, occasionally lightened by humour or playfulness' (1973, p. 178).

The basis of the direct instruction approach has been described by Bateman (1973) as that of 'clean teaching'. Task-irrelevant behaviour is reduced so that spontaneous exchanges between teacher and children are few in number and the efforts of all concerned are focused upon the specific task at hand. The pace is fast and the pressure intense, but only one lesson in each of language learning, arithmetic and reading is demanded on a single day. There is very heavy emphasis upon the elicitation of verbal responses which are usually required of the children in unison and all teaching is set up in planned sequences of small-step, instructional units. Heavy demands are placed upon the learners, no relaxation of intensity is permitted during the twenty-minute instructional period and there is little tolerance for inattentive behaviour or slipshod performance. Token exchange procedures are not considered necessary since the teacher's approval for correct responses or her severe rejection of incorrect or inadequate replies is regarded as sufficient to ensure the preschoolers' application to the task.

The key to the direct instruction approach is its one-to-one relationship to subsequent expected patterns of successful behaviour in the regular school system. If the system to be entered by the child demands skill in language use and in the logic of conception then, Bereiter and Englemann argue, it is up to the Head Start programme to supply these basic skills to those children whose prior experiences have not been of the kind likely to reach the level expected of school beginners.

The orientation to compensatory education reflected in the Bereiter/Englemann direct instruction pedagogy is not, as might be readily assumed, entirely behaviouristic. Despite Spodek's (1973) classification of the approach as an example of a behaviourist model couched in an application of associationistic learning theory, the essence of the method lies in a distinctly cognitive language learning theory. While the instructional methodology is undeniably stimulus-response, the expectation of the effect upon the learner as a result of his experience in the programme is a complex system of vertical transfer through which the learning of lower-order skills facilitates the processing of successively more complex material within conceptual systems.

It is perhaps interesting to note that while Englemann has continued in the strongly associationistic, direct instruction approach to reading and arithmetic and has developed several programmes in kit form, Bereiter has turned more towards the researching of conceptual skills and the development of the Open Court Kindergarten (Bereiter et al., 1970). This programme is based on the premise that the child's home and neighbourhood experiences need to be supplemented if he is to 'think constructively rather than merely to absorb' and to develop a 'consciousness of learning' (Bereiter et al., 1970, p. v).

The current version of the original Bereiter/Englemann programme is embodied in the commercial direct instruction arithmetic and reading programmes (DISTAR) which, with their emphasis on 'no nonsense', clean teaching, are far removed from the compensatory education direction taken by the Piagetian-orientated Ypsilanti Early Education programme.

The Ypsilanti project is predicated on a Piagetian view that the aim of education is the creation of possibilities of invention and discovery for the child rather than in attempting to transmit ready-made structures of knowledge. The stress in the programme is placed on cognitive development through the sensori-motor period to the level of conceptual thought (Laing, 1968) and four basic educational/developmental objectives have been established. These objectives include cognitive, perceptual motor, socio-emotional and language development and, while each is considered essential to the success of the compensatory programme, it is clear that the basis of the approach and its special quality are to be found in cognitive development.

The strong influence of Piaget is evident in the cognitive development objectives which include physical knowledge, logico-mathematical knowledge, social knowledge and linguistic representation. Physical knowledge is linked to the observable material properties of objects and phenomena. Dropping, squeezing, throwing, stretching, smelling, knocking and many other physical explorations of the properties of objects are encouraged in order to structure knowledge from the direct feedback available from real objects. This procedure is designed to develop the child's repertoire of actions in the confrontation of familiar objects as a prerequisite for finding out the physical nature of new, unfamiliar objects. This, in turn, is claimed by Kamii (1972) to assist in the creation of an attitude of curiosity and anticipation which will subsequently lead to an increased ability to define cause and effect relationships.

Kamii suggested that the second cognitive objective, logico-mathematical knowledge, is structured through the interaction of the child's coordinated actions with the results of these actions. While physical knowledge demands exploration of the specific properties of a given object, logico-mathematical knowledge derives from the relationships between and among objects. The essence of the point is that these relationships are constructed by the learner, rather than by evident, external reality. Three basic areas of logico-mathematical knowledge, classification, serialization and number, are to be found in the Ypsilanti curriculum and in each of these stress is placed upon the child's exploratory activities as a means to the achievement of mobility of thought.

Social knowledge, the third cognitive objective, is expected to be developed by interaction with other people. Again, the feedback principle is applied. Children are not directly instructed in social behaviour as would be the case in the Behaviour Analysis classroom; instead they learn from acting upon the real world of social interplay. This interplay is also the basis of the development of linguistic competence. Unlike the direct instruction method, the Ypsilanti programme does not recognize the centrality of language as the source or cause of learning. Rather, it is regarded as a tool of precise communication and the exchange of opinions (Kamii, 1972). At best, linguistic competence is seen as a stimulation of cognitive development through the structure of its symbolic qualities and its representational usefulness, but it is never considered the central issue in compensatory education.

The socio-emotional objectives of the Ypsilanti programme arise out of Piaget's integration of cognition and affect. According to Piaget (1954), affect provides the energy that produces cognitive development, therefore affectivity can accelerate, retard or prevent intellectual growth. The Ypsilanti project classroom attempts to provide a range of experiences for children so that their socio-emotional development will be conducive rather than disruptive to cognitive development. This is an important point in view of the proposition that the child in the compensatory classroom is often emotionally unprepared for learning, and it reflects a basic difference between the Piagetians and the direct instructionalists. In the Ypsilanti orientation the children are expected to develop competence in making their own decisions based upon their own interpretations of reality. They are encouraged to exchange rather than to receive information and opinion, and are expected to control their own behaviour rather than have it controlled for them by adults. Curiosity, disputation, exploration, independent decision-making, self-responsibility are at a premium in contrast to the acceptance, agreement, sequential conditioning, appropriate response-making and controlled behaviour demanded in the Behaviour Analysis Classroom.

In essence, the strategy of the Ypsilanti approach emphasizes procedures for the discovery of reality and for the integration of familiar social concepts. Its curriculum builds tasks according to the individual's learning style and does not impose preset objectives upon him, nor does it insist upon him getting 'right' solutions for such tasks. It respects and examines the logical structure of number and the sequential structuring of spatial concepts, and it encourages the development of temporal reasoning. Above all it engages the children in socio-dramatic play in order to provide them with an opportunity to construct the Piagetian key to intellectual performance—symbolic representation.

To most cognitive psychologists, the Ypsilanti approach to compensatory education represents a positive and accurate application of developmental theory to educational practice.

Before concluding this description of the Ypsilanti programme it must be noted that, despite its 'whole child' orientation, its compensatory education bias is towards structuring the child's environment so that his play and interaction with adults is largely aimed at preparation for subsequent activity in the elementary school. Hence, it is quite clearly objective-based, and it attempts, through a step-by-step progression, to achieve limited, preset goals. As such it is distinct from the Play School orientation which has had such powerful recent influences in British and American compensatory education.

The soul of the Play School approach exists in the spontaneous play of children experiencing materials, people, fantasies and themselves. It is often determinedly informal and avowedly pupil-centred. Play itself is seen as the principal means of learning in early childhood and it is argued (Plowden Report, 1967) that, through play, children become able to develop causal relationship concepts and obtain power to make discriminations, judgements, analyses and synthetizations. Furthermore, play is seen as the common factor in all children that leads to imagination and creativity. Play also has social development properties and supporters of the approach suggest that through it children can 'reconcile their inner lives with external reality' (Plowden Report, p. 193). Academic achievement is considered of relatively low importance in the Play School concept, and warmth, openness, flexibility and informality are at a premium.

The concept of openness has given rise to the *Open Plan* classroom, the contemporary innovative fad in North American compensatory education, which has incorporated the basic principles of the Play School. This plan has been extended into the elementary systems and currently much of its programming and research is more concerned with the non-disadvantaged child in the regular system than with the recovery of lost play opportunities. Nevertheless, it has become an almost mandatory feature of Head Start classrooms in Canada and in many States of the Union.

Essentially, Open Schools are orientated towards providing for personal experiences which MacDonald (1973) has defined as transactions in time and space in which the past and future are together integrated with the inner subjective space of the person and external, objective, cultural space. In short, the Open Plan school is committed to the principle of the whole person involved in a transaction which is functionally open through the perceptions and actions of the participants, and is independent of the goals of an observer or a non-participant.

Despite their insistence upon flexibility and freedom, Open Plan schools do have a contrived environment based upon the structuring of what MacDonald (1973, p. 95) called 'a living situation with a wide range of educative alternatives'. The structuring leads to planned 'accidents' or 'happenings' which are derived from 'the inner subjective and outer objective potentialities of situations'.

In action, the Open Plan compensatory programme is characterized by much 'messing about'. Usually there are two key teachers and often a number of aides in the classrooms and the children move freely among a wide variety of activities in which they became involved of their own volition. Order, neatness, control and precise objectives are not valued, and reinforcement schedules are, of course, heretical. The teachers interact with the children, supply the necessary materials to feed their play and interest, provide reading and writing opportunities, and generally try to develop an air of relaxed purposiveness. No curriculum is considered sacrosanct and regard for the individual's growth and development through his own experience is paramount.

But there is a problem, as Barth (1969) pointed out. The problem lies in the fact that the selection of learning material and the inevitable differential reinforcement of behaviour that occurs whenever groups of teachers and children interact effectively control children's learning. Consequently, the major problem confronting open education is the definition and determination of the division of responsibility for instruction. If the compensatory aspect of the Open Plan school is specifically considered, this problem becomes critical, since many disadvantaged children are identified by their apparent inability to engage in the very activities considered essential to the success of the Open Plan approach. As a result teacher leadership is of very great importance and the structuring of the programme often has a marked directing function.

It is as yet unproven that play, involvement, experience and activity in random packages wrapped in warmth are the full answer to the disadvantaged child's educational problems. As Yeomans (1969) has suggested, there may be a danger to the child of excessive shifting of activity which might readily lead to uncoordinated random behaviour and actually prevent the child from developing the very cognitive structures sought by the programme. There is also the difficult problem of assessing the effectiveness of a compensatory programme of this type. If the child does not continue in the Open Plan approach will he have achieved the concept development, however defined, necessary for success in whatever classroom he encounters? Who is responsible for the subsequent outcome if he does not?

The hidden flaw in all grouped, institutional attempts at compensatory education might well be concealed in the lateness of their delivery. There is an exceptionally large literature (most of it equivocal) on the likelihood or otherwise of the child's potential for education being substantially determined by the end of the prelanguage period. If indeed it is late in the day at three years of age, compensatory education may well be limited in its success to specific, short-term, small-step goals. This would force the conclusion that compensatory education delivered to the four-year-old disadvantaged child is an incorrect approach doomed to probable failure. The alternative orientation would then be preventive education aimed at the child prior to his experiencing the situations that would otherwise result in his inability to profit from normal educational provisions. The next two approaches to 'compensatory' education adopt such a position and argue that no child needs to be educationally disadvantaged if his early childhood experiences are noted and if his interaction with his earliest environments is properly encouraged. One of these orientations, that of the *Harvard Preschool Project* developed by Burton White (1969) and his associates, is parent/child centered. The second orientation is proposed by the present author in collaboration with Silverman, and is predicated on the assumptions that cultural deprivation is a misnomer, that all children whatever their cultural background have experiences in their commerce with life which are eminently amenable to education and that these experiences should form the basis of the curricula in the elementary schools. In its construction, the O'Bryan/Silverman orientation draws upon White's (1971) formulations and accepts Baratz and Baratz's (1970) proposition that the correct course for preventive education is the adoption of the experiences of the children as they occur in their actual life style as the basis of instructional curricula and teaching procedures.

The Harvard Preschool Project is a vigorously researched and markedly innovative study and application of mother/child relationships in the development of competence in very young children. Initially, research was conducted to determine the details of everyday experiences of two- and three-year-old children who were developing well and of those who were developing poorly. The researchers looked for the various competencies displayed by children and attempted to list the environmental factors which appeared to influence development in significant ways. Two basic types of abilities were found and these were classed as Social and Non-social abilities.

Social abilities, such as being able to get and maintain adult attention through socially acceptable means and subsequently to use adults as resources, were considered basic to good development. The highly competent two- or three-year-old was found to be able to express affection and hostility to his peers and to adults; to compete with, lead and follow his peers; to show pride in his achievements and generally to give evidence of meaningful involvement in adult play behaviour.

Non-social abilities were grouped into four categories. The first of these, linguistic competence, included grammatical capacity, vocabulary, articulation and extensive use of expressive language. The second category was rather more difficult to delineate in that it involved intellectual development depending upon such skills as the anticipation of consequences and the sensing of dissonance. Children who could deal with abstractions, who were able to take the perspective of one another and who were capable of making interesting associations, were considered to be high performers in intellectual competence. Executive abilities, the third category, were marked by skill in planning and carrying out multi-stepped activities through the free and ready use of available resources. Attentional skills such as the ability to maintain concentration on a central task and monitor peripheral activity were considered by White and his associates to be the remaining requirement for children to develop an adequate level of performance. Interestingly, in view of the recent heavy emphasis upon the development and recapitulation of sensory motor abilities in young children as a basic compensatory and remedial education practice, White found that differences in such capacities between children of high and low competence were, in fact, quite modest (White, 1971).

Having defined, to their satisfaction, the behavioural dimensions of competence in three-year-old children, the investigators turned to the delineation of early child-rearing stratagems which appeared to them to be most effective. Two major events emerged as significant to successful early child-rearing practices: the development of locomotor ability (walking) and the emergence of language. The mother's response to her child's increasing locomotor mobility, the degree to which she allowed freedom to the child to satisfy its curiosity, to explore and to engage actively in the environment, appeared critical to the development of competencies. As language emerged, the mother's response to the child's burgeoning verbal facility became highly significant to his development. Since both these events occur towards the end of the first year and move ahead dramatically in the second and third years, early involvement and intervention become critical to the child's ability to reach maximum levels of competency.

The Harvard Preschool Project was defined by its researchers as a natural experiment, the purpose of which was to learn the details of excellent child-rearing for the second and third years of life and White (1971, p. 86) presented the proposition that the mother's 'direct and indirect actions with regard to her one- to three-year-old child are . . . the most powerful formative factors in the development of the preschool child'.

What then are these direct and indirect actions? First of all, they are set in a physical world full of small, manipulatable objects which are themselves visually detailed. Some of these objects are toys manufactured for children, but most are normal household items such as bottle tops and jam jar covers, knobs and bobbins, containers and squeezable tubes: virtually anything that a young child can physically manipulate. There are chairs to climb, sofas to roll on, often (but not necessarily) larger mechanical toys to ride, and structures to swing on. The elaborately designed, expensively equipped playroom is nice but non-essential, for it is the use made of the objects by the mother and her child which is supposed to be the key to the effectiveness of early childhood development.

Preliminary conclusions, or 'best guesses' as White calls them, indicated that the most effective mothers did not devote the bulk of their day to rearing their young children. Instead they seemed to perform as designers and consultants. They were responsible for and interested in the provision of a rich and varied physical world in which the child is allowed full range for his curiosity and exploratory tendencies. The effective mother encouraged her child's readiness for exploration and responded with interest and enthusiasm when he sought help, advice or support. Her teaching was brief, pointed and occurred usually at the child's instigation. She talked a great deal to her infant, toddler or young child at an understandable level. The mothers are consistently energetic and are themselves actively engaged with their own environment.

In essence, the Harvard Preschool project takes the position that the ultimate educational die is cast by the mother/child interaction in the environment shared by them during the first three years of the child's life. While the project does not make the claim that subsequent compensatory education is unlikely to be of any value, it is clear that the orientation in this project is towards prevention through a highly developed analysis and application of what White (1971) has called 'Excellent Early Educational Practices'. Whether or not the project will make headway in the exceptionally complex problem of preparing the potentially educationally disadvantaged child for a successful venture into the school systems remains to be demonstrated, but its attempt to instruct mothers to take full advantage of their children's spontaneous curiosity and activity is certainly one of the more interesting recent orientations to early childhood education.

A programme currently being developed in Indian education in Canada is the O'Bryan/Silverman *Indian Education Project*. This project, which is expected to commence in the spring of 1974, is intended to be an application of Baratz and Baratz's (1970) orientation to compensatory education, which argues for curriculum recognition of the learner's prior cultural experiences. The project arose out of a series of studies conducted on an Ontario reservation by O'Bryan in 1969 (O'Bryan, 1972) in which it was found that the cognitive development of Indian children as measured by a series of tasks and scales drawn from Piaget (1952), Gesell (1925) and Uzgiris and Hunt (1966) proceeded comparably with white middle-class children until the Indians reached approximately the age of four. At this time a small deficit in comparative cognitive performance became apparent, and a continued decline ensued until the five-year-old Indian child entering the kindergarten was slightly but significantly behind his middle-class white counterpart. The difference at this time, however, could quite reasonably have been attributed to the fact that the test materials and procedures were more familiar to the white children. Indeed, an earlier investigation by O'Bryan (1966) had indicated that when test procedures and materials were drawn from the experiences of the Indian children then they outperformed a comparable group of white children. In any case, after one year in school on the Reserve, large cognitive development deficits appeared in the Indian pupils who were markedly unsuccessful in coping with the standard of the Ontario kindergarten curriculum. Some startling results which indicated that a number of children had actually *regressed* in development led O'Bryan and Silverman to conclude that it was the kindergarten programme, rather than the children, which was faulty and that the prior learning of the children was being neglected to the extent that five years of experience became a handicap rather than an asset.

It followed that a revision of curriculum materials, teaching procedures and the structure of the kindergarten should be carried out to take advantage of the early childhood experiences of the Indians and that this might best be done by a detailed study of the Reserve environment as it applied to children. This assumption led O'Bryan and Silverman to take an orientation in compensatory education which denied that compensation is the necessary mechanism in effectively educating children from groups which habitually produce the 'disadvantaged' learner. The implication is that compensation is necessary only when the child's prior experiences and adequately developed processes are ignored or rejected by the curriculum builders and goal setters of the educational systems. A further assumption was made that every child in a given definable group has had educably relevant experiences which can quite properly be the content of the elementary classroom. It was also assumed that the persons most likely to understand and accurately interpret the early learning experiences of children would be members of the group from which the children were to be drawn.

The O'Bryan/Silverman programme is planned to begin with a training programme for Indian aides to early childhood. From a Reserve in which there are thirty-two children between the ages of one and three years, four Indian girls will be trained first in the recognition of experiential potential in the environment of the Reserve and subsequently in non-directive interaction with children of the age range in question. The training for interaction with the children is based primarily on the ideas generated by the Harvard Preschool project but it also incorporates the approaches suggested by the Ypsilanti programme. The aides are also to be trained in observational techniques from the application of which will be constructed logs of the children's activities as they grow towards school entrance. Materials with which they play, the fantasies that they invent, the transactions they engage in, the language development that occurs and the logic of their world will be the basis upon which their first- and second-year elementary school programme will be designed.

Essentially the approach is twofold. On the one hand, it is aimed at providing an increased opportunity for the young Indian children to develop a greater awareness of themselves and of their environment through the assistance of the aides to early childhood who will work with them as baby-sitters for at least ten hours a week for each child in interchangeable groups of not more than five children. On the other hand, the children's experiences will be recognized as a valid source of curriculum material which is expected to avoid the learning shock presently transmitted to such children when their prior experiences are largely or totally ignored.

The approaches to contemporary compensatory programmes so far discussed all involve the contact and interaction of adults with children, either in a direct instructional or indirect environmental manner. No review of modern orientations in this field would be at all complete without consideration of electronic approaches in which adults, puppets, cartoon characters and talking symbols *present* compensatory programmes to children on a mass viewing basis. Indeed, there are as many different theoretical models underlying the television compensatory programmes as there are underpinning the classroom approaches. However, the writer has had direct experience in the development of one major programme, *Sesame Street*, a children's programme produced by the Children's Television Workshop of New York, and it is proposed to review in some detail its orientation to compensatory education.

The original intent behind Sesame Street was to provide a direct educational experience for three- to five-year-old disadvantaged children using the medium of television. The programme was specifically designed to incorporate psychological, educational and sociological theory and practice in a format that would permit the delivery of a specified educational package with punch and considerable precision.

Basically, Sesame Street has three areas in which it makes an active attempt to teach. These are symbolic representation, problem-solving and reasoning, and familiarity with physical and social environments.

Symbolic representation calls for the child to recognize basic symbol forms such as letters, numbers and geometric forms and use them to perform simple operations. This implies that the successful learner will be able to do such tasks as recognize differences in the use of numbers and letters, select appropriate letters or numbers from others under a variety of conditions, provide verbal labels for letters and numbers and match geometric forms (usually squares, circles and triangles). In addition, it requires the child to complete a number of secondary tasks such as reciting the alphabet and counting in sequence.

Under the general heading of problem-solving and reasoning, Sesame Street's instructional goals required the child to learn to deal with objects and events in terms of classifications, relationships and temporal and spatial ordering. He is expected to develop some reasoning ability and to acquire some skills in inquiry and problem-solving.

The goals are initially approached by encouraging perceptual discrimination (through the identification and labelling of body parts), visual discrimination (through matching and modelling) and auditory discrimination (through matching words on the basis of rhyming sounds and the perception of rhythms). In addition, the children are expected to learn to make classifications through grouping like and unlike objects and to gain skills in sequential ordering through the use of size and time-of-presentation criteria.

Problem-solving and reasoning are tackled on three fronts: inferences and causality, the generation of solutions and attitudes towards inquiry and problem-solving. Inferences and causality call upon the child to infer possible antecedents and consequences and to order causal sequences. If, for example, the child is shown Humpty Dumpty leaning over a high wall, he could infer that he had either climbed the wall or had been placed on it for a variety of antecedent reasons and that if he leans too far, there will be certain consequences. Should the scene show a broken Humpty at the bottom of the wall and a picture of him falling, the child should be able to recognize the causal relationship between the fall and the broken shell.

Two main approaches to the generation of solutions are used in Sesame Street. In one, the child is called upon to suggest multiple solutions to simple problems; in the other he is asked to select the most relevant or complete solution from a set of possible solutions. On the whole, this is a rather simplistic and narrow view of problem-solving, even though the stated aims of the programme include attempts to encourage 'useful' attitudes such as persistence, inquiry and reflection in problem-solving situations.

Of less difficulty for Sesame Street is its attempt to teach children about the natural environment, natural processes and man in his world. Through presenting various aspects of life and living, Sesame Street asks the child to learn about the function of nature and machines, society and self, and the cooperative aspects of modern life. Some attempts are made to recognize the often abstract concepts of justice and fair play, and the differences in points of view that exist among individuals and groups of individuals.

Sesame Street relies heavily on humour and incongruity, which are perhaps the most pervasive techniques used in the programme. In view of the non-captive nature of the audience, the humour element is useful in that it entertains and holds the attention of not only the younger children but also of older siblings and parents, who are potential channel-changers. The value of humour as a vehicle for instruction is less easily established but the producers argue that it serves several psycho-educational purposes. They contend that it provides motivation, so that the association of 'Wanda the Witch' with the letter 'W' makes learning more fun (there is a danger, of course, that the learned material is the joke, not the letter). Further, it is claimed that humour induces attention, especially through the use of incongruity. Since the highly repetitive content of the programme could easily result in boredom, the presence of unexpected and humorous twists in the repeated sequences is thought to provoke curiosity, attention and expectation. Yet another function of the humour technique is the affective quality it may possess for disadvantaged children, especially in language learning, which is presented as a pleasurable and personal social art.

An integral part of Sesame Street's technique is claimed to be its encouragement of the participation and anticipation of the viewer. This claim may be something of a surprise for several critics who have complained of the 'passivity' of the programme. The participation inducement technique appears to rely on the child's identifying with a particular performer in his attempts to label, classify, find relationships and solve problems. There is some research evidence (Fowles, 1973) that children sing and talk along with favourite performers, attempt to assist them in their tasks and compete with one another in solving problems presented to them.

A sense of participation and anticipation may also be generated by another extensively used technique: exact repetition and repetition with variations. In this technique speech is used economically and jingles, rhymes, rhythms and alliteration abound. Repetition with variations is used in two forms. In one, the content remains constant and the format is varied; in the other, the content is varied while the format remains unchanged. Several other techniques of instruction used on the programme utilize child and adult models, celebrities and puppetry and cartoon characters, which provide vehicles for a given educational segment largely through the entertainment and identification value of the personality or puppet concerned.

The goals, procedures and even the morality of Sesame Street as a compensatory programme have been subjected to a great deal of criticism. Not the least of this criticism has been levelled at a perceived stress on mechanical memory training and rote learning and the ignoring of the more generalizable conceptual development that unstructured, free-wheeling and open-ended activities are presumed to furnish.

Another criticism which is often offered deals with the rapid-fire, fragmented patterning of the material, especially in segments dealing with numbers. There may, in fact, be some truth in the claim that *Sesame Street* is not conducive to the development of attention in children, since it constantly avoids segments requiring lengthy concentration. It *is* aggressive and it *does* present very noisy sequences. Furthermore, it makes use of pleasure, surprise, anxiety, and humour in rapid succession. Whether this is actively detrimental to the development of a child's attention span is questionable for indeed the concept of attention itself is very much of an open question in psychology.

Concern has also been expressed over the question of the affective or emotional qualities in Sesame Street presentations. Essentially, this criticism centres on the adult and child actors, who have been accused of woodenness and of treating feelings and emotions too dispassionately. This is a difficult point on which to comment since the perception of others' feelings is a notoriously difficult task. Its difficulty is further compounded when an adult tries to assess a child's interpretation of the reaction of other adults, children and cartoon characters to emotions.

Other criticisms concern the lack of activity demanded of the viewer, the possible stifling of the creativity that might occur if the child were not so tightly structured by the programme, and the possibility of impaired parent/children relationships engendered by proud parents demanding that their children learn from Sesame Street.

Despite the criticisms, *Sesame Street* continues to be a phenomenally successful television programme whose specific goals, according to Ball and Bogatz (1970), have been substantially achieved.

The well-endowed and sophisticated programmes of preschool education described in the preceding pages are in the vanguard of a massive assault on the problem of inadequate early childhood preparation for success in the elementary schools. Each represents a particular theoretical approach to the problem and all of the currently operating programmes can provide substantial evidence that successful short-term gains in performance have been achieved. Indeed, the research indicates that every one is a highly successful approach that has clearly achieved its objectives and is obviously worthy of continued funding.

The problem of the disadvantaged child has thus been solved: simply send him to any one of the programmes and he will be fine. It is important to be certain, however, that the compensatory programme chosen for him is matched to the ensuing elementary school programme. It would probably not do for the well-behaved and appropriately conditioned product of the Behavioural Analysis Classrooms to find himself responding to the needs of an adult teacher in an Open Plan school. Neither is it probable that the free-wheeling, open-ended play schooler will enjoy his penalty periods in the time-out chair should he exercise independence in the grade one behaviour classroom. It would probably be appropriate, also, to warn the

Sesame Street viewer to avoid undue precocity in the naming of numbers in the Play School kindergarten, lest he be regarded as immature and developmentally restricted. Better to send him to a direct instructional school where his ready willingness to provide repetitions will be appreciated. 'Horses for courses' is an old handicapper's cliché that seems unpleasantly appropriate when the matching of the child's preschool experience to the school curriculum is the issue. The point, of course, is that many current orientations to compensatory education are slaves to the prevailing educational system rather than servants to the children experiencing them.

As Evans (1971) pointed out, various mixes of philosophical and psychological thought underly the goals of several compensatory programmes. Furthermore, an element of competition exists between them, and some bitter debates have occurred in the learned journals over the correct approach to early childhood education. Yet common problems confront each orientation. What, for example, is the proper relationship between the compensatory programme and the subsequent school experience? Who is entitled to make the decisions on how the child's preschool experience will be structured? What is the nature of 'cultural disadvantage'? Does it exist or is the question one of educational neglect or irrelevance? What is 'good' and what is 'unacceptable'?

Compensatory education has moved quickly from its beginnings in the public conscience to a stage of elaborately programmed instructional theory and practice. Its descent from enthusiasm to reality has been sharp and, in the short-term sense, fruitful. Nevertheless, a guiding philosophy has not been formulated. Until such a one does arise it is unlikely that compensatory education will transcend the various orientations and fulfill its promise to its dependent children.

CHAPTER 4

Specific Learning Disabilities

K. WEDELL

The development of special education has been characterized by a progressive differentiation of children who are failing to make normal behavioural and educational progress. At first, a child's failure to make progress was regarded as the direct outcome of his level of ability, which, in turn, was regarded as a genetically determined, immodifiable capacity. Gradually, it became evident that low achievement might be the outcome of other causes, such as emotional disturbance or environmental deprivation. Similarly, work with children who had sensory and motor deficits revealed that their low achievement might be due mainly to the limitations these handicaps set on their capacity to express themselves or to receive information from their environment.

The recognition of these specific causes of children's failure was based mainly on the comparison of children's levels of performance under different circumstances. The effect of environmental deprivation on a child became apparent when his behavioural and achievement level rose after he was given a more stimulating environment (e.g. Clarke and Clarke, 1973). The effect of motor handicaps on the cerebral-palsied child was revealed when methods were found to by-pass his inability to express himself either orally or by writing or drawing. In the case of these and of other types of handicapped children, it was the finding of discrepancies in the children's levels of performance under different circumstances which led on to the identification of specific causes underlying their failure to achieve behavioural and educational expectations.

More recently, interest has come to be focused on a further group of children who show discrepancies in their functional levels, but in whom further investigation of these discrepancies has not led to evidence of the types of causes mentioned so far. The children have not shown evidence that sensory or motor deficits, or emotional or deprivational factors, have had a primary limiting effect on their behavioural or educational progress. Furthermore, the unevenness of the children's performance levels, the fact that they were good at some tasks and poor at others, has also indicated that the children's problems could not be attributed to a generally low level of abilities. By analysing the pattern of the children's areas of high and low achievement, it became evident that there were different cognitive, perceptual or praxic functions underlying each. So what had appeared to be paradoxical discrepancies turned out to be disabilities, produced by deficiencies in functions common to the various areas of low performance. The child whose verbal performance was poor was thus seen to have a deficit in language—either of an expressive or a receptive kind, or both. The child who failed to copy patterns accurately was seen to have a deficit either in perceiving the shape or in organizing his movements in copying it, or both.

A category of deficits was thus identified, in functions which were thought to underlie the particular areas of achievement in which the child was failing. These functions were thought to be those by which a child derived meaning from his experience, and those through which he organized his movement in accordance with his intentions (Wedell, 1973) and the finding that these functions could be selectively impaired fitted in with the growing scepticism about the view of 'intelligence' as a unitary concept. The causes of these kinds of discrepancies in performance levels were therefore conceived as residing within the child and so the concept of 'specific learning disabilities' developed, and brought with it another orientation in special educational approach. This lay in a recognition of the need to make specific analyses of these children's performance levels in different areas of achievement in order to identify the functions underlying the areas of low performance. Since such functions were often hypothetical, the classification of learning disabilities often varied, and still varies, with the theoretical orientation of the individual special educator.

The present situation is one in which there is little agreement about the definition of specific learning disabilities. The following definition, quoted by Kass (1969) is one arrived at by a committee in the U.S.A.:

'Children with special learning disabilities exhibit a disorder in one or more of the basic psychological processes involved in understanding or in using spoken or written language. These may be manifested in disorders of listening, thinking, talking, reading, writing, spelling, or arithmetic. They include conditions which have been referred to as perceptual handicaps, brain injury, minimal brain dysfunction, dyslexia, developmental aphasia, etc. They do not include learning problems which are due primarily to visual, hearing, or motor handicaps, to mental retardation, emotional disturbance or to environmental deprivation.'

It is evident that the conditions are described in a variety of terms: supposed organic disorders (e.g. minimal cerebral dysfunction), psychological dysfunctions (e.g. perceptual handicaps) and disorders described mainly in terms of syndromes of presenting symptoms (e.g. dyslexia). Cruickshank (1966) lists 19 different labels used in the literature to refer to children with learning disabilities. The subject of learning disabilities is currently in a considerable state of confusion. Protagonists of different theoretical orientations not only prescribe correspondingly differing special educational remedies, but also claim conflicting areas of generality for the particular causes of educational failure which they espouse. At the same time, pressure is being directed at governments to legislate for the provision of appropriate special educational facilities, and legislators in their turn are demanding definitions of the conditions for which such provision is to be made.

The concept of specific learning disability consequently represents an important issue in special education at present. In what follows, an attempt will be made to trace the development of some of the main approaches to this topic and to examine some of the assumptions underlying them. The origins of the concept will be discussed under two main headings, Clinical Neurology and Functional Analysis.

CLINICAL NEUROLOGY

One of the origins of ideas about specific learning disabilities lies in the findings of specific functional loss made among adults with localized brain injuries. Following the early studies of Broca, in which he showed that speech functions were subserved by particular areas of the cerebral cortex, there was a steady accumulation of findings about functional loss associated with localized cerebral lesions. These showed that intellectual functions could be selectively impaired (Goldstein, 1948; Head, 1926). The mass of evidence provided by gunshot injuries to soldiers in the First World War was of interest to clinical neurologists not only because it indicated that the functions of many different parts of the brain could be identified, but also because it indicated what some of these functions were. On the basis of these, and of earlier studies, language loss was analysed into deficits of expression and of comprehension (expressive and receptive aphasia). Similarly, disability in the organization of intentional movement (apraxia) was identified, as also were deficits in the sensory localization of body parts ('body image' disturbances). Critchley (1953) devotes an entire book to the review of findings about functional loss consequent on lesions of the parietal lobes.

Strauss (Strauss and Lehtinen, 1947; Strauss and Kephart, 1955) related these findings on adults with brain injury to children. They were well acquainted with the work of Goldstein and noticed a similarity between some of the symptoms he reported among brain-injured adults and those among the mentally retarded children with whom they were working at the Wayne County Training School in Michigan, USA. Strauss and Lehtinen were particularly concerned with the perceptual and perceptuo-motor problems of their children, and with their attentional deficits. Strauss and Lehtinen demonstrated that some of their children showed difficulty, for example, in figure-ground discrimination and in copying patterns, and so they were concerned to find out whether there was evidence of brain injury in the histories of these children, which might account for their deficiencies. They carried out a series of studies, in which they compared the performance of children whose records showed evidence of brain damage, with the performance of children without such evidence. The evidence they used was records of conditions suffered before, during or after birth, which were known to be associated with brain injury. Comparisons of the performance of these two groups of retarded children tended to show that the 'brain-injured' children (whom they called exogenous) showed more specific disabilities than the 'non-brain-injured' (whom they called endogenous).

Strauss and Lehtinen subsequently came to place an increasing amount of weight on findings of specific cognitive deficits as evidence of brain damage in children, so that they ultimately reached a point where they regarded these deficits as evidence of brain injury in their own right. They were thus led to a circular argument, in which symptoms associated with brain injury were themselves used as evidence of it.

This kind of reasoning has been perpetuated in the use of the term 'minimal cerebral dysfunction', which is currently applied by some to children with specific learning disabilities. The word 'minimal' is included usually to imply that there is no direct evidence of brain injury, but that this is inferred from behavioural and other aspects of the child's performance.

Specific reading disability was another form of specific deficit which was recognized by clinical neurologists, in adults with localized lesions. Orton (1937) studied these and developed theories about their underlying causes. He carried these theories over to his study of children who had difficulty in learning to read. He found that many of the children who were referred to him were cross-lateral (e.g. they were left-handed and right-eyed). Since Broca and other clinical neurologists had shown that language functions were located in the dominant cerebral hemisphere, Orton argued that the children's failure to read had resulted from a language deficit, which in turn was consequent on a failure in the establishment of cerebral dominance. He regarded the children's cross-laterality as evidence of their failure to establish cerebral dominance. Orton built up a complex theory, particularly designed to account for the letter reversals in reading and writing shown by many of the children he examined. He even coined a term for this type of difficulty ('strephosymbolia' or 'twisted symbols'). His rather speculative theory proposed that images of letters were stored in mirror-orientation on the opposite side of the brain, and that the lack of ascendance of the dominant over the minor hemisphere resulted in the wrong image being applied by the child to his reading and writing. More recent work (Zangwill, 1960) has shown, however, that the association between hand preference, cortical dominance and cerebral localization of language function is more complex.

These early lines of thinking among clinical neurologists are still reflected in some current approaches to the explanation and treatment of children with specific learning disabilities. Delacato and his associates (Delacato, 1963), for example, place great emphasis on the importance of the development of lateral preference. They regard cross-laterality as an indication of inadequate neurological development. A central feature of their programme is the establishment of asymmetrical patterns of motor skills (such as the alternating movements of arms and legs in crawling). They see the neurological development of the individual child as recapitulating the phylogenetic development of man, and propose that neurological development can be fostered by teaching the child to go through movements characteristic of these successive stages. As the child with learning difficulties advances through these stages, unilateral preference is established, so it is claimed. Unilateral preference is also furthered by forced use of one hand, and one eye, on the assumption that this will have neurological effects conducive to language improvement, and thus to reading improvement.

These theories of Delacato and coworkers have been criticized and the American Academy of Cerebral Palsy issued a rebuttal of the views put forward. Criticism was directed at the hypothesis about neurological development, and about the relationship proposed between cortical function and the role of lateralization. Delacato *et al.* (1966) published reports of collaborative studies supporting the effectiveness of their methods, but other workers failed to confirm these. Robbins (1966) for example found that, after four months of training, a group of second grade (7–8-year-old) children showed less lateralization of motor skill than at the start. Kerschner (1968), in a study of retarded children, showed that an experimental group given five months of Delacato's training were slightly better at creeping and crawling than a control group, who were given a general physical education programme. But he found that there was no difference between the groups' performance on the Oseretsky Motor Development Test (a general motor skill test).

Motor training with the aim of modifying neurological functioning has also been advocated by some other workers, notably Ayres (1968), but evidence of improvement in intellectual function has not been forthcoming.

Knowledge about the relationship between the neurophysiological state of the human organism and its functioning is still relatively limited. Studies of brain injury in adults have undoubtedly begun to indicate associations, but again and again clinical experience has shown that it is very difficult to predict the exact nature of functional loss likely to result from a specific form and location of brain lesion. In children, the problem becomes infinitely greater, since one is concerned with a developing organism. Not only is one confronted with the problem of assessing the exact nature of a particular form of brain injury, but one is faced with uncertainty about the state of development of the organs concerned and about the level of integration of neurophysiological functioning achieved. Few would deny that ultimately all behaviour has a neurophysiological base and that deficits in behavioural and intellectual function must in some way be reflections of underlying organic dysfunctions. However, the present state of our knowledge hardly justifies our regarding such an association at other than a hypothetical level.

Clearly, clinical neurology has provided very useful models of functioning. The study of patterns of language deficits associated with various forms of neuropathology, have, as was mentioned above, helped to indicate some of the ways in which language functions might be subdivided. Johnson and Myklebust (1967), for example, have used such models in describing children's learning disabilities. 'There are many types of learning disabilities, but a basic underlying homogeneity is derived from the fact that it is the neurology of learning that has been disrupted.'

They have applied models derived from clinical neurology to distinguish deficits in the comprehension and expression of language in children, and have found them helpful in explaining some of the discrepancies between children's abilities and disabilities. The process of communication plays such a basic role in everyday behaviour that a model of this kind offers a wide range of application. It seems important to remember that, however plausible and all-embracing such a model may appear, it nonetheless remains a model, and does not preclude us from looking at behaviour in terms of other models at the same time.

Another model to be applied has, not surprisingly, been that of the normal developmental sequence in the child. The implications of development have clearly to be considered in evaluating the likely consequences of specific disabilities affecting the child at various stages in his growth. For example, a deficit which may be regarded as specific at an early stage may be supposed to have a handicapping effect over an increasingly wide area of the child's functioning as he grows older. As a result, many workers have regarded it as important that a child should progress systematically through successive stages of development, achieving adequate levels of functioning at each stage before being allowed to progress to the next. Delacato's theories include this notion, as is illustrated, for example, in his emphasis on the fact that children need to go through a crawling stage.

FUNCTIONAL ANALYSIS

The term 'functional analysis' is used in this context to describe those approaches which are directed at analysing the characteristics of the child's functioning, without extending this to assumptions about the organic processes which might underly the functions studied. These approaches tend to use models derived from experimental psychology and also from psychometrics. It is interesting to note that the types of distinctions made between various kinds of functions often appear analogous to those derived from clinical neurology. Functional analysis approaches to learning disabilities also, of course, have to pay particular attention to the developmental model, and this is well illustrated in the views put forward by Kephart (1971).

Kephart was particularly interested in perceptuo-motor functions, because he was concerned with the question as to how the child developed his concept of a stable physical environment. He had worked with Strauss at the Wayne County School and therefore his interest in perceptual deficits is hardly surprising. Kephart's particular concern was with the 'perceptual motor match'; with the way in which the child comes to direct his actions appropriately to the situation in which he finds himself. Kephart maintained that the child derived his concepts of the spatial aspects of the world around him through movement. It was only by moving his body through space that the child was able to learn about the spatial relationships between objects: movement, so to speak, formed the connection. Consequently, the 'match' between what the child perceived and his actions depended on the way his experience of movement was built up. He based his ideas partly on his interpretation of the work of the psychologist Hebb.

Since the child built up his ideas of the space around him through the movement of his own body, the child's 'knowledge' of the spatial coordination of his own body—front, back, up, down; left, right—formed an essential point of reference. Kephart consequently placed great emphasis on the adequate development of the child's 'body image'. ('Body Image' is a term which has been used in a variety of ways, and was a term already used by the early clinical neurologists.) For Kephart, an important feature of the child's body image was the 'body midline'. It was in relation to this that the child came to distinguish 'left' and 'right' in his surrounding space.

Kephart regarded adequate perceptuo-motor development as essential not only to the development of the child's concepts about the world around him and to the development of the child's general behavioural adequacy, but also to the child's subsequent success in learning at school. He devised an extensive programme of motor training, to cover various areas of performance. The activities contained in the programme are grouped under different headings: posture and the maintenance of balance, locomotion (moving around), contact (manipulation), and receipt and propulsion (e.g. catching and throwing a ball). Training in these areas might also be combined; for example, the child might be required to bounce a ball while balancing on a board. Kephart's programme leads up to writing exercises via 'chalk-board' exercises. He felt that inadequate development of a child's body midline might handicap him, for example, in making an arm movement from left to right, or in correctly drawing a reversible figure. Similarly, he felt that poor left–right discrimination might lead to reversal and transposition errors in writing.

Kephart was mainly concerned with the child's acquisition of competence in general movement. Another worker, whose work has become very well-known, directed her perceptuo-motor programmes at activities nearer to the pencil and paper tasks involved in everyday school activities. Frostig (1963) is probably best known for her Developmental Test of Visual Perception, although her more recent work has been directed more at general movement programmes (Frostig and Maslow, 1973). Frostig was concerned with the functional analysis of performance in tasks such as pattern copying, and divided the component skills into 'eye-motor co-ordination', 'figure ground discrimination', 'form-constancy', 'position in space' and 'spatial relations'. Her test is designed to assess each of these areas with some degree of specificity, and her programmes are directed at specific disabilities in these areas. Frostig was concerned, through her work, to demonstrate that a child's failure to copy a pattern might, for example, be due to a deficit in one or more of the functions she had differentiated. Correspondingly, remediation would need to be directed at the specific function or functions impaired. She placed considerable emphasis on the analysis of a child's profile of performance on her test, through which the exact nature of his deficits might be identified. She placed a great deal of emphasis on the degree to which deficits might be limited to certain areas of function. Frostig also pays considerable attention to areas of the child's functioning other than those to which her own test applied. She pays particular attention to language abilities and the potential for compensation they may offer the child. She recognized, for instance, that the child may well be helped to improve visual discrimination through verbalization.

One of the most extensive applications of functional analysis to specific language disabilities is that developed by Kirk, McCarthy and Kirk (1968). They based their approach on the model of communication devised by Osgood and constructed a battery of tests designed to assess specific aspects of communication in children. The Illinois Test of Psycholinguistic Abilities attempts to assess communication through the visual (pictures), vocal, auditory and motor (gesture) 'channels'. Communication is analysed into 'decoding' (receptive), encoding (expressive) and association processes, and these are categorized into different levels of complexity. Kirk, McCarthy and Kirk illustrate the processes included in their battery by means of a three-dimensional model, where the levels of complexity, the processes and the channels each represent one of the dimensions. This scheme of evaluation is clearly very ambitious and Kirk (1966) admits that he and his coworkers only partially succeeded in producing subtests which discreetly measured the language functions in the cells of his model.

The aim of the I.T.P.A. is, clearly, to identify areas of specific deficit in a child's language skills, and Kirk (1966) has provided case histories to show how language programmes can be designed to remediate specific deficiencies. Dunn and coworkers (1968) devised a system of programmes of language training based on this model of communication, called the Peabody Language Development Kits. These programmes are aimed at children with retarded language, resulting from environmental deprivation, mental retardation or other causes. The programmes are very detailed and provide complete lesson plans, in a progressive arrangement. The content of the lessons is intended to cover the various areas of language, and the items are carefully graded to ensure maximal success on the part of the children. The programmes can be geared to the needs of individual children by varying the rate of presentation.

Cruickshank and coworkers (1961) based their special educational approach on the methods originally put forward by Strauss. Strauss and Lehtinen (1947) had devised experimental educational methods designed to help their 'exogenous' children to overcome their attentional and perceptual deficits. They stated that educational methods should be directed at 'manipulating and controlling the external overstimulating environment' and at 'educating the child to exercise voluntary control'. Strauss and Lehtinen felt that it was not possible to achieve these aims in an ordinary classroom setting and therefore provided a 'distraction free' classroom for their children. This approach was further developed by Cruickshank and coworkers, in an experimental educational study designed to evaluate these methods. The aims of their approach were to help children over hyperactivity and distractibility by reducing the degree of stimulation of the classroom setting, and by supporting the children with a highly structured routine. Both these supportive resources were then gradually withdrawn, as the children began to be able to cope. The classrooms were specially designed to be of uniform colour, with floors and ceilings sound-deadened and windows glazed with frosted glass. The children were provided with cubicles in which they did their work, in order to avoid distraction by others.

The educational materials were, by contrast, designed to be as stimulating as possible, but they were presented in carefully planned sequences, with each task designed to be completed within the child's attention span. The number of children in the class was kept small. As the children began to cope with their work, and to be able to attend for longer periods, they were allowed to work outside their cubicles, and later in groups. Cruickshank et al. developed very detailed methods for each aspect of their teaching programme.

Although Cruickshank's approach was based originally on the work of Strauss and Werner, with whom he had worked, his methods have been mentioned in the context of functional analysis because this seems to be more characteristic of their emphasis. Furthermore, the methods are directed not only at improving the children's deficiencies, but also initially at the features of the environment which made these deficiencies a handicap to the child. For example, reduced distraction, reduces the extent to which the child's poor attention makes it hard for him to cope.

These approaches to the functional analysis of learning difficulties, although probably the best known, represent only a few examples of the very large number which have now been devised.

The main question which one asks about the above explanations of learning disability is, of course, whether they have any practical implications for remediation. The limitations of explanations in terms of supposed underlying organic deficits have already been discussed.

Explanations in terms of functional analysis have clearly had more direct implications for remediation. Programmes have been devised to remedy specific deficits in any of the component functions of the model on which the explanation was based. For example, Frostig has produced workbooks containing activities appropriate to each of the five areas of perceptuo-motor functioning measured by her test. The aim of these and similar programmes is to improve the relevant component function or functions, with the assumption that such an improvement will, in turn, make the child better at performing in whatever attainment he was found to show a learning difficulty in the first place. Training in the underlying skill was assumed to 'transfer' to performance in the 'target' task.

An increasing number of studies have now been carried out, with the aim of evaluating whether specific programmes are effective. These studies and their findings have been reviewed by Cruickshank and Hallahan (1973), Myers and Hammill (1969), Cratty (1970), Wedell (1973) and others. Cruickshank and Hallahan carried out one of the most systematic reviews of perceptuo-motor programme evaluation studies, in which they also examined the experimental control achieved. They found very few studies which could be regarded as adequately controlled, by Campbell and Stanley's (1963) criteria. For example, the progress of a 'treated' and an 'untreated' group of children might be compared without taking into consideration that the extra attention which the treated group received might itself have contributed to any improvement found. Where adequate controls had been applied, the findings tended not to support the effectiveness of perceptuo-motor training programmes bringing about greater improvement in the 'target' basic educational attainments. Studies comparing the effectiveness of perceptuo-motor training with that of ordinary reading instruction would typically show that both types of training resulted in improved attainment, but that perceptuo-motor training did not have a significantly greater effect.

Wedell (1973) suggests that there is a need for clarification of objectives. The more specific the objectives, the more specific the training has to be. The special educator is concerned to help the child achieve certain goals of achievement, or 'target' tasks. Basic educational attainments such as reading, spelling and handwriting involve the correct manipulation of a relatively limited series of symbols, and achievement in these areas requires that a child should learn, for example, to apply his perceptuo-motor and other skills to a particular task. Above a minimum level of skill it then becomes more important that a child should learn *how to apply* that skill to the relevant task. In learning to read, for example, improvement in visual discrimination above a minimal level is not so important as that a child should learn what are the most useful aspects of letter and word shapes to notice. General training for the improvement of visual discrimination will be likely to have only limited benefit since the task to which the child is required to apply it is so specific.

A further relevant point is one which has already been mentioned earlier. We do not as yet know the exact pattern of skills which a child needs in order to be able, for example, to read, and it seems likely that different children attain the same achievement through different combinations of skills. One reason for these individual differences in learning lies in the fact that children try to compensate for their deficits with their assets. So even the requisite levels of underlying skills may vary, since one child may have more compensatory abilities than another. This point was brought out by Keogh (1971). Given that a child is failing in a particular area of educational attainment, one can apply functional analysis to trace the causal chain of impaired functions backwards, until one comes to the lowest level of function impaired. One can then plan a programme of remediation upwards to the target task, with transfer of skill to the target task as the prime objective. In our present state of ignorance, we would rarely be justified in assuming that a child, who had a given underlying deficit, would on that account fail to achieve a target task such as reading.

We can argue backwards to a learning disability, but not forwards to educational failure. Such a view has implications also for tests designed to identify children with potential learning difficulties. It seems fairly obvious that the prediction of later failure in educational attainment, made on the basis of a child's earlier deficiencies in underlying functions, is likely to be very uncertain. We cannot know how the compensatory resources available to a child (in the form of other abilities, supportive parents or good teachers), may help him to overcome his deficiencies. Moreover, one might justifiably argue that accuracy of prediction implied inadequacy of teaching, since teaching is presumably meant to improve the child's attainment. It seems more appropriate to direct such testing to finding out whether children have achieved the level of skills which a teacher takes as the starting point for her programme of instruction. For example, the infant teacher who reads a story to her class assumes that her children can sit still, listen and understand the words she is using. Such an approach puts the emphasis on the assessment of a child *as he is* at a given moment and on relating this to the level of 'entry skills' assumed by a teacher.

When it comes to making a functional analysis of a child who is failing in basic educational attainments, one uses the assumed hierarchy of skills necessary for the particular 'target' task as the model for one's analysis. The child who has difficulty in handwriting may not know letter shapes, may not be able to discriminate shapes, may not be able to organize his hand movements, or may not be able to hold a pencil. At this basic level of educational achievement, such an analysis of the task depends very much on assumptions about more general underlying functions such as, for example, visual perception. It has been argued by some (Bateman, 1973) that effective teaching is more concerned with presenting what is to be learned by the children in sufficiently carefully graded steps, rather than by gearing teaching to individual differences in children's abilities. Given the form of analysis outlined above, it becomes evident that a carefully graded approach does in fact cater for children's individual strengths and weaknesses. Insofar as each child is taken through those stages of the hierarchy of skills which he needs to master, he is being taught to acquire and then apply the skills relevant to the task.

The functional analysis of language disabilities and their remediation are related in a similarly close way, since oral expression and comprehension constitute a clearly definable system of target tasks. This is illustrated by the Peabody Language Development Programmes, which are based on both a syntactical and a communication theory model.

An underlying issue in deciding the form which remediation should take is the question of generalization. In the case both of training in basic educational attainments and in language, the teacher is concerned with teaching the manipulation of relatively specific elements in a given system. Admittedly, one might question whether a child will learn to use language in a creative way; whether he will generate sentences he has not been taught. Such a consideration, however, brings in other abilities than those concerned with the basic functions involved in the production of language. The problem of generalization of skills arises more when one considers remediation of the general motor skills involved in everyday social competence tasks, such as, for example, dressing, finding one's way about, and so on. If one considers the problems of the 'clumsy' child, one realizes the infinite variety of tasks in which he may perform badly. These are clearly too multifarious to train individually. Here the need for generalization suggests the need to search for common underlying skills, from which the child may transfer to competence in a variety of specific tasks. One might therefore argue in favour of using underlying skills themselves as objectives for training (for example, Kephart's four areas of motor skill mentioned above). The effectiveness of spontaneous transfer from such skills has yet to be validated, however. Unfortunately, as Quay (1973) points out, validation studies of programmes such as Kephart's tend to be carried out either in relation to objectives in basic educational attainments, or in measures such as the Purdue Perceptuo-Motor Scale, which are based on the types of performances involved in the training methods themselves. More appropriate criteria for validating the effectiveness of these programmes for improving the behavioural adequacy of children would seem to be ratings by teachers and other observers of the children's social competence.

Such studies would need to be evaluated in comparison to those where training was directed at very specific social competence skills. It might well be argued, for example, that a child who was trained to put on a cardigan correctly would effectively transfer this skill to competence in a variety of other dressing, and to other even less similar tasks. Such comparative evaluation studies do not, however, appear to have been carried out as yet.

One problem associated with the training of supposedly key underlying functions is that of knowing the level of proficiency that is acquired for adequate transfer. Training in balancing, for example, is admittedly likely to transfer to many locomotor skills, but clearly the objective would not be to make the child a tight-rope walker. And yet, perceptuo-motor training seems sometimes to be carried out with objectives such as 'the achievement of a good body image' or other such hypothetical construct, when we do not exactly know how this is relevant to everyday behavioural adequacy.

CONCLUSION

The foregoing discussion has hopefully shown that the study of specific learning difficulties in children raises issues central to Special Education. There is little doubt that there are individual differences among children, which can only be accounted for in terms of deficits in the psychological 'equipment' with which a child attends, perceives, acts, communicates, and so on. Our knowledge of these processes on the one hand, and of the skills involved in the achievement of behavioural and educational adequacy on the other hand, is still rudimentary. Even more rudimentary, however, is our knowledge of the relationship between functional deficiencies and underlying organic defects.

The postulation of specific learning disabilities does not imply that a child has an irreversible or unremediable handicap. Specific learning difficulties should be seen in the context of functional analysis, by means of which a child's assets and deficits can be identified, so that he can be helped not only to improve those functions which are deficient, but also to mobilize other functions as a compensatory resource. In other words, it seems evident that teaching should not be directed only at the areas of the child's disability.

At the start of this chapter, attention was drawn to the disagreements about the nature of learning disabilities. Some of these disagreements are very similar to the age-old controversies about the nature of intelligence. It seems essential that those working in this area should constantly use the actual tasks which children are expected to perform as a reference point, both in the functional analysis of children's difficulties and in the evaluation of remedial methods.

CHAPTER 5

Behaviour Modification in Special Education

J. WARD

INTRODUCTION

An impressive and rapidly expanding literature reflects the use of behaviour modification techniques in most areas of special education. It is now evident that programmes of intervention based on psychological learning theory can be applied successfully to a wide range of problems both in the suppression of undesirable behaviour and the teaching of new skills to individuals and groups of children within a variety of institutional settings. The current popularity of behaviour modification is hardly surprising: at a time when resources are clearly inadequate to satisfy the demand for professional help it is now established that an effective range of educational and management skills may be taught fairly easily to those in primary contact situations, such as parents, teachers, nurses and peer groups. For behaviour modification technology places the emphasis firmly upon the individual behaviour as a function of circumstances in the environment and does not require acquaintance with esoteric theories of causation or the symbolic meaning of behaviour. Instead attention is focused directly upon specific problems and the manipulation of environmental contingencies by which they can be approached. The resulting educational therapeutic programmes are truly special in that they are tailored to the needs of individual children and, when carefully designed and applied, can usually show positive results. Moreover, systematic analysis of the problem and continual monitoring of behaviour means that when difficulties do arise their sources are more readily identifiable.

The explosion of published material on behaviour modification in special education has involved the writer, like other reviewers, in considerable problems of organization and selectivity. A primary impulse was to classify reports of research according to the broad theoretical background which they exemplified: for example, operant conditioning; respondent conditioning; social modelling. This was found to be unsatisfactory as so much recent work contains elements of several theoretical approaches. Likewise a speculative 'taxonomy' based upon the techniques predominantly used, (e.g. punishment, operant conditioning, etc.) was abandoned since many classic studies, (e.g. the work of Lovaas and his colleagues with autistic children) employed several such concepts concurrently. It was decided therefore to follow the well-tried behaviourist principle of concentrating on problem areas and the chapter will proceed on this basis. Its general aims are as follows.

(a) To describe the concepts and techniques typically used in the application of behaviour modification methods in special education.
(b) To review representative work carried out in the following major areas:
  (i) autism or child psychosis;
  (ii) mental retardation;
  (iii) deviant and delinquent behaviour;
  (iv) perceptual handicaps;
  (v) large-scale programmes in compensatory education and intervention.
(c) To discuss the various theoretical and practical issues raised by this work with particular respect to its effectiveness.
(d) In conclusion, to consider some of the ethical issues surrounded by the use of such methods.

The bulk of work cited will be based on operant theory although a limited number of studies using respondent conditioning will be reviewed.

HISTORICAL AND THEORETICAL BACKGROUND TO BEHAVIOUR MODIFICATION

Despite the fact that, following pioneering work by Watson and Pavlov, the stage was set for widespread application of behaviour modification principles almost 50 years ago, it was not until quite recently that systematic attempts to use learning theory to solve problems in special education and institutional management were made. This is exemplified by the early operant studies of Bijou, Ellis, Staats, Ferster and others.

Indeed, most reported work in special education has been within this tradition but, as Kanfer (1973) and other reviewers have pointed out, there are at least four recognizable trends in behaviour modification. The first is primarily concerned with the control of stimulus conditions which elicit conditioned reflexes and to date has generated strategies mainly for therapeutic rather than educational use. Even so, one such strategy, systematic desentization (Wolpe, 1969) has been successfully used in the behaviour management of school phobia, e.g. Ayllon et al. (1970); Lowenstein (1973). This work is classified under the heading of respondent behaviour. By contrast, most of the research to be described is of the operant type. Operants are responses or behaviours whose frequency of occurrence can be functionally related to the presence of certain reinforcing events in the environment. For example, it has been demonstrated many times (Becker et al., 1967; Madsen et al., 1968; Ward, 1971) that teacher attention and praise delivered directly after adaptive classroom behaviours can increase their frequency and duration. Such teacher behaviour is therefore defined as positively reinforcing and in the absence of such reinforcement a child's production of such behaviours may tend to decrease. Similarly, an all-too-familiar situation may operate in which children produce desired behaviours to remove the threat of painful consequences, or to rescue themselves from continual nagging: in which case their behaviour is negatively reinforced. Fundamental to the success of this approach is the discovery of stimuli and events in the environment which can be used to discriminate and reinforce desired behaviours and which can maintain them at acceptable levels. The logical extension of this procedure involves decreasing the frequencies of undesirable behaviours by aversive consequences or by allowing them to extinguish, whilst at the same time strengthening responses which are incompatible.

Both respondent and operant conditioning involve some form of direct experience of contingent reinforcement. Bandura (1969), however, pointed out that an important pervasive means through which new learning takes place in humans is that of observation of another person's behaviour and its consequences for them. This is termed 'modelling' and allied processes such as imitation, identification and copying as 'vicarious learning processes'. This third approach has generated considerable interest in imitation, particularly in the area of language acquisition in severely subnormal children, e.g. Lovaas (1966); Risley and Wolf (1967).

A fourth and more recent type of behaviour modification is concerned with teaching subjects to control their own behaviour by observation, continual monitoring and some form of self-reinforcement, the rationale for this being that both overt and covert responses obey the same behavioural laws as the more directly observable operants (Drabman *et al.*, 1973).

Methods of behaviour modification derived from these approaches are therefore used singly or in combination in order to

(a) reduce the frequencies of behaviours which when excessive may be inimical to normal functioning;
(b) increase the frequencies of adaptive behaviours to within normal limits and
(c) initiate and maintain new forms of response.

They are all directed towards ascertaining and providing the optimal learning situation for individuals, since the distinctive feature of the educational philosophy generated from behaviour modification is the considerable, if not absolute, degree of responsibility accepted for the learner's performance. Since learning may be defined in terms of responses to discriminative stimuli under conditions of reinforcement and since teachers are charged with the task of arranging these so as to promote learning (Skinner, 1968) it follows that in a very real sense learning is held to be contingent upon teacher behaviour. Many would consider this to be a simplistic view of human learning but the optimism it epitomizes has led to much effective and provocative work.

THE BEHAVIOUR MODIFICATION PARADIGM

The core of any programme for behavioural change, whether carried out with individuals or groups, or with simple or complex behaviours, is the functional analysis of the problem. A number of variations upon Skinner's original formulations are available and the analysis may extend to much more general systems of educational development, e.g. Bricker and Bricker (1973); Zifferblatt (1973). However, the procedure consists essentially of the following operations:

(a) Identification of the universe of behaviours to be controlled or instituted, often involving identification of hierarchical relationships in the target behaviours and a statement of intermediate and terminal goals.
(b) Observation of existing target behaviours in terms of their frequency and intensity of emission together with an analysis of the stimuli, environmental conditions and consequences which may be functionally related.
(c) Identification of methods by which the behaviour may be modified or elicited and their results evaluated; the analysis may then lead on to
(d) implementation of a programme,
(e) continuous monitoring of the target behaviours, sometimes varying antecedent, environmental and reinforcement conditions systematically,
(f) terminal evaluation, possibly with some attempt to establish stimulus and response generalization for new behavioural patterns.

These six components will now be discussed in more detail.

(a) Identification of the behavioural universe or problem area

The problem areas represented in behaviour modification research range from the initiation of simple bar-pressing behaviour (Bailey and Mayerson, 1969) to comprehensive systems for linguistic development (Bricker and Bricker, 1972) and large-scale intervention projects such as Operation Follow-up (Becker and Engleman, 1973). It is noteworthy that although behavioural modification, like systems analysis, would claim that one of its main strengths is the objective statement of target behaviours, in practice these are often initially couched in rather vague terms, particularly in programmes applied in institutions. Thus the consultant may be asked to reduce the level of disruptive behaviour and increase the quality of school performance. However, in the case of new learning such as self-help skills in the severely retarded or language acquisition in autistic children a finely detailed analytic approach is crucial. Even so, the postulation of terminal goals based on normative data is simple compared with the identification of component skills or intermediate stages in the acquisition of complex behaviours like spoken language or reading. In the vast majority of areas in special education the existence of a problem is beyond dispute as is the need for innovative and experimental work.

(b) Observation

The second stage is the collection of baseline data relative to the problem behaviours. It is essential that this should be, as far as possible, representative of the range of stimulus, setting or environmental conditions and reinforcement events which obtain. Accuracy of observation and recording is of course fundamental to scientific enquiry in both experimental and natural settings and this has been a prime concern of psychologists interested in the experimental analysis of behaviour.

The methodology of observation is now considerably augmented through this work and that of the ethologists (c.f. Blurton-Jones, 1972) and experimental social psychologists in their studies of the minutiae of social interaction.

There already exist general techniques for studying group interaction (Bales, 1950) and parent or teacher/child interactions (Flanders, 1970). To these may be added the techniques of industrial job analysis (Whelan, 1973) and various other means of analysing skilled behaviour (Connolly, 1973).

In some experimental work observational and recording devices are built into the equipment and also into the accommodation. Generally speaking however, observational variables may be classified as falling into two categories:

(a) the means by which information is obtained, e.g. human observer, videotape, film, sound recording etc. and

(b) the recording systems in use, e.g. check lists and event recorders of varying degrees of sophistication.

Human observers possess inherent unreliability which is exacerbated when they are asked to record too many behaviours simultaneously or are required to exceed the normal bounds of their attentional capacity. Checks upon reliability can be made when film or videotape recording can be carried out simultaneously; more commonly, however, the level of agreement of two observers of the same behaviour is assessed. Reliability may be affected by the feasibility of the recording system used, and the time-sampling methods, especially the nature of the time intervals into which behaviours have to be entered. Some workers insist upon extremely exact recording, e.g. Watson (1968), but most observational techniques in special education are designed for paraprofessionals such as teachers and parents and must be sufficiently robust to pick up useful data without placing excessive training demands upon the user.

These procedures will often specify a set of behavioural categories combined with a time scale, often divided into fairly gross intervals such as 10 seconds. The procedures can be varied as to the time sampling required, some users observing continuously for, say, 20-minute blocks, others alternating observing and recording. By overlapping, estimates of inter-observer reliability may be obtained. Thus Observer A might record for 6 minutes then rest; Observer B commences at minute 5 and records for 6 minutes, a measure of agreement being available for minutes 5 and 6. A simple recording sheet of this type is illustrated in Figure 5.1 below. Many

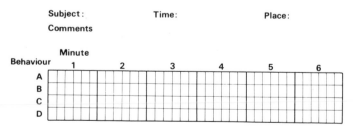

FIGURE 5.1. Behaviour observation recording sheet

similar sheets have been evolved, some using logarithmic scales (c.f. Haring and Phillips, 1972).

This method can be used for observing individual children of particular interest, representative 'target' children and, if necessary, for randomly sampling behaviour from an entire class.

(c) Identification of possible methods

The functional analysis should identify some of the antecedent and setting stimuli which are important and also the range of possible reinforcers which can be used to shape behaviour. It is then evident that minor reorganization or advice on handling is all that is required to effect substantial improvements in problem behaviour.

Antecedent events

Essentially antecedent stimulus events provoke and guide learning so that reinforcement can take place. In educational settings these include the curriculum, the teacher's behaviour in directing learning, and the organization of the classroom so as to facilitate the emergence of specified behaviours, for example the engineered classroom described by Hewett (1968). Even in special education this is by far the greatest source of behavioural control. Indeed, the first impact of operant methodology was felt in this area through the programmed learning approach in the late fifties. The obvious questions raised here are: is the sequence of behaviours to be learned relevant and interesting? does the learner possess the basic repertoire of behaviours upon which this new learning can be built? is the teacher effective in communicating the task requirements to children?

However, the ways in which these issues are resolved in the normal classroom may not operate successfully with children with special educational needs, whose programmes have to be fully individualized.

Setting events

Bijou (1973) suggests that setting factors are conditions which endow stimuli with functional characteristics such as a reinforcing property, and may derive from the child, his family, the teacher, the classroom and so on. These can include the physical state of the child, his home background, his teacher's attitude and expectations, and the physical appearance of the classroom. Though difficult to explain, these factors are readily observable in educational situations when, for example, the teacher who has good control over the children in her class, takes them into the classroom of a teacher who has poor control, and sees very different behaviour. For many children in special education the whole educational setting is aversive.

Consequent events

Events which can serve to increase the probability of responses are usually designated as reinforcing and those which decrease the probability of responses as punishing. Both positive and negative reinforcers therefore strengthen behaviour, and punishment weakens it. This can be schematized as follows:

	Positive reinforcer	*Negative stimulus*
present:	positive reinforcement (behaviour strengthened).	punishment (behaviour weakened).
remove:	punishment (behaviour weakened).	negative reinforcement (behaviour strengthened).

When behaviours are unreinforced their frequency decreases owing to the process of extinction. At the beginning of extinction, behaviour may show a temporary increase in frequency and then decrease consistently. It is conventional to classify extrinsic reinforcers as *primary*, (e.g. food, water etc.) and *secondary* or derived, (e.g. praise, attention, knowledge or results, rewards etc.). Primary reinforcers are used mainly in basic discrimination training and in teaching self-help skills, when the behavioural repertoire and consequently the range of effective reinforcers is very limited. Since autistic or severely retarded subjects may be required to be continuously reinforced at first, the satiation value of food reinforcers like Smarties is very important. To overcome this problem, alternative reinforcers such as vibration have been proposed (Bailey and Mayerson, 1969) in the research cited. Sometimes children's tastes in primary reinforcers are highly idiosyncratic, e.g. cheese, raw vegetables, particular sweets, etc.

Social reinforcers represent a vast and often untapped area of behavioural control for teachers, parents and other change agents. Becker (1973) in fact claims that the majority of behavioural problems in special education can be ameliorated by effective use of social reinforcers. Where excessive disruptive behaviour occurs, it is usually found that little contingently applied positive reinforcement is used by the teacher, his positive comments being delivered non-specifically and at the wrong times. Frequently the teacher's main style of control is aversive, with the possibility that this increases rather than decreases the amount of undesirable behaviour (Madsen *et al.*, 1968). Often observation of a target child will quickly reveal examples of deviant behaviour being reinforced (Becker *et al.*, 1967; Ward, 1971).

In classroom situations undesirable behaviours can be allowed to extinguish unless they are too extreme for the limits normally accepted. This, together with the use of social reinforcement, gives rise to a simple set of rules applicable to a variety of contingency management problems. These are:

(a) state the behaviours expected, often in the form of clearly understood rules;
(b) give, as far as possible, behaviours incompatible with these;
(c) reinforce the desired behaviours promptly and as frequently as possible, preferably at the same time as incompatible behaviours are occurring elsewhere.

Most of the manuals for precision teaching embody this type of basic system

(Meacham and Wiesen, 1969; Madsen and Madsen, 1970; Haring and Phillips, 1972).

Punishment

Punishment consists of the application of consequences which will suppress or reduce the frequencies of undesirable behaviour. The distinction is usually drawn between less aversive methods and strong, aversive stimuli such as electric shocks and physical restraint which have been used in the 'suppression' of self-injurious behaviour, e.g. Bucher and Lovaas (1968); Tate and Barroff (1966). A number of studies using aversive stimuli are reviewed by Gardner (1971).

Punishing stimuli available to teachers include *verbal reprimands* which may act to suppress undesirable behaviour; *suspension of privileges*, particularly if the child concerned is given 'time-out' from a positively reinforcing classroom situation and finally, *response cost*, which can involve taking away accumulated reinforcers such as in a token economy, or making offenders work to regain a privilege.

Token economies

Systematic administration of the types of reinforcers mentioned above involves considerable difficulties, particularly in school or institutional settings where the procedures are vulnerable to many sources of inequality and interference. Many of these may be overcome by the use of point systems or token economies, involving the award of points, stars, poker chips and symbols of various kinds contingent upon the production of desired behaviours. The tokens are then accumulated and can either be exchanged for various back-up reinforcers of the child's own choice or used to purchase privileges such as free time or highly attractive activities. Token economies have been set up in special classes for the retarded (Birnbrauer *et al.*, 1965), for the emotionally disturbed (O'Leary and Becker, 1967), in special schools (Bijou, 1973; Haring, 1968) and residential units for delinquents (Cohen and Filipcjak, 1971).

Activities as reinforcers

The reinforcement value of attractive and highly preferred activities has always been recognized by parents and teachers. Recently, however, this has been formulated in an elegant way by Premack (1965) who stated that, given two behaviours of differing probability of occurrence, the more probable behaviour may be used to increase the probability of occurrence of the other. The principle has been used in several researches (Homme *et al.*, 1963; Lovitt *et al.*, 1969; Wasik, 1970) and obviously possesses great potential as a source of behavioural control.

Reinforcement scheduling

Although many complex forms of reinforcement scheduling exist, the topic receives minimal discussion in most experimental accounts. Virtually all programmes directed towards the learning of new behaviours use *continuous reinforcement*, i.e. reinforcement following every response, but since such learning is easily extinguished, move towards *intermittent or partial* reinforcement. Examples of regular partial reinforcement are the *Fixed Ratio Schedule*, when reinforcement is contingent upon production of a given number of responses and the *Variable Ratio* schedule, when the number of responses before reinforcement varies round an average. *Fixed Interval* Schedules involve delivery after a fixed period of time whatever the number of behaviours, and *Variable Interval* schedules also vary around an average time interval for reinforcement. In general, variable ratio and interval schedules approximate best to reinforcement patterns in the natural environment and therefore are more likely to produce stable learning (c.f. Gardner, 1971 for a discussion of these issues).

Strategies for producing new behaviour

The procedure for identifying terminal and intermediate goals generates two important strategies for producing new behaviour. The first of these, *shaping*, is particularly suitable for children with limited behavioural repertoires since it involves gradually securing and reinforcing the best approximations to the desired response so that the final behaviour can be reinforced normally. Shaping typically uses imitation and positive reinforcement, the best illustrations being in the area of language acquisition.

The second procedure, *chaining*, refers to the establishment of behavioural chains in which each response acts as a stimulus for the next. Although the elements of a chain may form part of a logically ordered behavioural pattern, as might be involved in learning to dress oneself, e.g. Minge and Ball (1967), this is not necessary. In fact any temporal sequence can be thought of in this way and, as Haring and Phillips suggest, activities may be arranged so as to capitalize upon Premack's reinforcement principle. Thus high probability behaviour such as games can be used to reinforce low probability behaviours such as number work and spelling.

(d) Implementation of a programme

Whatever the level of complexity of target behaviours, the types of subjects and institutions involved, the following issues emerge in programme implementations.

(a) Administrators, teachers, parents, nurses and others who may carry out contingency management must agree with the basic aims and methods of the programme.

(b) Thorough training needs to be given to those administering reinforcement, and their performance monitored regularly. Adequate consultation should be available.

(c) The programmes should be sufficiently flexible to allow deployment of alternative strategies when difficulties are encountered.

Agreement with aims

The difficulties vary from, say, those of the parent of a retarded child who views consistency in reinforcement practices as unnatural and an abrogation of her right to show affection, to those of head teachers and administrators called upon to implement programmes with unacceptable aims. Many of these problems can be resolved by effective communication but sometimes more fundamental principles may be involved, such as whether teachers should allow the widespread employment of paraprofessionals in teaching roles. Then again, in the pursuit of innovation for its own sake, programmes are set up hurriedly and without adequate provision for consultation and support. Frequently, real differences in management philosophy emerge and those in previous contact situations may be unconvinced of the necessity for change. Unfortunately, these failures and the problems which they may cause are rarely documented (exceptions being the occasional article like 'How to make a token system fail' (Kuypers *et al.*, 1968).

Training

The extension of behaviour modification into so many institutional and natural settings has created a considerable demand for training at every level. There have been many reports of training teachers and parents of handicapped and emotionally disturbed children, e.g. Salzinger *et al.* (1970), Allen and Harris (1966), Hawkins *et al.* (1966), and also a number of books and programmed texts based upon behavioural principles have been published, e.g. Madsen and Madsen (1970), Patterson and Gullion (1968). Several excellent reviews of this work exist (Patterson, 1971; Gardner, 1973; Guerney, 1969). Similar training is of course required for nurses and child care staff (Watson, 1973).

Training college students have often been used as paraprofessional aides, e.g. Sloan *et al.* (1968), and several recent studies have explored the possibility of teaching peer groups to use reinforcement, e.g. Solomon and Wahler (1973).

Most work reported on training is descriptive rather than experimental. In the writer's experience, approaches which involve regular practically orientated seminars, fairly immediate try-out of the methods, and feedback on progress, work best with primary contact personnel.

The need for flexibility

Effective application of an operant approach should allow for variations in response to stimulus and reinforcing events and should provide for a range of alternative strategies. Difficulties often arise as a result of inflexible commitment to particular materials and methods, such as reading materials which are manifestly uninteresting, or to unworkable point or token systems. A parallel set of problems may be caused by using up all the options, as it were, early in a programme, with the result that potent reinforcers like praise and activities are degraded by comparison with expensive back-up reinforcers.

(e) Monitoring

The state of affairs indicated in the preceding paragraph emphasizes the need for adequate experimental controls. However, concentration upon single cases obviously involves many difficulties in design and evaluation. Most simple applications of behaviour modification use a quasi-experimental design such as *A B*, where *A* represents behaviour under baseline conditions, *B* behaviour under the experimental conditions. Teachers, parents and care staff who obtain a clearly demonstrated effect from the programme will often be unwilling to return to the pre-experimental condition even if this were possible, as Baer *et al.* (1968) point out in a discussion of these issues. A more effective indicator of experimental results is afforded by the so-called reversal or *ABAB* design and this figures prominently in fully experimental work. However, for cases where reversibility is not feasible, Baer suggests the *multiple baseline* design which is particularly appropriate where several behaviours are to be brought under control. Here experimental procedures are applied to one of these at first. If change is observed, and if the other behaviours do not change concurrently, the procedure is extended to a second behaviour and so on. In appropriate circumstances multiple baselines and reversals can be combined, an example of this being Kazelin's (1973) study of the effects of vicarious reinforcement on attentive behaviour.

Whatever the design used, continuance of adequate observation is vital, this being more easily achieved where formally defined behaviours such as academic achievements are involved, which can be objectively tested.

(f) Evaluation

The dominant criterion by which behaviour modification programmes must be judged is whether the target behaviours have been taught to acceptable levels or, in the case of surplus behaviours, brought under control. Associated with this is some assessment of the relative efficiency of the programme in reaching the criterion in terms of length of time, number of trials required and the level of reinforcement required to maintain desirable behaviour. Since evaluation by the personnel directly concerned is subject to contamination, some objective assessment of its reliability is normally included.

Psychologists evaluating programmes are normally concerned with the generalizability of behaviour to extra-experimental settings, and with its stability or further development under 'natural' conditions of reinforcement (Tharp and Wetzel, 1969). Evidence of *stimulus generalization* might include performance of self-help skills at home as well as in the institution within which these were learned: evidence of *response generalization*, performance of a limited behavioural repertoire which generalized to a wider set of behaviour. In evaluating outcomes psychometrically, the behavioural engineer may use criterion-referenced tests to assess the specific aims of the programmes (Popham and Husek, 1969; Ward, 1970) and norm-referenced tests to give information of generalizability. As in the programmed learning techniques with which it is frequently associated, evaluation in behaviour modification is fully personalized; it is the individual's response to various environmental events which is of interest, not differences between individuals.

APPLICATIONS OF BEHAVIOUR MODIFICATION

Autistic or psychotic children

Some of the most provocative and wide-ranging uses of behaviour modification are reported by Lovaas and his colleagues, working with autistic children at the Neuropsychiatric Unit, U.C.L.A. (c.f. Lovaas and Kogoel, 1973, for an overview of their many researches). Such children typically exhibit symptoms of extreme withdrawal and isolation to the extent that they are suspected of blindness or deafness. They frequently are unresponsive to parental affection, have little if any functional speech and are profoundly retarded in the acquisition of normal social skills such as toileting, feeding and dressing themselves. Along with these may be shown disturbing self-destructive behaviour, bizarre rituals of self-stimulation and stereotypy. Whilst recognizing the existence of a large number of possible causes of autism, these workers have assumed that the behaviour of autistic children can be brought under the control of environmental events and that their problems can be attacked by means of a learning theory approach.

Probably the most distressing problem behaviour is self-mutilation in the shape of head banging, biting, scratching and chewing flesh, necessitating heavy sedation or physical restraint. Despite the irrational nature of these acts, Lovaas considered them to be straightforward learning behaviour, highly discriminative as to the place of occurrence and clearly related to forms of social reinforcement by parents and institutional staff. When these behaviours were allowed to extinguish without intervention, the frequencies of self-destructive acts reached a peak and then gradually reduced to zero. However, the ethical and medical dangers of this procedure are obvious, Lovaas reporting that some children produced several thousand acts and injured themselves quite badly. In an attempt to avoid this, painful electric shocks were given, contingent upon self-mutilation. This was immediately and remarkably successful in reducing the frequencies of self-mutilations to near zero, although there was no evidence of any dramatic changes in other behaviours. The effect has also been observed by other researchers (Giles and Wolf, 1966; Risley, 1966).

By contrast with self-mutilation, the basis of stereotyped movements, various forms of self-stimulation and obsessionalism is less clearly understood. It is obvious that whilst children are behaving in this way, they cannot attend to discriminative cues for new learning, and therefore these activities must be suppressed as far as possible.

Extending the very limited behavioural repertoires available to autistic children presents a considerable challenge to teachers. One of the reasons for these children's failure to learn may be an inability to develop normal motivation based upon generalized reinforcers. Many workers point to the high idiosyncratic nature of functional reinforcers in autistic children. Moreover, it seems that although there may be no direct indication of partial sensory deficits, such children are unable to integrate information coming from several modalities. Instead, they may be overselective in responding to cues, fixating, for example, upon the teacher's face, but paying no attention whatsoever to the sound of the words they are being required to imitate. Lovaas and Koegel note that the use of prompting to guide discrimination learning in ordinary children may be precisely what makes learning so difficult for the autistic child.

A major emphasis in the special educational treatment of autistic children has been placed upon language acquisition (e.g. Hewett, 1965; Lovaas, 1966). The procedures typically include discrimination and training, bringing attention under stimulus control, and imitation, both non-verbal and verbal. The Lovaas programme goes on to teach a wide variety of sounds, words and sentences resulting in some cases in the production of reasonably normal social language. It is stressed, however, that initially mute children rarely reach this stage, the greatest success being obtained with echolalic children.

A considerable body of similar work has been reported: Nordquist and Waler (1973) describe their successful treatment of 'Joey', a four-year-old, variously diagnosed as mentally retarded, schizophrenic, brain-damaged, aphasic and autistic. Reviewing the results of experimental work of the Lovaas type, they remark upon the lack of evidence of generalizability to the natural environment of behaviours learned in experimental settings. This issue has been taken up by Lovaas and his collaborators in a very important recent article (Lovaas et al., 1973). Following up the progress of 20 autistic children treated at various times in their programmes, they note that children discharged into institutional care tended to regress towards former levels of psychotic behaviour. On the other hand, those returning home maintained their new behaviours and in some cases improved. Not unexpectedly, some parents proved to be better behaviour modifiers than others and it is instructive to note that these were

(a) willing to use strong consequences, i.e. food deprivation and spankings;
(b) willing to deny that their child was ill and
(c) were willing to commit a major part of their lives to their child, which might involve some degree of contingency management throughout the day. In other words, that they were able to continue the methods used by the researchers.

With appropriate maintenance by parents it therefore appears that some effects generalize over time and, as judged by improved IQs and Vineland Social Quotients, there is evidence of definite response generalization. However, the issues surrounding stimulus generalization remain to be resolved, particularly if the autistic child is eventually to be integrated into normal classrooms. Nonetheless, it is claimed that no other educational approach to autism has enjoyed comparable success and that for some aspects of educational treatment, behaviour modification is the technique of choice. Despite this, as Rutter and Sussenwein (1971) and others have observed, reduction of surplus behaviours has been rather more successful than remediation of behavioural deficits such as language.

Mental retardation

It is evident from even the most cursory scrutiny of the available literature that retarded children constitute the largest and most important group of subjects for behaviour modification programmes. Although, aetiologically, they form an extremely diverse population, the most commonly held view (Heber, 1961) is that mental retardation originates in the developmental period and results in impaired or maladaptive behaviour. Possible contributory factors may be classified under the three headings: biological, sociocultural and psychological. Bijou (1973) states that views about causation give rise to two basic theories; the 'defect' theory being mainly associated with biological factors and the 'deficit' theory being derived from socio-cultural and psychological factors. Neither theory has proved to be conspicuously successful in generating special programmes. To Bijou then, the specific behaviours defining mental retardation are not taken as 'indicators of pathology, but as the basis for planning a teaching programme, remedial or compensatory'.

For the present purpose it is convenient to adhere to the two main categories of *trainable mental retardates* (corresponding in the U.K. to the severely subnormal) and *educable mental retardates* (corresponding in the U.K. to the educationally subnormal, for most practical purposes).

Work with the severely subnormal

Operant work in this area has now been in progress for over fifteen years and has resulted in much more favourable perception of what can be achieved with these children. Thus, as Gardner (1971) observes, there has been a shift from basic care and life maintenance to rehabilitation and training in more advanced social skills.

Although it may be demonstrated that behaviour in the subnormal is functionally related to environmental change in relatively normal ways, Gardner lists a number of specific factors.

(1) Limited behavioural repertoires, important consequences of this being the difficulty of integrating new behaviour into existing patterns. Also very little adaptive behaviour may be available to compete with undesirable responses.
(2) Limited availability of reinforcers—particularly secondary reinforcers, as associative learning may occur so slowly.
(3) Difficulties in establishing conditioned aversive stimuli such as 'stop' or 'no'.
(4) Limitations in expressive and receptive language.
(5) Poorly developed imitation skills with the result that learning may not occur unless positively reinforced.
(6) Skills in attending to relevant cues are poor, resulting in faulty discrimination learning.
(7) High-rate disruptive behaviours are frequently resistant to change.
(8) Low tolerance for frustration together with hyperactivity, making it difficult to attract attention.
(9) Difficulties over response generalization.

As the name of the category might imply, most operant work in severe subnormality has been directed towards training in self-help and social skills. A number of studies are cited by Williams (1973) who makes the important point that not only is an attempt made to change the behaviour of the retarded subject, but also to alter the demands and expectations of others in his environment. The second process is, of course, facilitated when the retarded possess normal self-help skills such as toileting, feeding and dressing. Considerable ingenuity has therefore been applied to training toileting behaviours. Mahoney et al. (1971), for instance, carried out an elaborate procedure to toilet train five retarded children (four male 4-year olds and one profoundly retarded 9-year old) and three normal children in the 18–21 month age range. This involved equipping the children with an auditory signalling device which generated an auditory signal to the experimenters after urine flow. The training programme consisted of teaching the sequence of behaviours which precede elimination, such as walking to the commode, lowering pants and sitting on or facing the commode. This was carried out by physical, visual and auditory prompting, the first two subsequently being faded out, leaving the child to respond only to the auditory signals from the experimenters.

The second half of the sequence included elimination, and clothing return, gradually fading the prompts and signalling, and practising the behaviour chain without the auditory signal. Success was obtained in four out of the five retarded cases and in all the normals. The amount of experimental time required to achieve successful performance of the whole behavioural chain varied from 17–48 hours. In an attempt to obtain generalization the parents were taught similar procedures and follow-up data from the home was obtained.

Language and general cognitive development. Many attempts have been made to inculcate generalizable cognitive skills culminating in the acquisition of functional language. Here a major problem has been the poor training histories of the severely subnormal, necessitating much greater stimulus control in the simplest of discrimination learning tasks (Johnson, 1973). Even so, a number of studies have demonstrated their ability to form learning sets for concept formation tasks under various conditions of reinforcement. Jacobson et al. (1973), for instance, found that both modelling and immediate feedback procedures were effective in training a group of retarded adolescents on two-choice concept formation problems. Moreover, response generalization was claimed in the form of increased IQ scores.

Deficits in response to verbal cueing have already been mentioned, and are an obvious source of difficulty for learning situations. Whitman et al. (1971), using food reinforcers, physical guidance and fading, were able to teach two severely retarded children instruction-following behaviour such as responses to 'sit down'; 'give me the pencil'; 'pick up the cup'; etc. With older children modification of similar behaviour has been carried out on a group basis. Zimmerman et al. (1969) used general rather than individually directed instructional procedures with seven retarded boys. This study employed teacher praise and token reinforcements with mixed, though mostly favourable, results.

Research into the teaching of language to retarded children has both practical significance and importance for theories of developmental psycholinguistics. Much work has been stimulated by Skinner's (1957) definition of language as verbal behaviour, the logical extension of this (Staats, 1968) being that even complex learning, such as the acquisition of grammatical rules, is the result of generalized differential reinforcement. In this tradition Sailor (1971) studied the production of plural allomorphs (voiced and unvoiced) in two severely retarded girls, obtaining generalized effects in support of the theory.

The most developed application of this work has undoubtedly been the comprehensive programmes for children with developmental delay outlined by Bricker and Bricker (1973). The 'Toddler Project' they describe consists of a basic educational system in five main areas of human development; sensory-motor behaviour, self-care, recreation and play, social behaviour and language. Each area has its programme, procedure and implementation 'lattices'.

In the context of this programme behaviour modification methods are used to produce discriminated behaviour at all developmental levels. This involves obtaining stimulus control, shaping and maintaining behaviour over long periods of time. Considerable use is made of both motor and verbal imitation. In an integrated approach to language training evolved over several years, the Brickers have shown that retarded children can benefit from formal instruction in language. Commenting upon this paper Yule (1973) makes the point that the work demonstrates that behaviour modification is a strategy rather than a discrete set of techniques.

Work with the educable mentally retarded

Since the bulk of retarded children fall into this category, there has been a great deal of educational interest in the application of behaviour modification principles in special classes and schools for the educable mentally retarded. A prototype for this has been the experimental class at Rainier School which for over ten years has been carrying out experimental education with a variety of brain-damaged, mongoloid and familially retarded children (Bijou, 1973). These programmes are fully individualized with continual monitoring of skill and behavioural development within an integrated curriculum. Although a token economy is used, considerable emphasis is placed upon organization of educational materials and correct classroom behaviour, to make the programmes intrinsicly rewarding. Thus punishment in the form of 'time out' and response cost is now rarely used and the classes have developed a considerable degree of normality. Bijou reviews a number of similar experimental projects which act as a laboratory for technical development and generate new instructional materials.

Possession of a relatively wide repertoire of behaviours means that secondary reinforcers can be used more effectively. A recent example of this has been reported by Dalton et al. (1973) who used token reinforcement (poker chips on a continuous reinforcement schedule) to teach elements of the Distar language and arithmetic programmes to a group of mongoloid children. This study used a follow-up after one year and found that, by comparison with a control group, learning under the reinforcement conditions was much better retained.

It is therefore clear that behaviour modification methods can be applied to obtain educational gains in this area, but the question of whether superior long-term results in achievement and adjustment accrue is still unresolved. (However, in visiting several such classes the writer was vastly impressed by the diversity of the curriculum and by the social poise of many of the children.)

Control of deviant and delinquent behaviour

A basic premise of all types of behaviour modification practice is the notion that 'emotionally disturbed', 'neurotic' or 'antisocial behaviour' is learned, varying perhaps from the normal in terms of intensity and frequency, but subject to the same forms of environmental control (Eysenck, 1960; Wolpe, 1969). This position is usually reiterated in order to attack so-called 'disease' models of disturbed behaviour, although recently some writers (e.g. London, 1972) have seriously questioned the need for further polemics in this area.

In fact most programmes concentrate initially upon the reduction of antisocial behaviour as a necessary precursor to the establishment of more desirable activities. It is often found that the undesirable behaviour has been, or is being, unwittingly reinforced by parents, teachers and other significant agencies such as peer groups. This can usually be modified, and adaptive behaviour instituted and maintained by the methods already used in the work of Becker, O'Leary, Madsen, Staats and their collaborators. However, for certain classes of antisocial and aggressive behaviour use of a more systematically planned environment is necessary. In many cases this has led to the use of token economies as the most effective method of bringing such behaviour dramatically under control.

Reports of the use of token economies in education have been reviewed by O'Leary and Drabman (1971), Krasner and Krasner (1973) and Kazdin and Bootzin (1973). Typically the procedure demands exact specification of target behaviours, setting up a point or token system which can be administered without too much difficulty or extra staff, and an effective range of back-up reinforcers. In essence the token economy succeeds for the same reasons as any other form of contingency management, although it does possess considerable inherent flexibility. It can, however, give rise to a number of difficulties in practice, particularly over the lack of generalizability of behaviours reinforced under the token economy. This is usually interpreted as a failure to programme adequately for stimulus generalization but many teachers in schools where special classes are housed and also neutral observers, have commented on the way in which special classes reinforce disruptive behaviour. Thus, when a student is bored, frustrated or antisocial, he or she behaves intolerably and is reinforced by being placed in a more rewarding and perhaps less demanding situation.

Token economies probably function best, therefore, in residential situations where there can be uniformity of administration and policy. One of the best-known programmes of this type has been the C.A.S.E. (Contingencies in Special Education) Project reported by Cohen and Filipczak (1971). The aim of this project was to increase the academic achievement and social development of a group of 41 delinquent boys through a specially designed learning environment. In many ways the system replicated the economic aspects of American society. Students worked for the C.A.S.E. Corporation and were rewarded for academic achievement by points which could be exchanged for a wide range of privileges, including more comfortable accommodation, free time and home visiting, etc. Gains in academic achievement of the programme were considerable but long-term follow-up of the participants on release showed that the programme did not significantly affect recidivism rates. Even so the C.A.S.E. project attracted monumental publicity and the contingency management approach to delinquency prevention has obtained a wide measure of community support. Cohen (1973) lists a number of such programmes. Most of these attempt to function in more natural environments or in the community by using various agencies as contingency managers. The 'Teaching Family' approach, for instance, needs highly trained professional 'teaching parents' in charge of family groups of 6–10 delinquent children (Wolf et al., 1973). The most significant agencies for behavioural change are, however, probably the families of delinquent children and a number of attempts to train these as contingency managers have been reported. Patterson (1973) reviews several small-scale studies into training the families of deviant children in contingency management. Some of the early results are promising but as yet no large-scale study has reported data. A fairly comprehensive review of the use of parents as change-agents has also been carried out by Johnson and Katz (1973).

In view of the fact that peer groups have been strongly implicated in maintaining antisocial behaviour it is hardly surprising that their potential for effecting positive behavioural change has been explored. Although the number of such studies is relatively few, several creative approaches are represented, among which are group contingency management and tutoring by peers. Children have been used as behavioural engineers (Surratt et al., 1969) and a recent study (Nelson et al., 1973) describes how emotionally disturbed children were used as behaviour managers for others. The location for this was a summer camp for disturbed children. Eight out of nine case reports indicated change in the target behaviours.

Uses of respondent conditioning

In the article by Patterson previously cited it is claimed that only about a third of reported behaviour problems involve aggressive acting-out behaviour; alternative strategies may be required for different problem areas such as lack of self-assertion and phobic reaction. Thus in view of the strong affective component in such behaviour, respondent methods based upon classical conditioning may be more appropriate. In particular desensitization methods have been shown to be effective in the treatment of phobic reactions and excessive fears in children.

Desensitization involves identification of situations which are highly anxiety-arousing and asking the subject to imagine a hierarchy of situations which, proceeding from an emotionally neutral base, become progressively more anxiety-provoking until the problem situation is reached. These are then presented to the subject in the order of the hierarchy whilst the subject is relaxing or receiving some kind of rewarding stimulation antagonistic to feelings of anxiety. He therefore proceeds gradually up the hierarchy as he reports that he can imagine progressively more threatening situations without undue anxiety. An account of a simple classroom application of the technique was provided by Kravetz and Forness (1971) who treated elective mutism in a highly anxious 6½-year-old boy in a hospital school. The hierarchy used ranged from 'reading alone to investigators' to 'asking questions or making comment' in a weekly ward meeting. A strong hero figure, Paul Bunyan, was used as a supportive emotive image. . . . 'This time imagine that your big strong friend Paul Bunyan is standing next to you in the group', etc. The subject was reinforced in the actual situation and afterwards was reported as adjusting satisfactorily in a normal classroom.

Similar techniques have been used successfully in the treatment of school phobia (Lowenstein, 1973), although an operant approach, defining school as a 'low probability behaviour', has been described by Ayllon et al. (1970) and was apparently highly effective.

Self-reinforcement

In the course of reviewing a large number of token economy studies, O'Leary and Drabman (1971) suggested several possible ways of maintaining desirable behaviours following the withdrawal of tokens. These included the teaching of self-evaluation and self-reinforcement skills. A limited but ingenious demonstration of the feasibility of this was carried out by Drabman et al. (1973) with eight emotionally disturbed children in remedial classes as subjects. Here the children were receiving point awards for good work and behaviour under a token system. At the beginning of the experiment they were asked to evaluate themselves in the same way as their teacher: they were then asked to match their points award with that of the teacher, children whose totals closely matched being allowed to keep the points. Exact matching received an additional bonus, inaccurate matching lost the points. Gradually the number of checks on self-evaluation was faded to zero: under the token conditions children's self-evaluation determined their reward. Surprisingly enough, although there were ample opportunities for cheating, this did not occur and in the control conditions (non-token reinforcement) the level of behaviour was relatively good. A number of associated factors such as continual social reinforcement might have affected this finding, the writers making the shrewd point that the proportion of token time to control time was very high, 3 to 1, thus favouring generalization to the control conditions.

Despite the conceptual difficulties which undoubtedly surround the return of self-control, the work cited above is extremely interesting and capable of further development, especially with the emotionally disturbed.

Perceptually handicapped children

There is, of course, no fundamental reason why perceptually handicapped children should not respond to appropriate behaviour modification techniques and a multiplicity of handicaps are represented in operant work with the retarded. Thus far the volume of published work in the general area is small, except in language development.

From time to time, however, fairly orthodox classroom work is reported: Osbourne (1969), for example, studied the reinforcement effect of free time on remaining in seat behaviour in six young deaf children. This is a clear example of the use of Premack's generalization on reinforcement in a school situation.

Visual attention to instructional stimuli is crucial to deaf children as they obviously require concentrated visual orientation, and in any event aural reinforcement may be delayed or absent. Craig and Holland (1970) carried out several experiments into this problem in a special school for the deaf. Here the twenty-one children concerned had lights installed upon their desks which flashed contingent upon attending behaviour. The number of flashes was recorded and food reinforcers and various grades of tokens issued. An interesting feature was that tokens could be saved in order to 'buy' some highly attractive books used to supplement the reading lessons. The authors reported that these were always in high demand, as was extra tutorial time. Positive results were obtained under three types of reinforcement conditions and it is concluded that similar training should be given to deaf children as early as possible.

There is obviously scope for self-help training with the blind and a very interesting single case study of this type was described by Stolz and Wolf (1969). The subject here was a 16-year-old retarded adolescent who had been diagnosed as retarded and organically blind. The experiments were directed at evoking nonverbal responses. It was first established that Fred's, the subject's, performance on a series of gross discrimination tasks was better than chance. A second series of tasks using 1"-high letters printed on cards showed that Fred possessed sufficient visual accuity to enable him to read suitable print. Via shaping procedures using food reinforcers, Fred was then trained in eye contact with an experimenter and also achieved a limited amount of generalization to other individuals. This training was extended to social behaviour and self-help skills in natural situations such as the hospital cafeteria. The relationship of Fred's new behaviour to reinforcing events in his environment was clearly shown. As in most other examples of new learning, it is essential that the new repertoire continues to be reinforced. The authors cite other work where, after being discharged as sighted, subjects revert back to being 'blind'.

It is evident that many other potential applications of reinforcement principles exist, e.g. for wearing hearing aids, for lip-reading instruction, and so on. Bricker and Bricker (1969) have devised a method of carrying out audiometric assessment through operant methods. This forms part of the language programme already mentioned and is an obvious area for future growth in work with deaf and language disordered children.

Many problems are encountered in the measurement of visual accuity in nonverbal retarded children. Macht (1971) pointed out that owing to difficulty in assessment, many retarded children with visual handicaps either remain undiagnosed or have to wait a considerable time before receiving help. Using operant methods involving a single lever press Macht was able to obtain accurate measures of visual accuity on standard tests.

LARGE-SCALE PROGRAMMES IN COMPENSATORY EDUCATION AND INTERVENTION

Since the application of conditioning techniques to specific educational problems such as reading disability is discussed elsewhere, it is not proposed to discuss their use in remediation programmes at great length. However, behaviour modification is one of the many strategies that have appeared in expensive attempts at compensatory education in the form of the Head Start programmes and latterly the 'performance contracting' movement. And its general utility must therefore be considered in the context of the failure of such programmes to produce clear-cut and generalizable results. The first major indication of the inefficiency of expensive educational processes appeared in the Coleman Report (1966) and some of the associated issues sprang into prominence following Jensen's (1969) controversial article in the Harvard Educational Review. The debates surrounding educability still continue (Jensen, 1973) and it is clear that for some educationalists at least the technology of behaviour modification has not fulfilled its early promise.

Among reasons given for this have been lack of funds, resulting in short programmes; poor morale and high staff turnover; failure to extend reinforcement of educational behaviours to the child's natural environment and a lack of follow-up programmes to consolidate and extend the existing learning. One of the few continuations of the Head Start programme has been the Follow-through Project (Becker and Engleman, 1973) and since this, for the writer, is one of the most provocative examples of psychology applied to education in this century, a brief account of the work follows.

'Follow-through' is predicated upon the idea that the basic problem in teaching disadvantaged children is to get *more* teaching going on in the classroom. Thus the programme features:

(a) Increased manpower (two teacher aides per classroom, mostly parents).
(b) Structured daily routine: highly organized learning experience with teacher and aides 'specializing' in assigned content areas.
(c) Programmed lessons: the programmes use the successful 'Distar' programmes.
(d) Efficient teaching, involving correct use of reinforcement, the various aspects of the teacher's role in learning are stressed: cueing, pacing effectively and reinforcing.
(e) Training for teachers and supervision: continuing in-service training and consultancy are provided.
(f) Continuous monitoring of the programme: independent tutoring is carried out every six weeks and the results are centrally recorded and monitored. Children on the programmes are frequently tested for mastery.

Preliminary results from the study ($n = 6641$ mostly 'poor' children from a variety of underprivileged backgrounds), indicated substantial gains, particularly in reading recording skills. For example, in all cohorts of the study the children progressively exceeded norm expectations for average children and on the basis of results at the end of the third grade were at least one year ahead in reading skills, indeed, one cohort is likely to be two years ahead. Similar, though not quite so dramatic, data were obtained from the results of the arithmetic programmes.

The programmes are generating considerable educational interest and spin-off in the form of teaching materials. A number of the features are controversial, not the least of which is the exceptionally high level of control over teacher behaviour. The results of this and a number of 'downtown' applications of the Distar programme suggest that an instructional technology exists which can effect substantial improvements in basic educational skills. However, the techniques involved need to be applied consistently and single-mindedly under conditions of effective training and supervision. (Whether they could be applied in the typically free classroom environments of special education in the U.K. is another matter of course.)

PRACTICAL CONSIDERATIONS

It would have been possible to extract from the literature cited a long catalogue of practical issues surrounding the use of behaviour modification in both experimental and practical situations. The following will refer to what the writer considers to be some of the more important of these and will include some personal observations.

Problems

The effective application of behaviour modification demands objective definition of a problem and agreement upon the means by which it is to be attacked. However, it is paradoxical that where a programme appears to be most needed, in a behavioural sense, the conditions creating the behavioural situation may conspire against an efficient application of the method. Thus, in the simplest case of difficulties over management, many teachers, parents and care workers are temperamentally incapable of consistent reinforcement. Poor leadership and communication may also play a decisive role in limiting a programme's potential effectiveness.

Experienced writers in the area of precision teaching now seem extremely cautious about comprehensive programmes (Madsen and Madsen, 1970; O'Leary, 1973). Like the writer they recommend that a number of techniques of curriculum rearrangement and social reinforcement must be tried before fully planned environments like token economies can be introduced. The writer infers that some bitter experiences lie behind this moderate approach, adequate consultation should reveal whether a real problem exists and whether, in the circumstances, resources exist for the new method to succeed. Sometimes attitudes towards behaviour modification are such that it would be extremely unlikely for a programme to function effectively. For example, some of the doubts and prejudices frequently expressed are that behaviour modification is unfair; it teaches children to be mercenary and selfish; it is concerned only with short-term effects; it can make children passive rather than active and creative and, most frequently of all, that it denies the student the right of self-regulation of behaviour. It is of course possible to deal with this issue constructively but the prejudices involved may be deeply entrenched. In the writer's experience full discussion of the problem and the employment of reasonably objective methods of observation are probably the most important aspects of the application of behaviour modification principles. Although it may seem common sense to carry out basic functional analyses of the times, places and social contexts in which behaviour occurs, most psychologists advising on problems find that the institutions concerned have omitted to obtain any of this important information. Sometimes there is even resistance to conceptualizing a problem in this way.

Observation

It is clear (Connolly, 1973) that the techniques of ethology have considerable general relevance for the functional analysis of behaviour; in special education particularly, analysis of non-verbal communication and proxemics may prove to be extremely useful. Having carried out a number of small-scale studies in this area, and on the basis of experience with behaviour modification projects, the writer would make the following points.

(a) Much of the interaction between children and adults may be lost by conventional recording devices: slight changes of expression, asides and movement towards children may be lost in recording. Often these are not discerned even by trained observers, but may possess significant reinforcement value.

(b) The notion that observers 'fade into the wallpaper' after a time may be mistaken. Despite strenuous efforts to extinguish approaches to them, observers have often reported that certain children continue to speak to them or attempt to involve them in classroom activities. Teachers may also refer to the observers and on occasions use them as disciplinary props.

(c) Sometimes the observed act of recording behaviour has reinforcement value. In certain environments such as token economies this may be planned. However, bad behaviour can be reinforced unwittingly when children become aware of the fact that they are the subjects of observation.

(d) In an unpublished study using observers of different ages, sex and appearance, the writer found differential responses by target children. Older, larger observers seemed to have a definite calming effect on bad behaviour, according to teacher reports, whereas young observers were often the centre of a great deal of attention and curiosity, at least in the initial stages.

Reinforcers

Behaviour modification programmes conventionally seek to produce behaviours which can be reinforced by normal means in the child's natural environment. Token economies possess obvious difficulties in this regard and even simple reinforcers like attention and praise may be hard to use naturally. A common error is to use excessive reinforcement when an activity is intrinsically reinforcing. Often mere proximity, smiles, nods and shoulder taps at a low level of presentation are sufficient as there is a possibility that overexposure to social reinforcement may be counter-productive in the long run. In special classrooms many opportunities to use Premack's principle are missed as favoured activities may be free to all at any time during the day. Observation of preferred activities can easily lead to a reinforcement 'menu' for each child or, if a hierarchy of reinforcement preferences is sought, paired comparison methods can soon supply the relevant data.

Implementation

Many initial difficulties surrounding implementation of programmes stem from a lack of objectivity and precision in formulating goals, the need for advice from professional psychologists with training and experience in the work being paramount in any large-scale exercise. Some issues involved in the training of parents and teachers have already been discussed; it is worth adding that, however acceptable their initial performance, their effectiveness as contingency managers tends to deteriorate and needs to be maintained via seminars or regular con-sultations. The writer has also encountered both parents and teachers who have been placed in a sort of double-bind situation by being given instruction in behaviour modification. In the past they could attribute their inadequacy to lack of knowledge or technique: a crisis came when they realized that they did not possess the personal qualities necessary to put the new information to use. Attempts to do so proved to be both unsuccessful and personally destructive despite considerable professional support.

DESIGN AND EVALUATION OF PROGRAMMES

For experimental demonstrations of functional relationships under reasonably con-trolled conditions, variations upon AB, AB and multiple baseline designs are probably adequate. However, it is evident that in many programmes reversibility of effect is neither practical nor desirable, and in any event may be virtually impossible to obtain: programmes of language development are cases in point, as language is heavily reinforceable outside experimental conditions. It may well be, therefore, that opportunities for demonstration of a specific effect diminish as both stimulus and response generalization occur. Consequently it is arguable that the strategies of behaviour modification belong more naturally to a system analysis than to a classically experimental approach; this view being explicit in discussions of the topic by London (1972) and Zifferblatt (1973) and implicit in the work of the Brickers (1973) and Glaser (1973).

Zifferblatt proposes that the stage is set for the extension of behavioural strategies combined with systems procedures into larger and more complex contexts. He points out a number of characteristics common both to the applied analysis of behaviour and to system analysis, in particular, specification of objectives, procedural control and explicit process phases. The purpose of behaviour systems is to harness the advantages of both types of approach in terms of precision and generability. Their goals are to achieve a given mission in the best way possible by attention to what is happening in the programmes, by representing this explicitly and by refining operations whilst holding the mission objectives constant.

From the design point of view this involves maximizing knowledge about variability rather than seeking full control over responses as occurs in the early stages of operant programmes, which then have to introduce generalization progressively. It may therefore well be that some difficulties over stimulus and response generalization are avoidable if variability is introduced into the system from the outset. This might well facilitate the use of parametric statistics for the single case although, as continual feedback and refinement are part of the process phases, experimental demonstrations of effect may be regarded as transitory stages in the system.

As behaviour systems are most often idiosyncratic, Zifferblatt suggests that models derived from Operations Research (OR) might guide their development. The OR paradigm is system-specific and does not attempt generalization to other systems, its basic aim being that of producing optimal solutions and alternative solutions to given problems. Concluding this excellent account Zifferblatt advances a design and analysis model which may have considerable heuristic value for programme construction in special education.

Evaluation

Evaluation consists primarily of ascertaining whether specified criterion levels have been reached with optimal efficiency. In special education this may involve criterion-reinforced tests constructed specifically for the programme and norm-referenced tests as evidence of response generalization. A feature of most special educational programmes is that diagnostic assessment leads to individualized instruction, the diagnostic and remediation processes being perceived as integrated. However, there is a general point to be made about the setting and evaluation of behavioural goals. Since learning is directed towards goals set by the teacher and since learning is held to be contingent upon teacher behaviour, for meaningful evaluation to take place the learning outcome must be testable. The danger inherent in this is that the suitability of subject matter for testing might dominate selection for programme content excessively, even in individual cases.

THE EFFECTIVENESS OF BEHAVIOUR MODIFICATION

Special education has traditionally functioned as a laboratory situation within which attempts are made to put psychological theory to practical use, thus its experimental nature is continually stressed (Burrello et al., 1973; Bijou, 1973). Early work in behaviour modification was carried out in this spirit and the results, though lacking in generalizability, were construed as being sufficiently important to justify widespread applications of the techniques. Implicit in this was the idea that education would become 'special' for each child or, in restated form, the need for special education in the conventional sense would consequently vanish. There has always been an aura of idealism and enthusiasm surrounding behaviour modification which has hindered objective evaluation of the results obtained.

Even so, the writer does not believe that global statements about the effectiveness of behaviour modification are yet possible, owing to the diversity of problem areas and techniques represented. What can be said is that, for certain types of child and for certain classes of behaviour, behaviour modification offers what appears to be a sound technology for achieving educational and management goals. In other words, within the context of particular views about the nature and purpose of curricula, teachers can be made to teach more effectively. The statement is qualified as the writer sympathizes to some extent with the view held by Scriven (1973) and others that the scientific status of some of the evidence offered by protagonists of behaviour modification is hardly impressive.

However, looking beyond the technical limitations of the work, a number of positive secondary results are becoming apparent. The first of these is the increasing commitment by academic psychologists to solve problems in the applied field and, with this, some confidence that these tasks can be accomplished. The second is the spread of management/training skills which allow handicapped and unhappy children to be perceived and treated much more positively and optimistically. Thirdly, the writer can only welcome the extension of functional analytic methods throughout problem areas in child psychology and education. And fourthly, there is evidence that the techniques and language of behaviour modification may act as a bridge which could result in much more effective communication between disciplines.

OVERVIEW

It is hoped that the foregoing has conveyed some of the range and flavour of behaviour modification work in special education and its surrounding areas. An overview of the many books and articles consulted gives rise to the following impressions.

(a) Attitudes in the field seem to have undergone considerable change. It is now no longer questioned that behaviour modification will work in appropriate cases, nor are there any particularly heated theoretical debates as to why reinforcement principles function in the way they do. The search is now for effective technology (perhaps, as London (1972) suggested, on the basis that good technology drives out bad theory).

(b) In view of the entrenched attitudes of some earlier workers in the field the focus of the work is surprisingly eclectic, subsuming concepts from dynamic psychology, cognitive growth and education which at one time could have been unacceptable as 'mentalistic'. Thus units of behaviour have become progressively larger and more complex. In a sense, therefore, potentiality for response generalization is being built into programmes as they proceed.

(c) In keeping with the enormous demand for a technology of behavioural control the main problems are seen as ones of stimulus generalization, necessitating the shift of experimental interest from tightly controlled experimental settings to the natural environment (Tharp and Wetzel, 1969; Bijou *et al.*, 1969). With this the need for training parents and para-professionals in behaviour modification principles increases correspondingly.

(d) The language and concepts of behaviour modification have passed into general educational psychiatric usage very rapidly in a manner analogous to the spread of Freudian terminology and, in a more restricted way, to the spread of programmed learning and curriculum objective ideas.

(e) The emphasis is still firmly upon using reinforcing rather than punishing consequences as sources of behavioural control. Johnston (1972) recently commented that reluctance to develop this technology may be due to the emotional connotations of punishment and the fact that personal feelings and moralities, rather than science, are involved.

ETHICAL CONSIDERATIONS

The application of behaviour modification in special education and residential institutions has stimulated a number of specific debates, for example, about the use of food deprivation, various forms of punishing consequences, restricted environments, etc. With severely handicapped children a strong technical case can be advanced for the differential use of these methods. However, it is the writer's view that the ethical considerations surrounding personal autonomy and extrinsic controls are the same in the long run for all children, regardless of developmental level. At what point in a carefully planned programme of self-held training does a severely retarded child acquire autonomy? Then again, parents of exceptional children who receive training in management techniques may apply them to all their children; workers in the area of delinquency prevention may press for the extension of behavioural controls to families, schools and entire communities.

The general issue of personal autonomy has of course been brought into recent focus by Skinner's (1971) challenging monograph 'Beyond Freedom and Dignity' which, as its author intended, has provoked important controversy illustrated in the discussions by Scriven (1973), a long-standing opponent of Skinner's viewpoint. Eventually, behaviourists might argue, the problems of personal autonomy may be resolved by the development of self-regulating behaviour. However, in special education two aspects of behaviour modification are of particular ethical concern. The first of these is the type of target behaviours postulated. For instance, is the child to be passive and acquiescent, or creative, questioning, occasionally rebellious? What areas of the curriculum are to be given priority? With technical advances in behaviour modification the right of a teacher to impose controls and teaching processes will be increasingly questioned. Secondly, the systematic use of extrinsic reinforcement to shape behaviour has raised real doubts in many educationalists' minds, in that behavioural science may be lending its methods to facilitate essentially dehumanizing processes. It might be considered that western society suffers from a surfeit of extrinsically motivated behaviour and that, in the United States particularly, the extension of methods of extrinsic motivation throughout education will prove to be even more socially divisive. The greatest social dangers may lie in the adoption of behavioural control methods on expedient grounds without the accompanying scientific evidence as to their long-term effects. Already there is some disagreement as to whether behaviour modification requires a theoretical underpinning at all. (Those acquainted with the history of the psychometric movement may recognize many parallel features with behaviour modification in this regard.)

Whilst recognizing the need for caution, the writer believes that we are only at the beginning of the growth of a scientific pedagogy in special education. The problems are immense, the possibilities for success and failure legion. At this stage, as in the advance of any form of science, risks have to be taken and in any event the ethical issues surrounding a highly efficient behavioural technology will be debated in a future and certainly different social context. The most important of these will probably be concerned with punishing consequences, in the writer's view a future growth area which cannot be ignored for long.

Behaviour modification offers a challenge to contemporary society in that there is now the possibility of a real science of behavioural control. Special education with its traditional concern for the handicapped and underprivileged individual will continue to be an important setting for the essential humanization of its concepts and practice.

CHAPTER 6

Task Analysis and Programmed Learning

P. WIDLAKE

INTRODUCTION

Programmed Learning first began to influence British educational practice in the early 1960s, though it had, even then, passed its apogee in the USA. As is well known, Programmed Learning draws on operant conditioning theory, emphasizes positive rather than negative reinforcement and has been much associated with the work of Skinner. However, it draws also on other educational traditions; early work rooted in behaviourist theory, embracing such issues as 'mode of response', 'RULEG versus EGRULE', 'linear or branching programmes', has already acquired an aura of antiquity. What has survived, and what even at the time made a considerable impact on attitudes to teaching, was the concern with defining objectives in behavioural terms and with defining the population for whom the teaching programme was intended. The positive side of this emphasis on stating what it is one is trying to teach is that a programme, however presented, can be empirically evaluated, and revised if the tests show that the objectives are not being achieved. The negative side, which was almost completely ignored in the heyday of Programmed Learning and is still seriously neglected by many psychologists with a passion for testing, is the extreme difficulty of bringing certain areas of the curriculum within the compass of an objective test. The dilemma has been expressed in a Schools Council publication: 'To define the aims of education in general terms is more or less meaningless; to do it more precisely is downright dangerous'. (*Curriculum Innovation in Practice*, 1968.)

The 'office management' side of task analysis, the Systems Approach, has its uses, but the plethora of boxes and arrows tends, in Lincoln's famous words, mainly to help those who are helped by that sort of thing. It is foolish to ignore the value judgements which lie just below the glossy coat of certainty which Programmed Learning enthusiasts apply to the surface of the educational problems they tackle; yet crude achievement criteria are readily accepted. 'When we say a pupil "appreciates" a particular type of music/art/literature, what we probably mean is that he can discriminate subtle fine points in it, and that he seeks out books, or goes to concerts/plays featuring that type, when he could be doing other things.' (Calder, 1970.)

To bring the discussion firmly within the list of objectives set for this chapter, it is now proposed to examine representative reading programmes in some detail. If the discussion seems somewhat critical, this is because it is convenient, within the space available, to concentrate on the task analysis to the exclusion of the actual teaching materials, which, it should be added, have been used with some success and considerable enjoyment by children on whom they were tried.

AN EVALUATION OF PROGRAMMED READING TEXTS

Many reading programmes have been published. For example, one produced for Sullivan Associates under the title *Programmed Reading* (Buchanan, 1963) is aimed at being a complete course, starting with prereading material and taking the infant, with a minimum of aversive experience, to a condition of fluent reading. The prereading material consists of alphabet and sound-symbol cards, a programmed primer for the students and a reading-readiness test to be administered when the students have completed the first three parts of the primer. The reading programme proper consists of linear texts attractively printed in colour and abundantly illustrated. By the end of the prereading programme, the children should be able to read sentences such as the following: 'I am an ant. I am a man. I am a mat. I am a pin. I am a pan. I am ten. I am thin. I am fat.' (Leavitt's *Easy Lessons in Reading*, 1823, used an alliterative approach—'Nathan Noonan knows his nose; no man knows I know he knows his nose; his nose knows he knows his nose' (Johnson, 1964).)

Such texts can be criticized on three grounds: the objectives, though clearly stated, are not really specific; the values sought are undesirable; the programming techniques are uninspired.

The objectives, though clearly stated, are not really specific

As an example, take the Student's Concepts defined on page 3 of the handbook to Sullivan Associates' *Programmed Pre-reading* mentioned above. Three stages are set out. In the first, the student learns that letters have names and learns the names of all the letters. Stage 2 deals with sound-symbol relationships and a list of student concepts is given:

A word is made up of sounds.
When we talk, we say the sounds that make up words.
Letters stand for sounds.
When we read, we say the sounds that go with letters.
When we write, we write letters that go with sounds.
We write words by writing letters together.
Sentences begin with capital letters and end with periods.
We leave spaces between words.

I questioned a group of non-readers whom I had inherited at ages 10–11, after several teachers had tried to teach them to read. Pointing to a letter and asking, 'What's this?' produced no answer at first and then after prompting: 'It's a sentence', 'It's a word'. There was not a glimmer of understanding of the essential relationships between letters and sounds nor of the blending of sounds into words. These were, of course, exceptional cases, but Joyce Morris's (1966) figures (page 300) showed 45% of children still requiring special help at the beginning of their primary school lives; 19% were still at the first primer stage, 26% had some mastery but not sufficient to enable them to make progress on their own.

The question of children's concepts of reading has been examined by Reid (1966) and he found many confusions. At a first interview, only one child began by saying that books contained words, most referred only to pictures. Many talked about numbers, no distinction was made between letters and numerals. When asked: 'Can your mummy and daddy read?', two out of 12 did not know. Trying to describe how they read, only one child mentioned symbols ('names'). Some knew that the part their parents read was black, but others were very vague.

Each child was seen three times during the first year of schooling. At a second interview some children could find further examples of a given initial letter, the rest could not. The tendency to call letters 'numbers' had almost gone but had been replaced by a tendency to call them 'words' instead. However, some children were becoming aware of the need for regularity and rule. At a third interview, when asked to show their reading books and what they did if they did not recognize a word, the children were eager to talk. Nine out of eleven had something to say. Words 'spell', 'sound', 'copy'—all referring to sounding—'you say one word at a time'—'m' is a word, 'u' is a word: 'm', 'u', 'st'.

Awareness of phonic structure was developing but a new classificatory confusion had appeared, in the assertion that some words were not words but names.

The task can be seen to be complex: (a) to discover words and that all language is composed of them; (b) to think of sounds and to realize that written words are spatially ordered groups of letters bearing a systematic relation to the temporally ordered sounds of speech. Though it is probably necessary, eventually, to be able to distinguish 'word' from 'letter' and 'sound', Reid would not, like Fries (1963) and Durrell (1956), support the teaching of letter names: he was merely concerned to stress the importance of having a term available with which to make the necessary distinction. These distinctions involve immediately an understanding of hierarchial structure in its simplest form (that of the notion of a class with two or more sub-classes). In short, the children have to come to see that language and pictures are two kinds of symbol, that letters and numerals are subclasses in the class of written symbols, that names form a subclass in the class of words, and that capitals form a subclass in the class of letters. The interviews showed that these steps are not easily or swiftly taken but that children groped towards the necessary ordering elements at varying speeds and with varying degrees of success. Programme objectives such as those quoted above do not seem to be sufficiently specific. It is important to recognize that, even at this level, a hierarchy of concepts has to be established.

The values sought are undesirable

Many of the early programmed texts were based on a phonic approach. As has been shown, it is a matter of controversy whether initial reading methods should emphasize the mechanics of reading in this way. Some writers have held that different methods start children on different roads to maturity (Gray, 1956). Gray stressed that reading is a meaning-getting process. McKee, in the teachers' notes to his Readers, discriminated three acts in reading for meaning, which to him, is synonymous with reading. The child must identify the strange words and recognize the familiar words contained in a given piece of material; he must do what needs to be done to arrive at the meaning intended by the writer by a given word, sentence, paragraph or longer expression; he must evaluate the ideas he gains from his reading in order to retain and make use of those ideas that will serve his purpose. The typical programmed text has not been particularly concerned with meaning; the vocabulary is selected on phonic criteria and the emphasis is upon identifying individual letters. We can hypothesize that the young children taught by such programmes will differ qualitatively from those taught by techniques stressing meaning, so far as their reading is concerned. Conversely, 'the nature and variety of attitudes and skills that should be emphasized during any reading lesson are determined in large measure by the values sought' (Gray, 1956). Programmers should show evidence that they have considered the values underlying the skills they are seeking to inculcate, as Umans (1963) pointed out in his *New Trends in Reading Instruction*. 'With programmed texts perhaps even to a greater extent than with textbooks, there is a danger that the programme will dictate the curricula.' The theory went that every learning step should be a constructive act of discovery based on an existing repertoire; new and low strength responses should be generated which lead eventually to a change of behaviour in the direction required behaviour is shaped. The more effective the teaching technique, the more important the question of values becomes.

Everyone is aware that it is very difficult indeed to establish empirically that one method is 'better' than another (Schonell, 1945; Morris, 1966; but cf. Gardner, 1966). There is, however, considerable support for using meaningful material. Underwood (1964) in the course of a thorough review of studies of verbal learning concluded: 'The higher the meaningfulness, the more rapid the learning; this principle holds across all types of verbal learning tasks'. Intuitive teachers like Ashton-Warner (1961) have reached the same conclusions: the so-called Language-Experience approach to reading emphasizes meaningful material (Carillo, 1964; Edwards, 1965) and Marianne Frostig (1972) has ingeniously incorporated such material within her own distinctive, highly structured system.

The programming techniques are uninspired

There is little by way of technical innovation. Two main types of responses are typically called for: filling-in of missing letters and multiple-choice selection. In the later stages of one programme, there are whole pages to read and on a typical page only five responses are required (e.g. supplying individual letters). Yet the unit of *ac-*

complished reading is 'the word, the phrase or even the sentence', (Daniels and Diack, 1956); and Taber, Glaser and Schaefer (1965) maintain that 'The primary function of a frame is to stimulate the student to engage in behaviour relevant to the total behaviour to be learned'. Even if letters constituted appropriate responses at the beginning of a programme, in later phases such responses could hardly be regarded as relevant.

SPECIFIC OBJECTIVES FOR READING PROGRAMMES

Programmes *can* be written that will be really helpful in teaching reading, but they must work to careful task analyses and take account of current research. They should abandon the use of global terms in stating objectives. It would seem obvious that a taxonomy of objectives for reading programmes must begin by distinguishing at least two uses of the term 'reading': (a) an initiating process, as witnessed in young children or older illiterates; (b) the remediation of unsuccessful learning, which should be based upon diagnosis of specific disabilities. It would be preferable to abandon the term 'reading' altogether in this context. Even an objective such as 'to improve the child's listening skills' is much too general. Wedell (1967) has given some idea of the subtle analysis that might precede good programme writing. To discriminate perceptual-motor impairment as one form of cognitive disability, is itself a fine distinction by the standards we have been discussing. 'But perceptual-motor ability is itself very complex, and needs to be analysed further. Copying a square, for example, depends on a large number of functions. The square has first to be seen; the child's *visual mechanism* has to be intact. The sensory input has then to be "organised"; the square has to be *perceived*. All of this will depend on whether the child is *attending* to the square and on whether he has already acquired the *concept* of a square.' *Control, eye–hand co-ordination*, and the ability to *organize* are also itemized, making seven specific subfunctions within this one area of intellectual impairment: and one need not stop there. Programmes taking as objectives suitable items of functional impairment from this list would be moving towards an operational definition.

The deepest levels of task analysis require a three-dimensional model representing 'cognitive, affective and modality-processing demands to be made by a particular task on a particular individual in a given setting' (Junkala, 1972). However, it is rarely possible to integrate all these elements and, for the most part, the discussion will be limited to the cognitive domain. Junkala has devised 'a schematic representation of the relationship between the perceptual, coding and conceptual demands of the cognitive dimension'. He maintains that successful coding operations depend upon proper perceptual functioning; conceptual functioning may include both coding and perceptual functioning, although not every conceptual task includes a coding component. Look–Say approaches to reading make most demand at the perceptual level, analytic approaches at the coding level. At the conceptual level, the task requires the child to *relate*—to classify objects or events, to draw inferences from them, or to make statements about their value.

I observed a teacher administering a quick drill on initial consonants, following instructions which were derived from Junkala's article. These words were written on the blackboard

| ball | cat   bird   dog   saw   bag

and instructions given as follows to a group of four children.

  (i) 'The word in the box is *ball*. Show me another that begins with the same letter as *ball*.' (All children found *bag* or *bird*.)
 (ii) 'Show me another word that begins with the same letter as *box*.' (Two children could do so.)
(iii) 'Show me all the words that begin with the same letter as the word in the box.' (All children succeeded.)

These results exactly paralleled Junkala's, although the teacher concerned was not 'sophisticated' enough to comment, like his, that the children were 'perceptually handicapped'.

The first task can be placed at either the perceptual or the coding level; it depends on the cues utilized which could be either visual or auditory. The second task demands coding skills, the third makes conceptual demands. Differential performances indicate achievements at different levels. An analysis on the lines indicated also shows clearly that there is a task as well as a student variable. A teacher who is informed about task analysis will be ready to provide 'instructional alternatives' which Junkala suggests can be either *lateral* (keeping the activity at the same level of complexity but changing the material nearer to the child's state of readiness at that time) or *vertical* (changing the level of complexity of the task).

EXAMPLES OF READING PROGRAMMES WITH SPECIFIC OBJECTIVES

1. Jones and Leith (1966) produced work based on the researches of Gibson and Harlow. Gibson (1963) had worked on the development of the capacity to discriminate perceptual forms akin to letter shapes and found that certain dimensions of these forms were perceived before others. Thus children were able to distinguish closed from open shapes (e.g. 'C' and 'O') before they could recognize the difference between a shape and its inverse (vertical displacement) or its reverse (horizontal displacement).

Building on these theoretical foundations, Jones has developed a visual discrimination programme, (*Left to Write*). In the experimental form of this programme there were 42 problems involving visual perceptual discriminations. These were followed by 24 frames requiring a choice between three geometric, letter or word shapes of increasing difficulty; and a set of 18 frames designed to set up a motor-perceptual habit by means of colour cues: from left to right the colours used were green, blue and red. A full account of this work is still worth looking at and can be found in Volume 1, Number 1, 1966, of *Remedial Education*.

2. Project HUMID

Work has been carried out at the University of Minnesota on teaching beginning reading to hearing-impaired children. The method was essentially non-oral, and all instruction was by means of visual presentations using a machine similar to the Touchtutor developed in this country. Our interest lies in the description of the programmes which were created for this very special population but it is encouraging to read that the machine worked satisfactorily with deaf five-year-olds (HUMID is a word constructed from the initials of the machine). There was also a remedial programme for 9–10 year olds. The level of *Instruction Objectives* can be assessed from the following samples.

Programme 1

Objective: to introduce the teaching machine through the use of picture matching to establish reinforcement conditions.

Programme 2

Objective: to increase the discrimination needed to make a correct response through the use of stimulus and response pictures of the same categories.

Programme 3

Objective: to introduce the concepts *Janet* and *Ben*, and to develop an appropriate response to two programming techniques.

Programme 6

Objective: to introduce the concept *sitting* within the context *Ben is sitting*.
Procedure: each of the new words is introduced with a descriptive illustration. Stimulus *Janet* appears with *Ben* as a distractor and stimulus *Ben* appears with *Janet* as a distractor.

3. The English colour code programmed reading course

Research conducted by Moseley (1972) suggested that if phoneme-grapheme relations were made explicit by auditory prompts and visual cues, the majority of slow learners would be able to make the necessary links. He has described both the research basis and the materials in some detail (e.g. in Southgate, 1972); the published material represents the most systematic attack on auditory deficiencies in reading currently available.

4. The Frostig programme for the development of visual perception

This work is now very well known and constitutes some of the most carefully considered prescriptive programmes so far produced, dealing with specific visual perceptual difficulties in five areas.

(i) Eye–motor co-ordination.
(ii) Figure ground perception.
(iii) Constancy of perception of shape and size.
(iv) Position in space.
(v) Perception of spacial relationships.

Although the tests themselves are two-dimensional, paper-and-pencil tasks, Dr. Frostig has insisted that 'None of the paper-and-pencil exercises should be attempted until the physical exercises or exercises with three-dimensional objects, described in the Introduction of each workbook, have been practiced.' Indeed, the work of the Frostig Centre for Educational Therapy in Los Angeles is concerned with a much wider spectrum of disabilities than is generally known. In the paper already mentioned, Dr. Frostig has set out a checklist and treatment chart as follows.

A. Sensory-motor functions.
B. Auditory perception.
C. Visual perception.
D. Language functions: receptive and expressive.
E. Memory.
F. Symbolization.

This must represent one of the most useful task analyses conducted in the area of learning disabilities. The chart format lends a most welcome simplicity. The following headings are utilized:

Symptoms Observed in the Classroom
Possible Underlying Deficits
Methods of Evaluating Deficits
Suggested Training Methods
Suggested Reading Methods.

The most surprising element in this prescriptive programme is the link with Ashton-Warner's work. There is also a direct appeal to the teacher not to behave as an automaton.

'The teacher methods that follow will of course be changed or amplified as new methods and materials become available to the teacher, and as she develops her own creative, personalised methods within a valid theoretical structure.'

TASK ANALYSIS IN OTHER AREAS OF THE CURRICULUM

A number of recent Schools Council project teams have completed some form of task anslysis before attempting to produce materials. At least one of these preliminary analyses has been a research project in its own right: the project on the language of West Indian children at Birmingham University, England. Others have benefited from on-going research programmes which have also had other products: *Language in Use* and *Breakthrough to Literacy*, for example, are programmes for different age and ability groups which both spring from M. A. K. Halliday's research project in linguistics at the University of London. Curriculum innovation which draws on current, or specially conducted, research is in one sense making use of the most sophisticated task analysis available. Such work fruitfully underlines the complexity of the task; a good example is to be found in the Gahagans' *Talk Reform*, formulated on the basis of research work undertaken by Professor Bernstein at the Sociological Research Unit, London University.

Some of this work has clear-cut applications to children with special learning needs. An examination of Schools Council projects by Gulliford and Widlake (1973) has suggested that many areas of the secondary curriculum, normally regarded as outside the range of 'disadvantaged' pupils can, with imaginative and skilful adaptation of methods and materials, be brought within the scope of this population.

A most elaborate, and successful, task analysis, has been completed by the Schools Council team known as *Science 5–13*. Following Piaget, Ennever *et al.* have delineated three stages in the mental development of children between the ages of five and thirteen years.

Stage 1   Transition from Intuition to Concrete Operations; Concrete Operations Early Stage
Stage 2   Concerete Operations Later Stage
Stage 3   Transition to Stage of Abstract Thinking.

Each stage is then subdivided under ten headings, such as: Attitudes, Interests and Aesthetic Awareness; Observing, Exploring and Ordering Observations; Developing Basic Concepts and Logical Thinking ... Acquiring Knowledge and Learning Skills; Communicating ... Interpreting Findings Critically.

Thus a fully worked out stage would read as follows.

Stage 2. Concrete Operations Later Stage
2.21 Awareness of Internal Structure in Living and Non-Living Things
2.22 Ability to Construct and Use Keys for Identification
2.23 Recognition of Similar and Congruent Shapes etc.

There are both advantages and disadvantages to this explicit approach. Great clarity of mind results, and it is possible to produce activities highly appropriate to the various analysed stages and substages. On the other side of the coin, it is obvious that once the task analysis has been carried to this point, anybody with a critical bent will find objections to the style and content of the analysis. It immediately leads into the continuing and fruitful debate about discovery, guided discovery, or unsupervised learning. However, Ennever's work leaves plenty of scope for the teacher with the desire to allow pupils to go beyond the structure provided; the whole exercise seems extremely worthwhile.

Finally, in this brief resume of the useful outcomes of programmed learning, one ought to mention the outstanding work of Davies (1971) and of others working within the strict limits of the discipline. Davies' book not only sets out the principles upon which such work in teaching and learning can be based, but admirably exemplifies the processes in its own presentation of material. According to him, there are three basic assumptions about the learning processes.

1. Many teachers and instructors overteach, overmanage the learning situation, define subjects' roles too narrowly, make too many decisions on their behalf.

2. Motivation: the well-documented absence of enthusiasm is more likely to result from the way in which the learning situation is managed than from intrinsic aversion in the student.

3. The subject's behaviour is always sensible to him.

If one's teaching is based upon such positive attitudes, it becomes possible to take an optimistic view of the potential of even the least able pupil. *All* bring some discernible skills to the task and there is considerable ground for optimism in the application of the central concept of 'Management by Objectives' to the learning problems of handicapped children. This concept is, in Davies' opinion, the recognition and realization of key tasks and their associated performance standards. As has been indicated, some progress has been made and the lines of research clearly indicated. What, for example, could be more relevant to teachers of educationally subnormal children than these objectives for skills analysis training:

'. . . to enable new trainees to become competent and confident workers, with the least waste of time and resources.

. . . to facilitate the integration of trainees into the socio-technical system of the workplace . . . to regain economic and social status . . . ?'

CHAPTER 7

Enrichment Methods

R. GULLIFORD

One of the problems in the education of handicapped children is how to provide them with a normal education. This statement may appear somewhat paradoxical but it expresses the important idea that as well as needing special kinds of teaching, handicapped children need as full and normal an educational experience as we can contrive.

To achieve this it is necessary to consider first, how the organization and provisional of special education itself can be arranged to avoid, as far as possible, and to compensate for, its possible limitations; secondly, how the content and methods of special education provide not only the special teaching required for children's particular disabilities but also the full educational experience required as they grow through different age or maturity levels. It is a basic endeavour of the good educator that he seeks to enrich his pupils' learning and experience. Enrichment is not an additional or alternative extra but an integral part of the educational process. It is in some ways easier to provide enrichment in special schools because of their smaller classes and their greater freedom from organizational and academic constraints. But it is necessary to keep continually in view the needs of handicapped children as *persons* growing through the normal stages of human development as well as children with handicaps requiring special teaching and treatment.

Many factors tend to narrow and limit the education of handicapped children. While special schools enable many children to receive a richer educational experience than would be possible for them in ordinary schools, special school or class placement often tends to cut children off from a full range of curricular experience, especially at the secondary level. The fact that special schools are small compared with ordinary schools inevitably means that the range of teaching interests and skills is less wide, though this is compensated for to some extent by the fact that teachers in special schools generally feel more free to pursue their educational enthusiasms. Aware of the need to widen pupils' opportunities, many special schools are attempting to increase their links with ordinary schools and it is becoming a common practice for pupils to attend nearby secondary schools part-time. Wherever possible it is an advantage for a special school to be located on the same campus as ordinary schools. Special *classes* are theoretically an obvious way of enriching and normalizing the handicapped child's education but if they are to become a sound method of provision, much more thought and effort is needed to ensure adequate supporting and advisory services, and to ensure continuity of educational development. The special school has a stability and a cumulative experience and expertise which can only be matched in ordinary schools if needs are really understood and additional resources are provided.

An important set of limitations on the normal education of handicapped children arises from the need to provide special teaching for particular disabilities. Such priorities as language and speech for the deaf, learning basic literacy skills in the educationally subnormal, acquiring other special skills and techniques in other handicapped groups, make inroads on the total time available for education. Absences through ill-health, hospitalization and special therapies make progress slower. Until the recent raising of the school-leaving age in the United Kingdom this factor was recognized by an extra year of schooling for handicapped children, which is no longer the case. One solution must be to increase the opportunities for further education of handicapped children, an issue to be discussed later (Tuckey, Parfitt and Tuckey, 1973).

It is almost inevitable that the special teaching requirements for different disabilities should be the prior concern of the teacher. It is an essential part of the special educator's expertise that he should be well-informed and skilled in those techniques and procedures required for enabling particular groups of handicapped children to learn as effectively as they can. These central concerns of special education are the focus of training and the continuing theme of discussion and interchange of ideas conducted through the meetings and journals of teachers' associations. By contrast, the scope and methods of educating handicapped children in some of the main areas of the curriculum (science, the humanities) have not been the subject of such thorough and systematic examination. This is not to deny that many teachers with enthusiasm, knowledge and skill in particular subjects and activities have done very interesting work. (The possibility of drawing more freely on the experience of ordinary schools is discussed later.) It is also the case that, in the literature of handicap, medical and psychological aspects are more adequately represented than the educational; indeed the education of some handicaps is very sparsely represented. It is to be hoped that curriculum specialists will turn their attention to the problems of curriculum development in special education and that more subject specialists will examine the methods of teaching of their subject to particular groups of handicapped children.

It is a reasonable prediction that one orientation in special education in the near future will be to look even more closely at the total educational process with a view to ensuring that both school and out-of-school experience are as enriching and normal as possible. Hence the current of opinion running in favour of integrating handicapped children in ordinary schools manifested in some experiments in the 'open education' of blind children, in the well-established units for partially-hearing children and in the increase in the number of special classes in ordinary schools. Boarding schools frequently operate on a five day a week basis so that contact and relationships with the family are less disrupted; though perhaps with some loss of the enrichment that can be provided at weekends in boarding schools. Boarding schools particularly have, for a long time, made a point of trying to become a part of the local community. Day schools have further to go in this respect; the concept of the community school has something to offer. In a few places this concept is taking practical form on campuses where there are educational, cultural and recreational facilities for a wide range of community needs. A discussion of the urban community school in Appendix 2 of Schools Council Working Paper 27 (1970) is written in the context of disadvantaged children but it is not difficult to see potentialities for handicapped children, especially if the campus included special schools or classes.

Increasingly, schools tend to see their role as including cooperation and work with the family. The emphasis is at present perhaps on achieving adequate preschool guidance and counselling, essential for optimum educational progress subsequently, and on continuing cooperation between home and school during the school years. But special schools, like ordinary schools, face the challenge of a closer and more integral involvement of parents in their children's education, both at home and in school itself. The need for this is obviously relatively greater in the case of handicapped children. The concern of most parents of handicapped children to know what they can do to help their child ensures their receptivity to such guidance. One problem needing further study is that of parents who appear to have little interest or ability to participate but who, as some research and experience suggest, are ready and able to help if given the right kind of assistance. In brief, there are immense potentialities for the enrichment of handicapped children's education in the awareness that the classroom is only a part of the pupil's learning experience. While the teacher's greatest contribution is making that part as efficient and effective as possible, this can only be achieved by exerting a positive influence in other aspects of the child's experience.

THE NORMAL STAGES OF EDUCATION

One of the predicaments for the special educator is that his pupils' development may be out of step with that of their age group as well as the fact that disability may result in wide discrepancies between intellectual, physical and personal/social development within individuals. This is most obvious in the educationally subnormal whose intellectual retardation means that what they need educationally is, as a generalization, comparable to that of normal children at a younger age. But with most groups of handicapped children it is useful, indeed salutary, to pose the question: what would normal children be learning and experiencing at this age, or stage, of education? For example, it is fruitful to consider what interests, problems and concerns of adolescents should be reflected in the curriculum even though in some respects their intellectual and emotional maturity is not on a part with that of normal adolescents. Special education is not a different kind of education. Its basis is good normal education with such modifications of aims, procedures and methods as are dictated by the requirements of particular handicaps. It is no doubt for this reason that the Department of Education and Science Report on Education No. 77

(Special Education: a fresh look) selected as one of four influential current ideas that 'special schools should be in the mainstream of educational thinking'. It is worth examining some developments in ordinary education and considering how they can enrich the education of handicapped children.

Preschool education for handicapped children

It is now widely accepted that preschool education should be provided for handicapped children, both for making an early start on special educational measures (such as auditory training, language and speech in the deaf; mobility, independence and environmental exploration in the visually handicapped) and to enrich the child's all-round development.

In January 1972 when the total special school population in the UK stood at 122,283 there were 3032 pupils aged two, three and four in special schools. An unknown number of handicapped children are in ordinary nursery schools, in day nurseries and in preschool play groups. It is certain that considerable development of provision will be needed. Nearly all new schools for physically and mentally handicapped children include provision for children before the age of five. The Vernon report, (Dept. of Education and Science, 1972) made strong recommendations for the preschool education of visually-handicapped children.

It is accepted that, where possible, handicapped children should be included in ordinary nursery schools, though with the important proviso that specialist advice should be available and given to the staff about the special needs of handicapped children. Without advice and consultation with special teachers, nursery staff might be overprotective or uncertain about how much independence to expect of children. More important, the normal teacher needs some insight into the consequences of the disability for the child's exploration of the environment and his interpretation of experience. There is, for example, much practical guidance that a teacher of the blind or the partially-sighted could give to a nursery teacher. In some places, partially-hearing units have been set up in nursery schools and in many places the service of peripatetic teachers of the deaf is able to give supervision and guidance. Such advisory services must be developed in relation to other groups of handicap. The initial reaction to placement of a very handicapped child in a nursery school is often to wonder whether he can be safely and properly cared for and helped in a preschool group. The real question is not whether he could be 'contained' but whether nursery experience could be made fully enriching and beneficial for him.

Where handicapped children are being educated together in nursery classes or assessment units in special schools, it is not easy to match the quality of ordinary nursery school experience. The groups are smaller and the range of ability and development may be narrower; there may be less social and intellectual interaction in the group. Less space may mean that the environment is not so well organized for different kinds of play and activity.

Perhaps most critical for the development of good preschool education for handicapped children is the question of staffing. It should be the aim in staffing these units and classes to employ nursery-trained and experienced teachers who have an interest in, and knowledge of, handicapped children. Yet as nursery education begins to expand, there is already a shortage of trained nursery-school teachers. While there are some primary-trained teachers who can approximate to what is required it should be realized that a real understanding of preschool development and the skills required to organize the nursery environment and children's activity is not the simple matter it is sometimes assumed to be. It is a common but mistaken assumption that it is easier for a teacher to move to teaching younger age groups than the reverse. Each age-range has its own special teaching skills, none more so than the genuine teaching skills for children of nursery and infant age.

A normal nursery school is not a place where children come casually together and are supplied with appropriate materials under the benevolent supervision of a teacher who is fond of young children. It is a good deal more purposeful and planned than that. In the first place, it is a structured environment in that materials are selected and arranged in different places within the nursery to facilitate a range of activities which contribute to various aspects of children's development. Thus materials for locomotor activity, dramatic play, creative work, prescientific play, constructional play, are carefully selected and arranged. Much thought goes into the supply of materials as topical interests and pupils' needs arise. While pupils may gain much from the spontaneous use of the materials, the full educational benefit depends on the teacher's active role as a guider and stimulator of learning, and particularly in developing language in relation to activity and experience. The nursery language in relation to activity and experience. The nursery teacher's training and experience have equipped her with schemas of the cognitive and personality developments she wishes to promote, with ability to assess the levels at which individual children are operating, and with an awareness of the activities into which individuals and groups can be guided in order to promote their further development. It is often wrongly assumed that the nursery teacher's role is entirely child-centred (whatever that vague term means!). This is not how nursery teachers see it. The following table shows the results obtained from an experienced, trained group of teachers when asked to say which of four roles approximated most closely to their own view of the nursery teacher's role. (Schools Council, 1972.)

Role	Percentage rating
Child-centred: child directed.	5·1
Child-centred: teacher directed.	12·4
Teacher-centred: child directed.	59·5
Teacher-centred: teacher directed.	23·0

It was interesting that older teachers (over 45) preferred the last role. Young teachers without children of their own preferred the second role.

It is an important issue how far the practice of nursery education outlined here can be applied in the preschool education of handicapped children. In general, handicapped children are less ready and able to respond spontaneously to a well-organized nursery class environment. They usually have less experience of play than normal children, partly as a result of their limited contact with other children. Physical handicaps may have limited the range of exploratory activity. Mentally handicapped children may be at a sensori-motor stage of development and, for a while at least, they may not be ready to benefit fully from the materials for symbolic and constructive play. Moreover, their limited conceptual and linguistic development implies that their spontaneous activity is less directed. There is the further difficulty that the number of children in the group may be smaller. Since all will tend to be limited both intellectually and in other ways, the stimulation and child–child interaction which is such a fruitful source of learning with normal children will be much reduced.

Kirk and Johnson (1951), describing a preschool programme for educable mentally retarded children, indicated some of the characteristics of these children's play which called for different emphases in the teacher's role. Play patterns tended to be more repetitive and less experimental in the use of materials and ideas, so that a greater amount of the teacher's attention and guidance was needed to extend the play and to continue it. In dramatic play the children were, not surprisingly, limited to everyday events and experiences. Much more repetition of activities was needed in order that the children learnt from them. These are not, in fact, major differences. Nursery teachers are accustomed to receiving children from socially deprived circumstances who need to learn to play, to explore the use of materials, and to progress from mainly locomotor activity to symbolic play. With mentally retarded, as with socially disadvantaged, children there is the need to consider methods of promoting language through greater adult–child interaction. With young visually handicapped children consideration needs to be given to the consequences of the handicap for exploring and comprehending the environment.

It is not too optimistic to hope that the increasing provision of preschool education for the handicapped will improve their educability and will alleviate some of the behavioural problems and learning difficulties which arise through inadequate help in the preschool period. At the same time, it is important to recognize that preschool education is not a panacea. The problems of handicapped and disadvantaged children are not solved at any one stage but require a comprehensive and continuous programme of treatment through the age groups.

Enrichment at the primary stage

Many handicapped children require a continuation of nursery education experience into the infant–junior school period. As they become ready to do so, there are many important developmental tasks to be faced and skills to be acquired in the period before them. Scholastically, there are the basic educational and communication skills. These require emphasis on special teaching procedures (e.g. Braille for the blind; language and speech for the hearing-impaired; the teaching of reading at a later age with educationally subnormal children) and often require remediation procedures to overcome weaknesses in preacademic or readiness skills (e.g. language and perceptual training programmes).

Such teaching should obviously be well-organized and sequenced but this does not mean that it should be narrowly channelled. It is necessary to examine carefully how a well-organized scheme of teaching basic skills can draw life and motivation from wider experiences. This is currently appreciated, for example, in teaching language to the deaf, communication to the severely subnormal and reading to the educationally subnormal. Likewise it cannot be thought that certain training materials, however well-devised or organized, can be the only resource for dealing with specific difficulties. The alert teacher will, like Frostig, be quick to see how many normal classroom experiences can contribute to remediation (e.g. through creative work, mathematics, science).

While a specific language programme may have value to particular groups of children and may also help the teacher to recognize what is involved in teaching language, it should be a part of a broader approach to language improvement. Every primary classroom should have a 'language programme' as an integral part of the learning and experience organized by the teacher: the language arising in early mathematics experiences and science activities, for example. (The teacher who does not know how to use such experiences in this way is hardly likely to get more than a minimal value from a scheme of unrelated language training.)

The phrase 'structured learning' is increasingly used in relation to the education of handicapped and deprived children, usually implying the opposite of spontaneous or incidental learning. It is a term which really needs definition since all teaching worthy of the name is structured in some sense and to some degree. The main point is that some children are so impaired in their ability to learn certain intellectual, language and educational skills that the steps to learning them have to be well-sequenced and taught in very carefully organized teaching situations. The word 'structured' can refer to different features of this process.

The most important meaning of *structured teaching* is that the teacher has a *conceptual structure* of the nature of the learning (its objectives, the sequence of subskills to be learnt) and the learning characteristics of the pupil. For example, any teacher teaching the early stages of reading or early mathematical concepts ought to have a thorough understanding of the nature of the skills and concepts and how they are built up. Very few children, if any, attain them spontaneously or incidentally. Intelligent children may learn adequately in spite of poorly organized teaching. Less able children whose learning is at risk are dependent on well-organized, well-sequenced teaching.

The teacher's understanding of the process of learning particular skills has then to be applied in the actual operation of teaching, which gives us three other senses in which the word 'structured' is used: (i) the organization of learning activities (ii) the construction or selection of materials (iii) organizing the learning environment.

The teacher cannot always be working on a one-to-one basis with pupils. Some of her aims for individuals can be achieved through the *activities* promoted for the class as a whole and even more by grouping children who are at a similar stage in different aspects of learning. This is a standard practice in infant schools. 'Setting' and cross-classification are other ways of structuring the organization of teaching to facilitate the teaching of material with a clear sequential structure.

Well-programmed *teaching materials* not only assist with the organization of teaching but help the teacher to achieve understanding of the sequence of learning. The good teacher uses such materials as a stepping stone for developing her own and adapting them to the needs of her pupils.

There is also a sense in which the *environment of learning* can be carefully structured in order to facilitate and promote certain kinds of learning. Examples of this are Hewett's (1968) 'engineered classroom' with centres or areas for order, exploratory or mastery levels of functioning. The open-plan principle in English primary education is a good example of an educational environment which is structured (in several senses: architecturally, educationally and socially) to facilitate the occurrence of certain kinds of learning experience. It is an organic development from certain principles and practices in structuring the environment which have been developing over a long period in nursery–infant education. It requires more, not less, organization by the teacher and more assessment over a wider range of pupil development.

In summary, it is suggested that we should not see structured programmes and enrichment activities as opposites or even as complementary. Rather, we should see the structure of learning as being based on a very clear conception of the general aims and even more the specific objectives of teaching particular groups of pupils. We can view the techniques of structuring as being on a continuum. At some times (and with some pupils more than others) it is essential to provide teaching which aims to achieve very specific objectives by well-planned techniques in well-controlled learning situations. At the other end of the continuum the learning will not be so closely organized but the environment and the activities have, nevertheless, been planned by the teacher. They can be used to extend, consolidate and practice what has been learnt. A conception such as this avoids the danger, on the one hand, of a collection of remedial activities which do not add up to education and, on the other hand, of an aimless activity which does little to tackle children's difficulties.

But the notion of enrichment at the primary stage has a more fundamental aspect in relation to the total development of the child as a person. During the primary stage, children acquire and extend elementary reasoning processes which enable them to organize their experience of the environment; they elaborate a great variety of gross and fine motor skills in physical activities and in manipulative and constructive activities; they develop social skills enabling them to function in and learn from the peer group; they differentiate emotional responses to a wider range of experience: they are interested in Man, in good and bad, in themselves and in other peoples' qualities and behaviour. It is a period of mastery in many spheres and significant for the development of self-concepts. As Erikson puts it, the child at this stage is 'acquiring a sense of industry and fending off a sense of inferiority', a polarity which is particularly relevant to the nurture of handicapped children. The problem is how to organize the classroom and the school to ensure these personal developments as well as the acquisition of the important basic educational and communication skills.

The practical developments and the theoretical discussions of primary education provide an ample source of ideas about normal methods, but there remain the more difficult questions of how 'normal' can the methods of primary education be for handicapped children? Should a limited range of objectives be specified for ESN children and do their weaknesses and difficulties in learning require a major difference in methods of learning and teaching? Do 'distractible' children require a less 'stimulating' classroom environment? Are team teaching and open-plan approaches appropriate for children whose progress has always seemed to depend so much on a close personal relationship with the teacher? How far much certain things be taught to certain groups of handicapped children which would be acquired incidentally by normal ones?

Both evaluated practical experience in the classroom and research into the learning deficits and the development of handicapped children should work towards answers to these and related questions. The tension in current thinking between, on the one hand, the desire to normalize the experience of handicapped children and, on the other hand, to identify and treat their special difficulties in learning and adjustment, should be productive of a new level of practice.

Enrichment at the secondary stage

Traditionally the secondary stage of schooling is viewed as one in which children begin to follow subject disciplines and are increasingly expected (if not always able) to manifest abstract reasoning and critical thinking. In most categories of handicap, selective secondary education is available for children capable of this level of academic work. With the remainder, as for below-average children in ordinary secondary schools, there is less agreement about the aims and content of their education.

One priority is the need to continue the process of acquiring basic literacy and numeracy skills and a second one is to develop social competence skills, culminating during the last years of school life in a more intensive effort to prepare pupils for the demands of working and social life. What else is contained in the curriculum tends to depend upon the particular interests of schools and teachers. Some emphasize practical activities, some give importance to creative work, others achieve interesting work in environmental and social studies. Schools are concerned to widen and enrich education and to provide normal experiences which handicapped children might otherwise miss. While much of value has been achieved, a coherent view of how the curriculum can be organized has not yet emerged. There have been, however, developments in the curriculum of ordinary secondary schools which have much to offer curriculum enrichment in special schools. The Newsom report (Ministry of Education, 1963), the Schools Council's programme of curriculum development (expressed in a stream of Working Papers) and a considerable number of curriculum development projects producing materials and resources with defined aims and objectives between them provide a rich source of ideas and practice. The special educator has always prized his freedom from the strait-jacket of subject specialization but in recent years there has been a marked trend in ordinary schools towards team teaching and the integration of subject matter. The special educator has always faced the problem of classes with a wide range of ability and attainment but the movement towards mixed ability grouping in ordinary schools requires practical solutions to a similar problem there. The impetus given by the raising of the school-leaving age has given much of the curriculum development a familiar social emphasis. These trends have brought the secondary curriculum closer to a condition, from which special schools can look to it for an infusion of new ideas, which can be adapted to the different groups of handicapped children.

There is another respect in which the ordinary schools curriculum has moved closer to what is required in special education. The methods of learning and teaching tend to emphasize the pupil's own activity; practical work and experience rather than reliance on the textbook (indeed many Schools Council projects provide teachers' guides and pupil resources rather than textbooks); talk and discussion rather than written work. The emphasis on starting from pupils' own interests and conceptual level rather than working through a set syllabus also commends many recent curriculum developments to the special educator.

For example, four Schools Council projects in science provide a great variety of content from which courses in Science could be selected for handicapped children. The Teachers' Guides of *Nuffield Primary Science* in fact quote examples of educationally subnormal children engaging in exploration and discovery. *Science 5 to 13* consists of more than fifteen teachers' guides, each of which provides the teacher with background information about units such as *Science from Toys, Coloured Things, Wood, Holes and Cavities* and *Minibeasts*. A feature of this project is its attempt to delineate the objectives of science teaching for pupils at various levels of mental development: intuitive, concrete-operational and the transition to formal operational thinking. These are examined in terms of what skills in observation, communication, questioning, developing basic concepts and logical thinking might be aimed for at different stages. *Nuffield Combined Science* and *Nuffield Secondary Science* provide courses from which topics to suit the interests and needs of different groups of pupils can be drawn. They have both proved valuable in work with slow-learning and disadvantaged children.

Work in science not only provides children with concepts which one might consider essential for their personal development (e.g. ideas about growth, health, reproduction, and many ideas contributing to personal and social competence) but also increases their awareness and makes a foundation of simple knowledge for the possible subsequent development of interests. We do not need to aim at a thorough and integrated body of knowledge so much as at an awareness which facilitates future learning and interest. It is the *process* of thinking and learning rather than the *amount* of learning which is so valuable.

This is also true of mathematics. In teaching less successful children we have tended to stress basic computational skills and social arithmetic valuable for functioning in society after school leaving. But we should also see mathematics as a means of enriching pupils' understanding of their environment and developing their ability to think and solve problems. There are many suggestions in *Nuffield Primary Mathematics*, in *Mathematics for the Majority* and in the latter's *Continuation*

Project which stimulate interest and promote thinking. Again there is not an obligation to follow a set course but an opportunity to undertake topics and units appropriate to particular groups.

One of the aspects in which many handicapped children most need enrichment is in an understanding of the community and the social environment. Recognizing this, many schools foster links with the community in various ways, sometimes receiving community service, sometimes offering service in the community. Environmental studies and social studies, in some form or other, figure in the work of many schools.

A number of curriculum development projects in this area offer methods of approach and techniques which could be incorporated in work with handicapped children, adapted to their particular requirements. The *Social Education* project, for example, sees social education as a process rather than as a subject with a specific content. Children develop social skills and awareness as they undertake their own chosen enquiries. One technique (Profiles) consists of making studies of social groups: the class, school, peer group and the local community. The reports published so far by this project seem to add a dimension to the term *social education* which is so familiar in special education. How far, and by what means, the project's intentions could be realized by groups of children impeded by handicaps in communication or mobility would be worth exploring.

Geography for the Young School Leaver uses the study of themes of interest and relevance to pupils; a consideration of the local environment and community as a basis for extending the study to more distant parts of Britain and the world. A study of leisure provision in the urban environment leads on to study of the countryside and to holidays and tourism. The topic is a familiar one in special education but the concepts and materials of the project provide extra help to the teacher and stimulus to the pupils.

The *Humanities Curriculum Project* provides collections of pictorial, taped and written evidence as a basis for discussions on such topics as The Family, Poverty, War, Education, Relations between the Sexes. A feature of the approach is that the teacher acts as an impartial chairman. While the materials are probably too difficult, both conceptually and linguistically, for many handicapped children, some aspects of the approach might well be used. For example, simpler collections of evidence making more use of pictures and tapes to initiate and support discussion could be prepared to cover the kinds of human and social issues raised by the *Humanities Curriculum*. These are issues which all save the most limited in ability should have the opportunity of considering and, in the course of doing so, they would gain both linguistically and conceptually.

One can profitably examine curricular developments in secondary schools for what they can contribute to that essential part of special education—the emotional and moral education of pupils. In this there have been developments of immediate relevance to handicapped children. For example, *Lifelines*, materials produced by the Schools Council *Moral Education Curriculum* project, views moral education as 'all education which helps a child to adapt a considerate style of life, to have respect for other's feelings as well as his own'. To achieve this, pupils are encouraged to discuss or to dramatize situations drawn from everyday life: 'Your father is critical of your hair and your clothes'; 'What might happen if someone locks a child outside from 2 to 10 at night'. A wide range of situations are available on cards in collections entitled *Sensitivity, Consequences* and *In Other People's Shoes*. The materials have been used with success with slow learners and with ESN children in special schools. One teacher who used it in an ESN school remarked that the approach was similar to informal discussions she had been accustomed to having with pupils, but the materials and the underlying aims of the project had proved a useful framework.

Both this project and the Social Education project stress the value of socio-drama (Slade, 1954). The Social Education Project outlines a graded approach to this activity, beginning with mime and moving from simple to more complex situations.

There are few schools which do not find some means of enrichment through music, dance, art and craft, and the work achieved is often of a high quality. It is not so much the quality, however, as the significance for the individual which is important. It is a means of personal development, in the intellectual as well as the emotional sense, which can compensate in some measure for limitations of experience and opportunity in other directions, and a means of communication and personal expression; all the more important for children who are limited in other forms of communication. This is well demonstrated by Bailey (1973) who exercised remarkable ingenuity in adapting and using a very wide range of musical instruments for use by physically and mentally handicapped children and also devised ways of teaching the elements of notation to pupils whom many would have considered unlikely to learn it. Although art and music *therapy* have a place in certain situations, in a school context we are concerned with the arts as a medium of *education*. Too often neglected in ordinary education, we can at least say that they have a higher valuation in special education.

All these and many other ways of enriching the experience of handicapped pupils represent an embarrassment of riches, and the embarrassment becomes acute when one considers that by the age of sixteen many pupils have not achieved basic skills in literacy, communication and social competence. 'We would like to do more of these things but where is the time?' is the cry. To some extent, enrichment and the teaching of basic educational and social skills need not be seen as mutually exclusive. Literacy skills could more readily be seen as taught and developed through general curriculum activities rather than exclusively through reading and writing materials. For example, opportunities for word study, reading comprehension and written expression arise in an integral and well-motivated way in science and environmental studies. An enriched curriculum provides both somthing to talk about and the motivation to discuss. We also perhaps have to face the issue of whether there are not certain educational priorities which in the last resort are more important than conventional literacy. In any case, we need to explore the uses of audio-visual resources as a means of complementing other methods of communication, and in some cases as the only method. We have to educate the intellect, the emotions and social awareness, not simply ensure basic skills.

Further education

One solution to the problem of how to achieve certain basic educational goals for handicapped children and how to educate them in as wide and rich a sense as possible must surely be an increasing provision of further education for handicapped children. The opportunity for education beyond the normal age of school-leaving is desirable for all children but for handicapped children there are particular circumstances which increase its desirability. Many pupils are still educationally retarded by the age of leaving school; many are still personally immature and would benefit from a longer period of education as well as from the opportunity to mix with other students in a college rather than a school atmosphere. Moreover, the range of choice in subjects would permit pupils to test their interests, discover new ones and find satisfaction in areas of learning previously unrealized. While their further education at present tends to include a vocational assessment element, it will be important, as facilities develop, to ensure that provision is made for a broad and enriching education both for those who will work and those who will require sheltered employment.

For some time special provision has been made for various groups of handicapped young people. In the UK the Spastics Society established a further education centre for cerebral-palsied children and a centre for heavily handicapped young people capable of a higher education level. The Star Centre near Cheltenham was set up to provide for a variety of handicapped school-leavers. For the visually handicapped there are a number of facilities; the issue is examined in the Vernon report (1972). At the instigation of the Department of Education and Science, Hereward College was set up in 1970 at Coventry, for physically handicapped leavers needing further education.

There has been for some time the practice of sending a few suitable pupils from special schools to further-education colleges, often on a part-time basis in their final year. The signs are that this is an increasing trend which raises the need to discuss how such work should be organized (one hopes not in rather segregated special departments) and staffed (should some further education staff be suitably trained?).

Burden (1969) describes an experiment in which pupils in their final year at an ESN school attended a College of Further Education, taking courses chosen from art, building, car maintenance, carpentry, cookery, needlework, painting and decorating and welding. The mean MA of the pupils successfully completing the course was $10\frac{1}{2}$ (range 7–11+ years) but it is of interest that the Mean IQ on the Morrisby Test of Mechanical Ability was between 85–89 (Range 65–108). The staff of the college were overwhelmingly in favour of the project, but what is of particular interest is that certain pupils were able to reveal and use potentialities which had not previously been recognized.

Hutchinson and Clegg (1972) describe a work orientation unit set up at the North Nottinghamshire College of Further Education. Within three years the enrolment increased from three to eighty students and included wide ranges of handicaps and ability. One course, 'Transition to Work', is basically a work orientation course for pupils who need further preparation for working life; another course, 'Training for the Future', is for intellectually more able students and is similar to a conventional course in a college of further education. The range of courses includes engineering crafts, building crafts, painting and decorating, domestic cooking and catering, needlecraft, fashion and shop window display and commercial crafts.

As the Vernon report (DES, 1972) remarked, 'The polytechnics and colleges of further education provide rich educational, technical, cultural and social opportunities'. Development in the use of these opportunities by handicapped children seems one of the most promising ways of enriching the education of handicapped pupils, many of whom are only just becoming ready at the age of school leaving to benefit from a wide range of social, cultural and learning experience. While such courses are likely to be undertaken partly with a vocational purpose in mind, it is to be hoped that recreational, cultural and broadly educational courses will increasingly be provided. This is particularly important for many handicapped young people since social interaction with other young people, and in the community generally, does not come easily, either because of difficulties in independent travel and in communication, or because of their immaturities and poor social skills.

CONCLUSION

Enrichment is viewed as part of a comprehensive and continuous approach to the education and care of handicapped children, beginning as early as possible in the child's life and continuing into adult life. This framework has been outlined in the National Children's Bureau's, *Living with Handicap* (Younghusband *et al.*, 1970).

Enrichment implies normalization; that is, as far as possible handicapped children should have normal experiences of schooling and living. Even though this may not always be possible, there is much that can be done through a broad curriculum and through further educational opportunities to enrich the scope and quality of their education. It is important that special education should maintain a close contact with the mainstream of educational thought and practice.

Schools Council Curriculum Projects

Information about publications and materials may be obtained from the Information Officer, Schools Council, 160 Gt. Portland Street, London. Curriculum materials of the projects mentioned are published as follows:

Collins	Nuffield Primary Science
Macdonald Educational	Science 5–13
Penguin Educational	Nuffield Combined Science
Longman Group	Nuffield Secondary Science
W. and R. Chambers	Nuffield Primary Mathematics
Hart Davis Educational Ltd.	Mathematics for the Majority
Heinemann Educational Books	Humanities Curriculum Project
(Lifelines) Longman Group	Moral Education Curriculum Project

Note: The Social Education Project has not produced materials; *Geography for the Young School Leaver* materials are in the trials stage.

CHAPTER 8

A Psychodynamic View of the Therapeutic Opportunities of Special Education

I. CASPARI

SPECIAL EDUCATION VERSUS GENERAL EDUCATION: SIMILARITIES AND DIFFERENCES

In its widest sense, education can be defined in terms of furthering the development of an individual so as to enable him to fit into his environment, to contribute to the best of his ability towards the well-being of society and to help him to adjust to the demands that his environment is going to make on him. This process can be examined in a variety of ways. A psychodynamic view explores the emotional implications of this process, focusing particularly on what people feel about each other.

The people most intimately involved in the educational process at school are of course the children and the teachers. This is as true of special education as much as of education in general. In either setting the children have to attend school, they have to concentrate on the tasks selected by the teacher as furthering the educational process, they have to relate to a number of peers with whom they have to share the teacher, and so on. This situation makes considerable demands on the intellectual and emotional resources of the children. By and large, this challenge furthers the children's development, but it can, of course, also cause considerable anxieties.

Similarly, teachers need to select and present the 'educational task' so that children can take it in, they have to look after the children's physical well-being, they have to control them so that they can express themselves safely in the group situation in which most of the children in schools are educated. This, too, is a challenge to teachers, and often a cause of anxiety, all the more so as the teaching–learning situation at school is far more difficult than is generally admitted, and as the skills needed to succeed in this difficult operation are often underrated.

In this process the teacher's understanding of the children's feelings towards him and towards each other, and the understanding of his feelings towards the children, is of fundamental importance. The better the teacher is able to understand these feelings, the more likely he is to succeed in this very difficult task. To this extent there is very little difference between special education and education in general.

However, children selected for special education have distinctive characteristics that single them out from their peers. They have been unable to meet the challenge of education. Sometimes they were excluded before they entered school, but the majority of such children have been tried in ordinary schools and have failed. This sense of failure, the experience of being rejected, naturally influences the children's feelings, so that it is harder for them to get on with the teacher and with their peers in school.

Moreover, their specific handicap often makes learning very difficult for them. In this respect the teacher of handicapped children needs even greater skills than the teacher in ordinary schools. He constantly needs to consider the educational process in relation to the child's handicap in an attempt to fit the child into society despite the handicap. In this way special education adds to the developmental process of education a therapeutic element and the teacher is therefore constantly working on the boundary between therapy and education.

For example, in the presentation of the teaching content to children with a physical handicap; special arrangements have to be made to present the material in such a way that these children can learn in spite of being blind, deaf, spastic and so on. Similarly, in schools for educationally subnormal children the syllabus has to be adjusted so as to suit children of low intelligence.

However, handicapped children not only have difficulty in learning, they also find it harder than other children to meet the emotional demands made on them. This is, of course, particularly true of maladjusted children whose handicap is generally connected with particular difficulties in relating with other people. Yet whatever the handicap the therapeutic task of special education needs to be considered with the child's emotional problems in mind, especially those arising from the handicap and from the experience of failure connected with it.

To this extent there is inevitably a psychotherapeutic component within the therapeutic task of special education and psychodynamic theories seem, therefore, especially suitable to explore the therapeutic task from this angle.

I see psychodynamic theory as a way of examining observable behaviour with special reference to the feelings connected with it, particularly to those feelings of which the individual is not aware. A simple example might illustrate what this emphasis means in practice.

Let us imagine that a teacher observers Johnny hitting Jimmy in a lesson. While doing so Johnny shouts and his face grows red. Most teachers would assume that Johnny is annoyed with Jimmy and that there was a reason for Johnny's behaviour. Jimmy might have teased Johnny. The teacher might have observed this for himself or the other children might tell him. On a much less obvious level, the teacher might deduce from Johnny's previous behaviour that hitting another child is one of Johnny's devices for gaining the teacher's attention. On previous occasions the teacher might have talked to Johnny. He might have reprimanded him, but at the same time he might have accepted Johnny's wish to have him, the teacher, all to himself. He might have demonstrated that in a classroom situation all children need to share the teacher and that he likes Johnny even if he sometimes does not seem to take any special notice of him. Each time Johnny might have insisted that the other child started the fight, although evidence suggested that this was not so. Each time Johnny might have promised that he would not do it again, but his behaviour had not changed. Again and again these fights occur.

In such a case psychodynamic theory would hypothesize that Johnny's behaviour is linked to feelings of which he is not aware, and that these unconscious feelings are far more powerful in determining Johnny's behaviour than are his more rational, conscious ones. One would leave the options open as to the precise nature of Johnny's unconscious feelings and these hypotheses would be examined and re-examined in the light of the evidence.

For instance, the teacher might have observed that Johnny only hits boys smaller than himself. It might also be known that Johnny's younger brother was born when Johnny was just starting school, and that following the brother's birth Johnny's mother was in hospital for some time. It could then be assumed that the fighting is to some extent linked to Johnny's jealousy of his brother and to his feelings that, at the time, his brother deprived him of his mother's attention. He, himself, might not remember this incidence at all. He might or might not be exceedingly fond of his brother. But this experience has lowered Johnny's tolerance for sharing an adult with other children and he expresses these feelings in school by fighting other, smaller boys.

At this point I should like to refrain from discussing the practical implications of this kind of interpretation of behaviour. The purpose of the example is to illustrate psychodynamic thinking.

By and large, the concept of unconscious feelings and unconscious motivation is quite readily accepted by teachers. It is, however, very unpopular amongst scientists. Winnicott (1971) puts one reason for this in a nutshell when he says 'A computer cannot be programmed to give motives that are unconscious in the individuals who are the guinea-pigs of an investigation'.

To the extent to which this is true psychodynamic theory must be considered as a hypothesis of behaviour supported mainly by circumstantial evidence. Personally, I support the psychodynamic point of view because it explains to me much of the paradoxical behaviour I meet in myself and in my clinical work with people.

Those who subscribe to a psychodynamic interpretation of behaviour such as Freud, Klein and Winnicott, are unanimous in attributing the origin of these unconscious feelings to experiences in early childhood, and often link unrealistic behaviour such as Johnny's attacks on other children to conflicts that could not be resolved at that time.

There are varying views about the relative importance of certain universal experiences. Freud, for instance, places much emphasis on conflicts arising from the oedipal situation while Klein concentrates on the feeding situation during the first weeks and months of life and on the relationship the infant forms with the most important people in his environment.

In this paper I am concentrating on three psychodynamic concepts which in my view are of special relevance to the educational process: ambivalence, sublimation and play. These concepts are, of course, frequently used without reference to any psychodynamic theory. Moreover, they are used in various ways by different authors, and even the same author might use these concepts differently at other times. I shall attempt to give some idea of the ways in which these terms can be used, concentrating on my own interpretation of these terms as I myself have experienced them in education, particularly in the education of handicapped children.

The term ambivalence was first used by Bleuler (1910), to describe contradictory feelings, such as the way an individual might love and hate the same person at the same time. This concept was taken up by Freud (1912), first of all in connection with these contradictory feelings as they appeared in Freud's patients during analysis. Later on (1926) Freud linked the ambivalent conflict especially to the oedipal phase, i.e. to that time of human development when the child is intensely jealous of the intimate relationship between the parents; when the boy, for instance, wants to take his father's place in relationship to his mother, but is, at the same time intensely afraid that he might succeed and might be eliminated by his father in revenge. These feelings are, of course, unconscious and in later life one does not remember the conflict experienced during the oedipal phase. However, observations of young children often substantiate the hypothesis, such as seeing children of 3–5 years squeezing between their parents and the various devices often employed by children of that age to attract their parents' attention at night.

In the more general way in which Bleuler originally used the concept ambivalent feelings are also more consciously experienced. One need only think of the prover-bial 'lover's quarrel' or the way even the most devoted mother will become impatient with her child at times. One always feels extremely guilty about these feelings of an-noyance, yet one also knows that the lover's quarrel does not necessarily destroy the relationship between the two young people. On the contrary, they may feel closer to each other than before. Having appreciated that they can be annoyed with each other without the relationship coming to any harm, they will feel much more secure, as each has experienced that the partner can bear the feelings of hate and that he or she has not been rejected.

The way in which an individual comes to terms with these conflicting feelings will contribute greatly to his healthy development. There are many ways in which this process can be facilitated. Bowlby (1958) for instance, suggests that the child can be helped most by his parents allowing him to 'express his hostile and jealous feelings candidly, directly and spontaneously' provided that the intensity of the feelings are within the limits that the parents can bear. Similarly and with equal candour parents might express their negative feelings towards their children, again within the limits that can be borne. The same principle can, of course, be extended to teachers. In this case the limits in terms of a 'safe framework' are important. If a child is in fact hurting the adult, the adult is inclined to reject him, and this confirms the child's worst fears and thus leads to a tendency to hide the hostile feelings. The same process would result if the adult expressed his hostile feelings to the extent of rejecting the child for good. In addition, different settings allow for different ways of expressing hostility 'safely'. Parents have opportunities denied to teachers and vice versa. Some hostile feelings might be expressed safely in a small group, but would destroy the 'safe framework' if expressed in a class of forty children.

The process of coming to terms with conflict situations is also helped by sublimation. Freud (1908) first used the concept of sublimation in an attempt to account for the experience of intellectual and artistic activities in terms of the theoretical model of behaviour he used at that time. This hypothesis underwent a number of changes. At first, for instance, Freud saw sublimatory activities solely in terms of displacement of sexual impulses. Later, as Jones (1957) reports, he contemplated that artistic and intellectual activities could also be seen as displacement mechanisms of aggressive impulses.

More recently the concept has been modified by a number of psycho-analytic authors. Klein (1929) uses the term, for instance, in connection with her 'objects' relations' theory which links all human relationships to the first experiences of the infant with the 'loved objects' in his surroundings, i.e. with his mother, his father and his siblings. In this theory she refers to the infant's feelings of hate towards his 'early objects', which might occur, for instance, when the mother does not satisfy the infant's feelings of hunger immediately. Naturally, most mothers cannot feed their infants the moment they cry. Therefore, this is a common human experience. Klein assumes that the infant's feelings of hate are accompanied by fantasies that these feelings might destroy the 'loved object'. Therefore, the infant has a great need to restore the 'loved object', and this restoration is done by the mechanism of sublimation expressed in later life by intellectual and artistic activities.

To some extent this explanation is somewhat nebulous. This is true of the use of this term throughout psycho-analytic literature and therefore I feel free to adapt the term 'sublimation' more closely to the educational process and to use it to denote the mechanism by which socially unacceptable feelings can be expressed in socially acceptable ways. For instance, a person might feel so angry with another that he feels he should like to kill him. Naturally, such action cannot be sanctioned by society. Sublimatory activities provide him with a variety of ways in which these feelings can be expressed and accepted. For instance, he can say something unpleasant to the person or he can 'beat' him in a game of chess. He could also paint a picture of a fight between two people, in which he might either consciously or unconsciously identify the victim with the hated person. Similarly, he can write a poem about his fight. He might also direct his efforts towards learning so that, in the long term, he would be able to beat the hated person intellectually.

In this way the sublimatory process can be applied to any impulse that for some reason or other cannot be satisfied and, in as far as school activities include all forms of artistic expression as well as learning, the educational process offers abundant opportunities for sublimatory activities.

Closely related to sublimatory activities is the concept of play. Its importance for human development has been known by educators throughout the ages. As early as 1909 Froebel pointed to the contribution of play towards healthy development of infants and young children and since his time play has been accepted as the basis for all nursery education and as a necessary activity for the development of children of all ages.

In this context play is often seen as a means by which the child can experience his environment. The child plays at being a doctor or a postman and experiences what these occupations would be like. He handles constructive toys such as bricks or plasticine and finds out how different materials can be used.

Psycho-analytic theory adds another dimension to the concept of play: the opportunity of experiencing feelings in the play situation and of communicating them to other people. Winnicott (1971) has given special attention to the uniqueness of the play situation and for the purpose of this chapter I should like to restrict myself to some aspects of his contribution to the theory.

To give an example: a three-year-old might play with her doll and might engage her mother in the play. The little girl pretends that the doll will not eat her dinner. She smacks the doll and pretends that the doll cries. She pretends that the doll is now eating her dinner and praises her for being a good girl. In this play the little girl is, of course, trying to identify with her mother and experiences what her mother's feelings might be when she punishes her for not eating her dinner. At the same time she is communicating to her mother, who watches her, what she feels about not eating, about being made to eat, and about the reconciliation afterwards. In this process the action is under the control of the child. To that extent the play represents the child's feelings. But the play is acted out in reality, it can also be experienced by the mother. So it is not only experienced by the child in fantasy, it is also experienced in reality. Yet it is the reality of play, not the reality of real life. In this way the mother can share the child's feelings, but need not react to them in the way that she would have to do if the child herself were to refuse the food.

Obviously such play could not occur if the child could not trust her mother to accept these feelings expressed. Nor could the child express these feelings if the toys were beyond her maturity level. Naturally the child would not engage in such play if the mother were not sensitive to her little girl's communications.

In play, therefore, feelings can be expressed indirectly and less intensively than in reality. The fantasies underlying the play can be tested out in a reality that can be controlled and is therefore less threatening than 'real life reality'.

THE CONTRIBUTION OF THE TEACHER–CHILD RELATIONSHIP TOWARDS THE PSYCHOTHERAPEUTIC TASK OF SPECIAL EDUCATION

It is, I think, not difficult to see that the characteristics of this kind of relationship are not so very dissimilar to some of the interactions that, in later life, take place between the child and his teacher at school.

Just as the mother creates an atmosphere of trust to encourage the kind of 'creative play' described above, the teacher fosters 'creative learning' by establishing a similar atmosphere in the classroom. Just as the mother encourages her child to play with a suitable toy, the teacher provides a variety of learning tasks that are within the grasp of the child's ability, and presents them in a way that the child can learn. Just as the mother permits the child to show his feelings in play, the teacher allows the children in his class to express their opinion even if they do not agree with him, but in such a way that they do not do harm to him, to each other, or to the classroom. Thus the learning situation offers the children ample scope for experiencing and communicating their feelings, provided that there is an atmosphere of trust between the teacher and his pupils.

The teacher has, therefore, a unique opportunity to help the child to come to terms with many emotional conflicts, including ambivalent feelings towards the people he loves, particularly as it is far easier for the teacher, in his more remote relationship to the child, to accept the frustrations and anxieties of the child's negative feelings than it is for the parents who are much more closely involved with him.

Of course a child cannot trust a teacher unless he likes him, and a teacher is unable to develop this atmosphere of trust unless he is fond of the children he teaches. This is not an easy task. No teacher can be fond of all the children he meets and children are not likely to be fond of all their teachers.

Institutions concerned with special education, however, usually make provision to maximize opportunities for positive relationships between the staff and the children. For instance, the classes or groups are smaller and there is often some opportunity to move a particular child from one group to another if he cannot get on with a particular teacher or if he is especially attached to another. Moreover, many teachers in special education receive an additional training. There is also a greater acceptance of difficulties and more opportunity to discuss these with colleagues or with specialists in other fields, such as doctors, social workers or psychologists.

This atmosphere of trust is particularly important for special education because the hostile feelings of these children are often more intense and less easy to control than those of children who are not handicapped. This is obvious in the case of maladjusted children whose emotional problems are often connected with such strong feelings of hate and destruction that they are compelled to express them in an antisocial way. However, it is equally important for children with other handicaps. If one sees the process of coming to terms with contradictory feelings as part of adjustment to society and life, any handicap, whether it be mental, emotional or physical, will make this adjustment more difficult. To this extent all children with handicaps are at risk, although some of them can adjust extremely well in spite of it.

In institutions for children with emotional problems these therapeutic elements become, of course, most evident. Brown (1962) gives a vivid description of how every member of the staff at the Mulberry Bush School, including the cook and the gardener, was used to help these very disturbed children. Yet it is not easy to find incidences to illustrate how this is done. Sometimes the event seems so matter-of-fact and unimportant that one hardly takes any notice of it. In an article on school consultation (Caspari, 1962) an example is given of a headmistress of a Primary School helping a very difficult 10-year-old boy in this way. The boy was constantly disrupting the class by his difficult behaviour and the headmistress frequently removed him from the class and had, in this way, given him an environment in which he could express his negative feelings to her without disturbing the activities of other people in the school. The headmistress was very fond of the boy, and he had become very attached to her. She always reprimanded him for his misbehaviour but she understood the reasons for his misdemeanour and did not punish him or reject him. In this simple way she repeatedly gave him the experience of being accepted, in spite of his attacks, by an adult he loved. On these occasions she often talked about feelings and how difficult it was to control one's anger. Gradually the temper tantrums decreased. Originally it had been considered necessary to place him in a day school for maladjusted children, but by the time he had to transfer to secondary school it was felt that he would be able to manage in a comprehensive school and this proved to be successful.

Sometimes the handling of such a child might even seem inappropriate. A headmistress of a day school for maladjusted children, for instance, repeatedly rewarded another ten-year-old boy with money whenever he had fights, destroyed something or ran away from school.

This was, of course, a very deprived boy whose ability to come to terms with contradictory feelings was greatly impaired by feelings that he was so bad that nobody could like him at all. So the headmistress had felt that the only way to help him was by 'rewarding his badness'.

In both cases the boys had to experience over and over again that their 'badness' could be accepted. In both cases the child was helped. Each time the insight and sensitivity of the headmistress had made this change possible. To some degree both headmistresses were aware of what they were doing, but neither of them would have put it in the way in which it is described here. From the psychodynamic point of view it could be said that both headmistresses understood the unconscious feelings of the two boys that caused their deviant behaviour, although to some extent their understanding was intuitive; in other words, unconscious. Through this kind of psychotherapeutic interaction they helped the boys to come to terms with some of their contradictory feelings. They would not have been able to achieve this goal if the interaction with the boys had not occurred in an atmosphere of trust.

THE CONTRIBUTION OF THE EDUCATIONAL TASK TOWARDS THE PSYCHOTHERAPEUTIC TASK OF SPECIAL EDUCATION

This psychotherapeutic process is also helped by 'the educational task'. The 'educational task', i.e. the acquisition of knowledge and skills, is often described as 'work' and it is expected to be arduous, and to demand effort and strain. Yet I think that the division between 'work' and 'play' in the school situation is rather artificial. For the child in an infant school there is very little difference between his 'play' with constructional toys and his 'work' with reading apparatus or Cuisinaire rods. Similarly, an adolescent might put as much 'hard work' into learning to 'play tennis' as he does into learning mathematics for G.C.E. 'O' level.

There are, of course, certain differences between learning and play. Play, for instance, is more often initiated by the child. In play the child examines his surroundings and experiments with them, and the adults who play with him are not unduly worried if he loses interest and stops playing. If play is initiated by an adult, by introducing a toy or an activity, most adults would not be too concerned if the child terminated the play. They can easily accept that something else might attract the child, that he might be tired or not yet able to handle the play material.

Learning, however, is much more frequently introduced by an adult who is concerned that the child should learn. If, for some reason, the child refuses to do so, the adult is likely to become anxious and to put pressure on the child to continue whether he likes it or not. However, the difference between the learning situation and the play situation can be greatly diminished if teachers are sensitive to the child's refusals and if they are flexible enough to plan and programme the material according to his needs. Many teachers handle this aspect of their work with the utmost skill. On the other hand, the demands of academic learning, particularly at the secondary school stage, are often not adjusted to the child's maturity and to his needs. Hence there is the general expectation that learning has to be performed under duress.

There is generally much less pressure on academic achievement in institutions for special education where most teachers and parents expect only limited academic success. Moreover, most handicapped children have experienced failure at school and thus tend to avoid learning situations. The teacher in special education therefore needs to take particular care to choose an educational task appropriate to the child's ability, and to introduce it in a way that arouses the child's interest. The teacher also needs to accept the child's refusal to learn as a matter of course. In this way the learning situation is almost identical to a play situation and from the psychodynamic point of view the child will profit from this kind of learning in the same way as he benefits from playing.

The educational task also adds to the psychotherapeutic opportunities of education as a sublimatory activity, which often helps a child to experience and express socially unacceptable feelings in socially acceptable ways. In literature, for instance, many characters are villains. Others express feelings that they are unable to accept. In discussing these characters and in scrutinizing their actions, the child participates in their feelings, which are often very similar to his own.

For different children, different feelings and characters will be relevant at any one time. Great literature, such as *Hamlet* or the *Canterbury Tales,* presents such a large spectrum of human experience that it is of almost universal relevance. However, all literature is relevant to some human situation and it would be impossible not to be able to choose the study of a particular piece of literature with the specific conflict of a certain group of children in mind. The children are, of course, experiencing these feelings by proxy, 'as if' they were the characters in the story, having their feelings and sharing the responsibility for their actions. To this extent the experience can be seen as a 'sublimatory process', the feelings being expressed in the 'reality of play' which was discussed earlier. This experience is naturally heightened if the teacher is sensitive to this aspect of the material and if the child is able to take a more active part in the process, for example, by either acting or miming the characters or by illustrating the story with drawings.

The relevance of this hypothesis to special education might be more easily understood if illustrated by an example. Claude was a 13-year-old West Indian boy, who had been referred for vicious temper tantrums at school. He was also underfunctioning, particularly in arithmetic. For various reasons he was considered to be unsuitable for analytic psychotherapy and was therefore treated by 'educational therapy'.

In the second year of his treatment he brought the comics of Superman to his sessions, and began to dictate to me a series of stories in which he was able to express many of his contradictory feelings. Below, I am giving some extracts of one of the stories called 'The Hulk's Fight with the Submariner'. The first refers directly to his temper tantrums:

'The Hulk is hunted by the army, but we all know that the Hulk is not really as bad as the army thinks. Rick Jones, the Hulk's companion, helps the Hulk all the time . . . The Hulk used to be a savage man whom the army used to hunt down, but ever since Rick Jones can control him by saying anything to him the Hulk is a completely different person . . . Sometimes the Hulk changes back to himself, that is why Rick Jones does not want to let him get away: because when Rick Jones sleeps he loses control of the Hulk and the Hulk reacts savagely again. If the army was to find out it would be the end of his other-self identity, Dr. Banner . . . There is another reason for Rick Jones' coming: he goes to the Hulk's stronghold to let the Hulk out and to see whether he is changing to his other self, Dr. Banner'.

I should like to suggest that from a psychodynamic point of view Claude used the characters to show what he felt about himself, although he was not aware that he was doing this. He was a very affectionate, likeable boy, full of good intentions, but he had these uncontrollable temper tantrums. The story indicates how strongly he felt that his 'savageness' needed to be kept under control. The Hulk–Dr. Banner theme was also one of his problems, for he was an intelligent boy with an above average IQ but incapable of using his intelligence. The description of Rick Jones also refers, I think, to the way he felt towards his therapist, the help she was giving 'by saying anything to him' and to the danger of her 'being asleep', i.e. not being there during holidays.

The second excerpt is connected with his problems about his colour; it is the story of the marriage of the parents of Namur, another character from the comics:

'His mother was an undersea princess. One day she came to the surface. When she came up she saw a ship. The captain of the ship was on the deck looking on the sea, thinking. Then suddenly to his surprise the princess came out of the water. He called to her and asked her what she was doing in the water. He looked at her strangely and he seemed to be in a sort of hypnotic state because her skin was purple . . . When he sort of recovered he fell in love with her. He told her he could not take her to the city because people would ask her a lot of questions and embarrass her'.

Subsequently they meet on the ship and are married by a vicar who is blindfolded 'without the vicar seeing the princess' face'.

The white captain can only have a close relationship with the 'purple princess' in secret. Nobody must know the colour of her skin, not even the vicar. This gives a glimpse of Claude's feelings that he cannot be accepted by white people because of the colour of his skin. It also refers again to his 'secret' relationship to his therapist, i.e. to the confidentiality of the sessions. These stories can be seen simply as essays and they could have been written during any English lesson at any school. At the same time they are communications. They told me how Claude felt. Whether or not the communications can be interpreted in the ways described above is, of course, debatable. One can never be completely certain whether or not one's understanding has been correct. To my mind this is not of overwhelming importance. The therapeutic process lies in the way that the child can try out his ideas, can show his feelings to the teacher and attempt solutions of his problems in the story. Sometimes one might discuss some of the characters' problems with the child. For instance, one might have talked about the captain who has to keep his marriage secret, and about the feelings of the princess who is unable to meet her husband's family. One might have discussed what would happen if the purple princess were to enter the city. Such a discussion would have offered an opportunity to look at the child's problems with the child at the 'once removed'. This is generally much less painful to the child than a direct discussion of his problems. Moreover, he will learn to use this indirect way of expressing his feelings as a means of coming to terms with them in a sublimatory way.

It is fairly simple, I think, to extend this principle of the emotional aspect of learning to other studies, such as the study of History or Geography. However, I should like to suggest that this principle can be extended to all learning activities, including the acquisition of skills such as reading, mathematics, foreign languages and so on. Some suggestions of this kind have been given in another paper (Caspari, 1970).

In this way the curriculum can help the child to come to terms with a variety of feelings including his ambivalent feelings towards the teacher. In Bowlby's view one of the conditions for coming to terms with contradictory, unacceptable feelings is the possibility of expressing them, but within the limits that both the child and the adult can bear. Openly aggressive behaviour, such as hitting other children or damaging the furniture, or even excessive verbal rebellion or rudeness, is usually outside the limits. However, the teacher has this possibility of diverting the negative feelings into the 'educational task'. If the feelings are expressed in a story or a painting the teacher can accept them, and by doing so he will give the message that feelings expressed in sublimatory ways are generally acceptable. To the extent that the educational task is carried out in relation to the teacher, all feelings connected with the task will also to some extent be directed towards the teacher. Claude did not just express his feelings about himself and his problems in his stories, he also told me what he thought of me.

A technique that we often use in the teaching of reading to children with severe reading difficulty might illustrate how negative feelings can be safely expressed in the learning of simple skills.

The teaching of phonic rules demands a certain amount of rather dull practice, such as reading a word list. We usually introduce this activity in the form of a game, in which the child scores all the words read correctly, while the teacher scores the child's mistakes. This game is only effective if the teacher is sure that the child will score considerably higher than he does. In this way the child is given the opportunity to 'beat' the teacher in the game. The beating is obviously an expression of negative feelings but in a game it is socially acceptable. The situation contains an extra bonus as the teacher is bound to be delighted with his defeat, since the child's victory in the game is at the same time a proof of the teacher's success in teaching the child to read.

Many practitioners in the teaching of reading will recognize this way of teaching as a fairly common procedure, without perhaps realizing what it might mean to the child in terms of his feelings. Moreover, this simple strategy may give opportunity for experiencing many other feelings: feelings in connection with authority, feelings about success and failure and so on. Very little attention has hitherto been given to this aspect of teaching and learning. The beneficial results occur, of course, whether one is aware of them or not, but it stands to reason that effectiveness is likely to increase if one knows what one is doing.

THE CONTRIBUTION OF THE SETTING TOWARDS THE PSYCHOTHERAPEUTIC TASK OF SPECIAL EDUCATION

Whatever the teacher can do directly either in the relationship to the child or through the curriculum will also depend on the setting in which the interaction takes place. This includes the bricks and mortar, the size of the unit, the relationship of a particular unit to the institution as a whole and to other institutions, the staffing ratio, the kind of staff employed, the regime and the expectations of the people engaged in the work and so on. Different settings will offer different opportunities, even if the children suffer identical handicaps. For instance, the therapeutic opportunities for educationally subnormal children placed in a class attached to an ordinary school will be different from those in an identical class in an ESN school. The former offers ample opportunity to mix with ordinary children. This prevents the child from feeling isolated, but it might increase the ESN children's feelings of being a failure. They will be spared this conflict in an ESN school, but will suffer from being far more clearly identified as an exceptional group. This does not mean that one setting is necessarily better than another. It is different, and the differences have to be taken into account to maximize the opportunities that each setting can offer. The greater the variety of settings the greater the opportunity to find a suitable surrounding for a particular child.

I should like to examine the link between the setting and the therapeutic opportunities by looking at a variety of institutions for the special education of children with emotional and behaviour problems. These institutions, of course, pay special attention to the children's feelings, yet each school can only be helpful within the framework of its setting. Each setting has advantages and disadvantages.

Some children, for instance, can be helped within the framework of an ordinary school. For example, in one comprehensive school children with behaviour problems were attached to one particular member of staff, who saw the child for at least ten minutes each day. In other schools this role is given to a 'counsellor', and in many cases these children are helped very effectively. Yet they have to be able to fit in with the large institution of a comprehensive school for the rest of the school day. They have to follow the school routine, go to the right classroom at the right time, share a teacher with a large number of other children and so on. Some children will be able to function within such a large setting if given this limited extra attention, others will have to be referred to a special school because their behaviour difficulties could not be resolved in this way.

There are various units that might cater for a child with behaviour disorders. The facilities vary greatly in different areas and only some are selected for discussion. For instance, there are the so-called 'tutorial classes' to which the child goes for part of his school day. These are small units of 6–8 children, sometimes situated in another school, sometimes placed in a flat of their own. There is usually one teacher in charge. Naturally, in this setting a child's conflict can be explored in far greater detail than in a large comprehensive school and there is much greater opportunity to help the child with his problems by adapting sublimatory activities to his needs.

Let us again take the example of Johnny hitting Jimmy in a lesson. In a comprehensive school all the teacher can generally do is to stop the fight. Usually he has little idea about the reasons for the fight, because in a group of 30 it is difficult to notice what would provoke such a situation. The provocation might, indeed, have been more in the attacker's imagination than in reality, and the teacher might realize that this is a particular area in which the boy needs help. Yet at that time his main occupation is to teach a group of 30, and the attention to the one boy would result in the neglect of the remaining 29. If Johnny attacks Jimmy in a tutorial class the teacher will have a much greater chance to find out what might have caused this behaviour, and if he finds that the attacker felt himself attacked without any obvious reason, there will be a much greater chance for discussion. The underlying, unexpressed reasons might also become much more apparent in other ways, through the boy's behaviour at other times, through his communications to the teacher in stories or drawings, through the fact that the tutorial teacher has more contact with Johnny than the teacher in the comprehensive school. Once the teacher understands the reason for such behaviour he can seek opportunities that might help the boy to come to terms with the underlying feelings, and these opportunities will be increased by the close relationship between Johnny and his teacher, by his teacher's special understanding and the greater flexibility provided by a small group.

However, if a child attends a tutorial class he will have to spend half of his school time in a larger setting where he will have to adjust to greater pressures. This changeover might be unbearable to him. He might need an environment that can give him this understanding and flexibility all day and every day. This opportunity can be provided in a school for maladjusted children, where the whole school day can be arranged with the children's emotional difficulties in mind.

Johnny might be helped within the framework of a day school. Alternatively, he might only profit from this kind of treatment within a residential institution which can provide a therapeutic community for 24 hours a day. However, the advantages of each setting need to be considered against the disadvantages. The more specialized the setting the more remote it is from the life of ordinary children. In the comprehensive school Johnny would live an ordinary schoolboy's life. Attendance to a tutorial class would take him out of this setting for half a day only. During the other part of his time he would continue to have contact with ordinary children. However, if Johnny were placed in a day school for maladjusted children this contact would discontinue, while placement in a residential school would involve a break from home.

The detailed arrangements in each unit could be scrutinized in a similar way. Everything is of importance: the size of a building, the lighting, the heating, the grounds and so on. Most teachers in special education are fully aware of this. They know the value of large, airy classrooms in new buildings, but they are also aware that for some children an old building with well-used furniture and walls that bear the mark of time is much more suitable. For the teachers it is mainly a question of making good use of the conditions they find and of realizing the limitations of their conditions. Again the important factor is the teacher's understanding of the possible influence these external conditions may have on the therapeutic aspect of their task.

Of the many other aspects of the setting which might be well worth discussing, I should like to single out the provision of food for more detailed scrutiny.

Eating and drinking plays an important part in all children's lives. For handicapped children eating and drinking is often also of great emotional significance. One tutorial teacher, for instance, reported that she considered the therapeutic process frequently started with the child making tea or coffee for himself and the staff. Many other people have made similar observations. Miller (1964), for instance, reports in some detail how much money was spent on the kitchen in the planning of the Northways project for ex-Borstal boys. He also argues that it was of the utmost importance that the boys should have access to the kitchen.

There are, to my knowledge, no systematic accounts that demonstrate the link between these detailed arrangements and the therapeutic opportunities that special education can offer. Much more attention has, of course, been given to arrangements made in connection with staff. The importance of the teacher–child relationship has been discussed earlier. However, the relationships of staff members to each other is of equal significance; so is the communication system between the teachers and the Head of the school. Do the teachers feel free to discuss their problems with the Head or do they keep them to themselves? Does the Head discuss administrative arrangements with the teachers, does he modify them in the light of the discussion, or does he just inform his staff what these arrangements should be? How does the Head relate to people the institition, to the Education Officer, to his Governors, to the School Medical Officer and so on?

This is such a wide topic that it would demand a paper in its own right. For the purpose of the present argument it will suffice to state that however trivial the detailed arrangement may be it will form an integral part of the setting and will therefore have a significant effect on the therapeutic opportunities of the institution.

THE LINK BETWEEN THE TEACHER–CHILD RELATIONSHIP, THE EDUCATIONAL TASK AND THE SETTING

A discussion like this unavoidably decides what, in practice, occurs simultaneously. The teacher interacting with a child in an educational situation uses the relationship with the child, the curriculum and the environment all at the same time. He does not, of course, always focus on the child's feelings. He is often concerned with giving factual information, with helping the child to acquire skills and with practical issues such as washing one's hands or doing up one's shoes. Yet even these mundane activities can be invested with intense feelings.

Similarly, a psychodynamic view comprises a far greater range than the three concepts of psycho-analytic thinking that have been discussed in this paper. This became obvious in connection with the discussion of Claude's stories which revealed a number of other conflicts, such as his problems about control and about secrecy.

The strength of special education lies, I think, precisely in the possibility of linking so many different aspects of human experience within one single institution. This variety of simultaneous occurrences makes it very difficult to isolate the single variables without giving a distorted picture of the enterprise, but at the same time it offers opportunities for therapeutic interventions that cannot be found outside an educational setting. Behaviour disorders, for instance, are often treated by psychotherapy or behaviour therapy outside the educational sphere. Frequently, this treatment is very successful. Yet with some children the change cannot be brought about without the educational element and all the therapeutic opportunities pertaining to the educational task. Still others will need the setting of a therapeutic community, where a certain amount of 'acting out' is permitted.

Unfortunately, at this point in time overall provision of therapeutic opportunities is somewhat haphazard. This is partly due to the scarcity of the provisions, and partly to our lack of knowledge. Yet, as our understanding of the problems increases, so does the provision of opportunities and some local education authorities have made great strides in this respect over the last few years.

The psychotherapeutic opportunities of special education are very widely recognized, but there has often been little awareness of the unconscious mechanisms such as those discussed in this paper. Yet from a psychodynamic point of view the effectiveness of a therapeutic endeavour is tremendously increased by awareness. If there is an understanding of the importance of any of the factors discussed and of a link between them then the therapeutic programme can be much more deliberately planned than if the therapeutic element is left to chance.

The benefit derived from the understanding of the therapeutic elements in special education can be put to an even wider use. The 'healing process' devised to counteract a disability is very similar to comparable processes that help the ordinary child to grow and develop. The handicap helps to make the process more explicit. Ordinary children, for instance, learn to read by any method, almost in spite of the teacher. When children do not learn, however, scrutiny of the process of learning to read becomes a necessity.

Workers in special education are therefore especially motivated to examine the educational processes and to increase their awareness of the psychotherapeutic opportunities they can offer. In this way they not only find more suitable ways of helping handicapped children, their experience and insight gained in the field of special education will also make a significant contribution to the effectiveness of education as a whole.

CHAPTER 9

Medical Approaches in Special Education

M. I. GRIFFITHS

Educational management becomes 'special' when a child has needs which differentiate him from his peers. This is likely to be the situation for approximately 5 to 6 per cent of children in Britain (Rutter, Tizard and Whitmore, 1970; Court, 1971). Children who have a disability, whether physical, mental or multiple, need special consideration in school although they may not necessarily need to attend a special establishment.

Thus the field of special education is one in which doctors and teachers meet on common ground. It is vital that each should make his unique contribution to the welfare of the child and in doing so should comprehend the extent to which their professional approaches are complementary. Educational problems may arise by reason of either a single severe handicap or a complexity of minor conditions and a knowledge of the organic basis of these is essential for planning both medical and educational management.

In this the role of the doctor can be seen as: first, presenting to the teacher a child who is as healthy in body and as alert in mind as possible; second, explaining the physical, mental and emotional aspects of the disability which may be a handicap in education; third, assisting to contrive physical and educational ways and means to enable each individual child to work to his full capacity.

The medical approaches involve far more than visits to a school to advise on medical treatment. An extensive preschool programme including early detection, diagnosis and comprehensive assessment must precede educational placement.

EARLY DETECTION

The early detection of handicapping conditions has several objectives. It makes it possible to start treatment for specific conditions as early as possible and to prevent complications; it helps to support the family; it alerts the health, social and educational services to probable future needs both for the individual and the community (Griffiths, 1973b). It is therefore important from the educational point of view that it should be done efficiently.

Some conditions may be obvious at birth. The majority, however, whether inherited or acquired, become manifest in some delay or deviation of development of skills or behaviour. This may not be immediately obvious to the parents, particularly in a first child, and they may hesitate to initiate further enquiries so that it is important that screening procedures should be offered in a way that will lead to ready acceptance.

The early detection of potentially handicapping conditions is at present carried out in two fields: by clinical observation and developmental testing in motor, visual, auditory and social functions, and by biochemical techniques which detect inborn errors of metabolism.

Developmental screening

Two approaches are possible: either a careful follow-up at regular intervals of children who might be expected to show disability as a result of known factors in their history (the 'at risk' group of children); or screening of the whole child population (at rather longer intervals). The advantages and disadvantages of both these methods are considered by Rogers (1971).

Davie, Butler and Goldstein (1972) describe two high-risk groups; the first, Group A, (1·4%) with severe physical, mental or multiple handicap and the second, Group B, (2·3%) requiring special schooling for educational backwardness. The first group are shown to be those with prenatal or perinatal complications, or family history of severe illness, whereas the second group is largely composed of children in families with social problems, leading to poor antenatal care with its associated obstetric risks, often conditioned by poverty, apathy or low intelligence in the home. It is clear that high-risk medical factors are largely responsible for Group A, and that social factors are more involved in Group B, the proportion of which (2·3%) is strikingly similar to the incidence (2·7%) of familial mild mental retardation quoted by Penrose (1963). The complex of poverty, malnutrition, infection, poor antenatal care, poor mothering and lack of stimulation in the environment makes it difficult to separate genetic from social high-risk factors (Brennan, 1973).

Knowledge of high-risk factors in a family which should lead to special attention to those in 'at risk' groups does not absolve the medical profession from the necessity to undertake careful developmental testing of all children in the population. The most useful results can be expected from a combination of particularly careful follow-up of high-risk infants and a programme for developmental screening of all (Forfar, 1968).

It is probably best for the infants 'at risk' from pre- and perinatal factors to be supervised by the paediatrician in attendance during the perinatal period, but other children may be followed in the community by well-trained public health nurses, supervised by experienced doctors.

Screening methods may vary but should comply with Sheridan's (1969) dictum that they should be simple to carry out and sensitive in selection with few false identifications. They must be based on records of careful observation of normal infants.

Normal development

During the first two years of life a child's development is largely dependent upon the maturation of the central nervous system, which allows a synchronous progression of skills in gross motor, fine motor, visual, auditory, language and social fields. These basic neurophysiological aspects of development are very clearly described by Prechtl (1971).

This pattern of infant development is similar in all cultural environments, so that the observations of McGraw (1943) and Gesell and Armatruda (1947) in the USA and of Griffiths (1954) and Sheridan (1960) in the UK can be applied to infants the world over. Some differences in rate of development between native Indian and white babies in Mexico was found by Brazelton *et al.* (1969) and acceleration of gross motor development in Jamaican babies was noted by Grantham-McGregor and Back (1971). Francis-Williams and Yule (1967) described differences between British and American infants in motor and social competence on the Bayley developmental scale, which they ascribed to differences in rearing practices. A wide time range in the development of skills was recorded by Nelligan and Prudham (1969) in a homogenous group of British infants.

Developmental scales therefore rely on similar items in development with some variation in methods of administration and recording, (see: Bayley, 1965; Caldwell and Drachman, 1964; Frankenburg and Dodds, 1967; Griffiths, 1954; Wood, 1970). It is particularly convenient to use profiles, as in the Griffiths and Denver scales in which skills are noted in several fields, so that discrepancies in ability can readily be seen.

Developmental testing identifies young children who have handicaps which may interfere with later learning and which may respond to specific treatment. Studies by many paediatricians and psychologists (e.g. Knobloch and Pasamanick, 1963; Hindley, 1965; Rutter, 1970; Freedman, 1971) have shown that the results of such tests are not accurately predictive of future intellectual ability although low scores are indicative of severe mental, physical or multiple handicap. In order to detect children who may need special schooling on account of educational backwardness, further testing just before school entrance on the lines described by Francis-Williams (1970) would be most useful.

Biochemical screening

Various screening procedures can be carried out. These consist of tests on small quantities of blood or urine which are able to reveal the presence of treatable inborn errors of metabolism (Raine, 1973). This type of screening may be applied to whole populations of newborn infants, to selected populations or even to selected families. When treatable inherited metabolic disorders such as phenylketonuria, galactosaemia, homocystinuria and histidinaemia are discovered in the first few months of life, dietary treatment can be introduced which may prevent subsequent brain damage (Raine, 1972).

In Britain, and many States in USA, screening, whilst universally offered, is not obligatory whereas in some States it is mandatory. The ethics of such procedures are considered by Lappé, Gustafson and Roblin (1972).

As a result of screening children can be divided into three groups. The first, and by far the largest, comprises those children with normal responses to the tests used. The second includes those children with results that indicate definite abnormality and in the third group are those in whom the results are doubtful. In the two latter groups further investigation for the purpose of diagnosis and assessment is essential.

Diagnosis implies the identification of a specific disease entity of which the cause can be defined, the future outlook known within reasonable limits and, in some instances, effective treatment administered. Implications for siblings and more distant relatives can be rationally deduced. The practical value of making such definitive diagnosis is the ability to undertake treatment and to initiate forward planning.

Assessment is essential whether or not the diagnosis has been established as future management, both medical and educational, depends upon evaluation of the child's disabilities in many fields.

COMPREHENSIVE ASSESSMENT

Assessment can be defined as evaluation for the purpose of management. Thus it is possible to consider a limited type of assessment (such as motor assessment) for a limited purpose (physical therapy), but for the needs of special education comprehensive assessment involving all fields of possible disability is essential.

It is envisaged that a three-tier system will operate in Britain (British Paediatric Association, 1972). Developmental screening as already described will be carried out by doctors and nurses working in the community. When delay or abnormality in development is suspected children will be referred to the paediatric unit of a hospital serving a population of 100,000 to 250,000, which will be equipped to deal with straightforward conditions. For children with multiple handicaps or obscure neurological disorders regional assessment facilities in association with University teaching hospitals will be available. This development has been actively encouraged by the Department of Health and Social Security and is described in more detail by Moore (1973).

Although it is probable that most comprehensive assessment units in Britain will be sited in hospital paediatric units, this is by no means essential. Some units have already been established in an educational setting and are equally successful. Other countries will have their own approaches. The *sine qua non* of successful assessment is teamwork, wherever the site and whoever the leader.

Comprehensive assessment needs a team in which the members have acquired a high level of individual skill and the ability to work closely and harmoniously with people of other disciplines. It cannot be undertaken by any one person in a single session, as a number of members of different disciplines will each need to apply their expertise either consecutively or concurrently, in order to arrive at a complete evaluation of an individual child.

It is sometimes necessary to play the child in an appropriate situation, often with a peer group, to observe his difficulties and his response to training and management. The actual team engaged in helping an individual child may vary according to the nature of the handicap, and a possible nominal roll has been suggested by Moore (1973) (Figure 9.1).

At this stage, and in a paediatric setting, it is probable that the paediatrician will be leader of the team but when the child advances to an educational setting the teacher or psychologist may take over that role.

Audiometrician	Ophthalmic surgeon
Ear, nose and throat surgeon	Orthopaedic surgeon
Family doctor	Orthoptist
Local authority medical officer	Paediatrician
Medical social worker	Physiotherapist
Nursery nurses	Psychiatrist
Nursery teachers	Psychologist
Nursing officer	Secretary
Occupation therapist	Speech therapist

FIGURE 9.1. The medical assessment team. Reproduced with permission from J. R. Moore in *The Young Retarded Child. Medical Aspects of Care*, (Ed. M. I. Griffiths) Churchill Livingstone, Edinburgh and London, 1973

Procedures suggested for cerebral-palsied children (Griffiths, 1962) can be applied to children who are found to be suffering from developmental delay from any cause.

Motor disorders should be referred to the physiotherapist for formal recording of muscle strength and weakness, tone and postural reflexes, and range of active movement. Response to treatment must also be recorded. The advice of a paediatric neurologist or of an orthopaedic surgeon may be sought in some cases.

Visual competence must always be assessed. The paediatrician can look for squints and field defects and undertake ophthalmoscopic examination but beyond this an ophthalmologist must be consulted. Visual cortical evoked responses are a most useful additional investigation, especially in young or mentally handicapped children (Harding, Thompson and Panyatopoulos, 1969; Harden and Pampiglione, 1970).

Audiological testing should be carried out in all children, giving special attention to those with delayed or abnormal speech. Most young children and many mentally retarded children will respond to conditioning techniques in free field audiometry but in severely physically, mentally or multiply handicapped children (particularly the deaf/blind), cortical evoked response technique (Barnet and Lodge, 1967; Rapin and Bergman, 1969) or sleep audiogram may be necessary. The role of the otologist has been summarized by Crabtree (1972); such expertise is essential, particularly in cases of conductive deafness which is preventible and treatable if diagnosed in time.

Disorders of speech and language. Hearing testing should always be carried out in any child with delay in development of speech or language. If the child's hearing is normal the next step is usually to compare language comprehension and expressive speech, as in the Reynell (1969) developmental language test. In children with a motor disorder of the speech mechanism or in children with an expressive dysphasia there may be a marked discrepancy between the two scores with comprehension well ahead of expressive speech. Mentally retarded children, on the other hand, may be more forward on the expressive than on the comprehension scale.

In older children the Illinois test of psycholinguistic ability (Kirk, McCarthy and Kirk, 1968) analyses components of communicative ability.

The most important team member for this work is the speech therapist who cooperates with the psychologist in testing and undertakes continuing treatment, advising either mother or teacher or both in their conversational approach to the child.

Disorders of perception. In a book such as this it would be an impertinence for a paediatrician to attempt to differentiate between the various tests, rapidly increasing in number, which can be used to probe a child's perceptual ability. It is the task of the psychologist to bring to light specific disorders in fields of visua-spatial perception, visuo-motor coordination, auditory perception, language and reading which are discussed in greater detail elsewhere.

The medical role is to investigate the organic basis of the disability and to correlate the neurological and psychological findings. These disorders may appear as the major manifestation in an educationally backward child or they may be present as an associated disability in cerebral palsy or hydrocephalus.

Mental subnormality. The decision as to the child's level of mental ability should never be made on the result of a single test wherever it is carried out. Many children have multiple handicaps (Komrower and MacKeith, 1966) and these children may need to attend a multidisciplinary centre for many months before their individual disabilities are evaluated and their potential for the future assessed; their overall retardation may give a false impression of mental subnormality. It is important that all children who appear to be mentally retarded should be fully assessed, as their difficulties are compounded if they have associated motor, visual or auditory disability. Special units with a high staff/child ratio for children with associated behaviour disorders are particularly useful.

The role of the teacher in preschool assessment units is important. Much of the diagnosis and measurement of disability is in the hands of doctors and therapists, as already described, but their work needs to be carried on in an environment that cares for the whole child and in which the day-to-day activities are created to enable progress to be made in social, perceptual and cognitive skills whilst the child is under continuous observation. Skilled nursery teachers and appropriate assistants are essential to create such an atmosphere.

The assessment centre building must be planned within the confines of the site and financial resources available. It may vary in size from a small prefabricated building to a multistoried Institute although the standard of services provided will in the long run depend upon the quality of the members of the assembled team.

The focal point of the building is the children's play area. This can be divided by low moveable partitions so that children can be allocated at times to small homogenous groups but there must be immediate access to toilet and washing facilities. A number of small quiet rooms are needed for individual testing and training, with observation through ordinary or one-way glass windows or by closed circuit television (Griffiths, 1974).

Facilities for diagnostic investigations such as X-ray, EEG, cytogenetics, biochemistry, audiometry and ophthalmology may be provided either in the centre itself or in the hospital to which it is attached. Facilities for speech therapy, psychological testing and for individual or group training should be available within the centre. In smaller centres, as illustrated in Figure 9.2, multipurpose rooms may be used.

This basic plan can be adapted to larger projects with the addition of extra play space, more training and testing rooms, offices for the staff and, where necessary, diagnostic facilities.

As a result of such wide-based continuing assessment individual formulae of ability and disability and varying programmes for management can be evolved for each child. The optimum educational placement is sought on a personal basis.

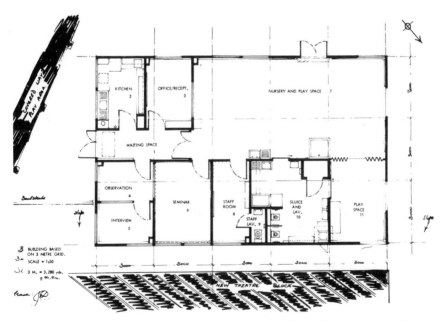

FIGURE 9.2. Plan of assessment centre, Birmingham Childrens' Hospital. Rooms 7 and 11, nursery and play space divisible by folding door. Rooms 4, 5, 6, observation suite, sound deadened. T.V. cameras and microphones in rooms 5 and 6, control console in room 4. The centre accommodates 12 children attending daily. Printed by kind permission of the United Birmingham Hospitals

Many factors must be taken into account; the paramount need for special education for specific handicaps, neighbourhood facilities, standards of the home and transport difficulties must all be considered in making a decision. The best place for a particular child may be the local ordinary school, or a school with special facilities which can be attended on a day basis, or a residential school which has highly developed expertise in dealing with the particular handicap.

MANAGEMENT

The length of stay in a comprehensive assessment centre is very variable. Two weeks is sometimes adequate to define the areas of strength and weakness in a child, but in more complex handicaps the period may extend to months or, occasionally, years. During this time the child's response to treatment and training is recorded.

Children who are too young to attend school at the end of the assessment period may need some form of interim placement, particularly if nursery classes are not available. Preschool playgroups have an important function in this field, as they provide help for handicapped and socially deprived children (Grantham, 1971; Joseph and Parfitt, 1973). When the majority of children in the group have physical or mental handicaps nursery teachers and therapists (occupational, physical and speech) are needed and medical and psychological surveillance should be available.

In the school the concept of teamwork developed in the work of the assessment centre must be carried on but other disciplines become subordinate to the educational goal. The role of leader of the team will pass to the teacher although doctors are still active members.

Although the services of the otologist, ophthalmologist, neurologist and orthopaedic surgeon may only be required from time to time, the paediatrician should be regularly and freely available not only for advice on intercurrent illness and similar problems but also to advise and direct aspects of medical treatment and regulation of activities in and out of the classroom.

Both medical and educational aspects of special education are constantly changing, and Figure 9.3 illustrates recent changes in the type of physical handicap encountered in special schools. This forecasts an increasing number of physically handicapped children with cerebral lesions and hence an increasing proportion of such children with specific learning difficulties.

Multiple disabilities are also common in the visually handicapped (Department of Education and Science, 1972) and in the backward child (Komrower and McKeith, 1966), so that the demands on special educational services are more complex. Although many children who previously attended special schools are now able to take their place in the normal educational environment, more sophisticated approaches are necessary both in educational techniques and in medical treatment for those children who require special education on account of multiple handicaps.

Handicapped children fall into three groups. First, those with a physical handicap that does not impair their intellectual efficiency, and who, with suitable medical treatment and some understanding of their disability, can take their place in

'CRIPPLED' CHILDREN IN BIRMINGHAM P.H. SCHOOLS

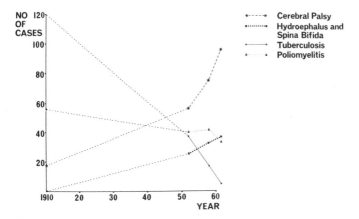

FIGURE 9.3. Prevalence of physical handicap. Admissions of children to day schools for the physically handicapped in Birmingham, England. Statistics provided by the head teachers of the schools and published by permission of Dr. E. M. L. Millar, Medical Officer of Health and Principal School Medical Officer

normal schools. Second, those with a physical handicap, whose disability may prevent ordinary social activities in a normal school, or whose associated disabilities are such that normal educational methods cannot be followed. Third, those children whose main problem is in the educational field.

Group I. Physical disabilities permitting normal educational placement

The majority of children in this category are those who in Britain would previously have been deemed 'delicate' or sent to an Open Air school. Most of them suffer from disorders, many of which can be treated, which may impair their general health or physical ability but have no effect on their brain.

Diabetes mellitus in the child needs energetic medical treatment, usually with a regime of insulin injections and dietary control. The diet is made as liberal as possible and intelligent children have a good knowledge of the type and amount of food they may take to counterbalance the insulin which they usually administer themselves. Occasionally excessive exercise or lack of food may cause hypoglycaemic reactions, which are rapidly corrected by administration of sugar or glucose, and with which the teacher should be familiar. In spite of this risk there is no indication for the curtailment of normal physical activities.

Disorders of growth, leading to short stature or obesity, should not be ignored. They may be manifestations of organic or emotional dysfunction which may need medical treatment and sometimes they are associated with organic disorder of the brain causing mental retardation. Occasionally, although they have no clinical significance, they may give rise to teasing or bullying and become the focus of un-happiness in school.

Hypothyroidism causes mental retardation and short stature. This can be prevented by treatment with suitable replacement therapy which must be carefully monitored and continued indefinitely.

Cardiac conditions can often be treated surgically in early life; the regulation of athletic activities is a medical decision and children should be encouraged to indulge in the maximum amount of exercise compatible with their clinical condition.

Disorders of the respiratory tract are less common than previously. Asthma merits serious consideration as attacks are frequently triggered by emotional stress which may be caused by too much educational pressure and which may sometimes need special educational placement. Fibrocystic disease is an inherited condition which is most serious in early childhood, but which cannot be cured, so that sufferers need energetic antibiotic treatment whenever they have a chest infection.

Haemophilic children should be able to attend normal schools unless they have already developed joint lesions. Biological control and prevention of the bleeding tendency should be adequate to deal with minor trauma, but prompt referral to hospital is essential when bleeding occurs so that it can be rapidly controlled.

Children with *fatal diseases* should attend normal schools as long as they are able so that their life can be as normal as possible.

Some children described in Group II may also be able to attend normal schools.

One advantage of the presence of a practising physician on the management team of the school health service means that the child's own medical attendant will divulge to his colleague details of diagnosis and treatment that are confidential. The school physician can then explain to the teaching staff aspects of the disorder and its treatment.

Group II. Physical handicaps which may need specialized education

Education implies the presentation to the child of a series of learning situations which depend upon his ability to see, to hear, to understand, to exercise his imagination and to respond. In dealing with children who need special education for specific disabilities one or more of these activities is impaired. It is the role of the doctor to diagnose and, where possible, to correct the physical disability to enable the teacher to help the child to use his remaining active unimpaired faculties.

In this group of conditions the medical aspects which impair educational efficiency will be considered individually although it must be understood that some children suffer from multiple disabilities, of which one or the other or a combination of them may determine the special education needed.

Cerebral palsy

Can be defined as a disorder of posture and movement caused by non-progressive damage to the brain which has occurred during its period of development. In this group of children, whose disability is due to an environmental insult to a potentially normal brain, there is a wide variety of total disability, ranging from the child with a moderate degree of motor handicap, normal intelligence and ability to compete with his peers, to the child with severe mental retardation who is unable to profit by any type of education. Although the actual cause is non-progressive, there may be clinical variability in the physical signs during the period of maturation of the brain.

The motor disorder in cerebral palsy varies in nature and distribution according to the anatomical site of the lesion; three pathways in the central nervous system control movement and posture, and lesions in these pathways have different clinical effects. *Spastic conditions* arise from interference with the pyramidal tracts or their nerve cells, and cause typical clasp knife rigidity with slowness of and difficulty in initiating voluntary movement; only one-half of the body may be affected (right- or left-half, hemiplegia; the legs only, diplegia), or all four limbs may be involved (quadriplegia/tetraplegia), often asymmetrically. Lesions of the basal ganglia in the mid-brain lead to disturbances of the extrapyramidal system causing *athetosis* or *dystonic rigidity* affecting all four limbs. Cerebellar disorders affecting balance and causing *ataxia* are least common and are often associated with a progressive disorder.

The motor dysfunction affects whole limbs rather than individual muscles, and usually involves the trunk. Finer movements may also be affected so that involvement of the eye muscles may cause squint, or involvement of the muscles of the cheeks, lips, tongue and palate may cause feeding difficulties and affect speech.

Associated disabilities due to the brain damage are very commonly present in children suffering from cerebral palsy and may be the major cause of educational handicap. These will be considered later in this chapter under individual subject headings.

Treatment. (i) *Physical therapy.* The pathways involving postural reactions are called into play in all activities and therefore treatment needs to be directed to better control in all circumstances. This concept has been elaborated by the Bobaths (1966 and 1967) and detailed for the use of parents and teachers by Finnie (1968). Physical therapy for the cerebral-palsied child involves more than passive movements and must be directed to whole-body activity which needs to be supervised unobtrusively throughout the day.

Undoubtedly the major impact of physiotherapy is in the first five years of life and habits of movement for good or ill are often established before the child commences formal education. For the first two years of life treatment of the child by himself is useless; the mother or mother substitute must be involved and shown favourable methods of handling and playing with the child. At a mental age of two to five years treatment can be given through play situations, and the child encouraged to move about first by rolling, then by crawling or shuffling and finally, if at all possible, by walking. In older children group therapy, with an element of competition, is often very effective. One very real problem is the decision whether or not to use a wheelchair. The younger child should be encouraged to crawl and to circumnavigate the classroom with support from the furniture. The older child may prefer the more rapid mobility afforded by a wheelchair; in this situation it is important to encourage movement around the furniture and ability to get in and out of the wheelchair to bed and toilet. In treatment of the motor handicap it is essential to consider the emotional and psychological factors in addition to the medical and educational aspects. For some children, especially if they are in normal schools, it may be better to allow unrestrained and relatively unsupervised physical activity with acceptance of the probable need for later surgery.

(ii) *Drug therapy* has its place in the treatment of the child with cerebral palsy (Denhoff, 1964). Epilepsy when present must always be controlled by medication and behaviour disorders need treatment in order to encourage concentration in the classroom. Drugs with a direct action on motor activity are still limited in their application. Diazepam may be indicated for athetosis and dystonic rigidity (Holt, 1964; Kendall, 1964). Recently, dimethothiazine has been shown to be a useful drug when given in short courses and for specific reasons to children with spasticity (Griffiths and Bowie, 1973).

(iii) *Orthopaedic treatment* has a limited place in the case of the young child but may become increasingly necessary as the child grows older. Many orthopaedic surgeons prefer to undertake surgical treatment as late as possible, although some procedures, such as adductor tenotomy at the hip or elongation of the tendo Achillis at the ankle, may be very useful measures in the young child.

The special educational needs of a child with cerebral palsy depend partly on his physical ability, partly on the severity of the associated handicaps and partly upon his nett intellectual capacity. School placement varies for each individual child. Whereas the aim will always be placement in a normal school, the strain of keeping up both physically and mentally may lead to frustration and unhappiness in many cerebral-palsied children and, for this reason, many do better either in special schools for children with cerebral palsy, in schools for physically handicapped children or, occasionally, in schools whose major concern is with one of the additional handicaps.

Spina bifida and hydrocephalus

At birth the incidence of congenital abnormalities due to failure of closure of the neural tube is much higher than the reported incidence of cerebral palsy. Owing to the higher mortality rate the number of children needing consideration for special education is lower than this (see Figure 9.3) although better survival as a result of successful surgical treatment has produced an increasing number of school-age children with this handicap. In these children the primary motor disorder is dysfunction in the lower limbs in which there is a wide spectrum of disability from a mild unsteadiness (15%) to complete lack of function in the lower limbs (60%) (Lorber, 1972). Most children need appliances in order to help them to walk. In some children the upper limbs are secondarily affected and involvement of the brain usually follows the development of hydrocephalus in 92% (Lorber, 1972). Although this can be treated by drainage of cerebro-spinal fluid either into the heart or into the peritoneal cavity, visual complications and specific perceptual disorders may ensue and will be considered later in this chapter.

Major physical difficulties in children with spina bifida centre around the problems of mobility and continence. Children with calipers, wheelchairs, or both, need schools with wide doors, ramps and lifts, all very costly items in buildings. Incontinent, often chairbound children, need care- or nursing-trained staff to help with toilet. These difficulties may prove insurmountable when questions of admission to normal school arise.

Other disorders involving the motor nervous system

These conditions will not be considered in detail but they deserve mention. Familial inherited conditions often involve the peripheral nervous system, the muscles, the motor nerves, the motor nerve cells and the spinal cord. Many are progressive and children may attend normal schools at an early age but later may need special schools on account of increasing physical incapacity. In some mental deterioration accompanies the physical deterioration and, in 20% of cases of pseudohypertrophic muscular dystrophy, mental retardation is present from the outset (Cohen *et al.*, 1968). It is unusual to encounter specific learning difficulties in these children but their emotional problems, particularly if they understand the nature of their disability, are often very acute.

Disorders of vision

Squint is a condition in which the two eyes do not move normally together. It is very easily seen in the classroom and it may be due to a variety of causes. (i) It may be due to an abnormality of movement of the muscles controlling eye movements. This may occur in children with cerebral palsy (Griffiths and Smith, 1963), or hydrocephalus. Operation is often necessary in order to straighten the eye. It is important to correct the squint because if the child actively uses only one eye vision in the other eye is gradually lost. (ii) Concomitant squint occurs when the two eyes do not learn to work together. As long as a child is using both eyes alternately, no harm is done as vision is not suppressed in either eye. Orthoptic measures may be taken to help the child to use both eyes together. (iii) The third cause of squint is an error of refraction. This may be nearsightedness, longsightedness or astigmatism and the child, at times, may squint. This type of squint can usually be corrected by glasses. (iv) Finally, blindness from any cause is usually accompanied by a squint as direction of eye movement is uncontrolled.

There is no evidence that squint in itself gives rise to any reading disability. It may, however, be associated with reading disability if it is due to a severe visual disorder or if there are associated difficulties of visual perception or visuo-motor coordination (Abercrombie, 1963). Children with squints may be encountered in the whole range of education and in every type of school and squint of itself is not an indication of need for special education.

Nystagmus is a condition in which there is an inconsistent and continuous flickering movement of the eyes, sometimes only at the extremity of movement but sometimes at rest. As with squint it may be an expression of blindness or it may be associated with motor disorders in which the muscles controlling eye movement are unable to hold the eyes completely steady. The child is often partially sighted.

Visual field defects are caused by a lesion either of the visual pathways or of the occipital cortex. The commonest type is a homonymous hemianopia associated with spastic hemiplegia and consists of inability to see objects on the same side as the motor weakness. This has a direct bearing on classroom activities, firstly because the child should be placed in the classroom so that his 'good' side is towards the centre of the room and secondly because a right-sided hemianopia may lead to difficulties in reading in languages in which the child has to scan from left to right across the page.

Severe visual disorder requiring special education may be due either to lesions of the eyes or to lesions within the brain. In the child with *partial sight* vision may be corrected to some extent by glasses but never sufficiently to read normal print or to see clearly at a distance. Such children are helped with 'low visual aids' such as large magnifying glasses for reading and small telescopes or binoculars for distant vision. Correct lighting of classrooms is essential, and visual acuity must be re-assessed frequently. Many of these children are classed as educationally backward and it is possible that this to some extent is due to inadequate knowledge and delay in identification of the visual condition. *Blindness* is present when a child cannot be educated by sighted methods although this does not necessarily mean that the child cannot see at all; most blind children have some perception of light and many are able to see enough of their surroundings to get about.

Visual handicap is very often associated with another handicap. Figures reported by the Department of Education and Science (1972) show that the proportion of blind children with other handicaps aged from 5 to 15 years increased from 42% in 1959 to 59% in 1970. The commonest complications were deafness, cerebral palsy and mental retardation. The figures quoted only take account of children receiving special education on account of visual handicap, and therefore do not represent the total of blind children with other handicaps, or those previously classified as 'ineducable'. Great difficulties are experienced by the deaf/blind child who is unable to communicate, for whom learning about the world is a slow and difficult process and by the blind/spastic child who is unable to explore the environment or to use the hands for learning Braille. The combination of deafness and blindness is so severe that children with this dual handicap need to attend special units. Hydrocephalus and spina bifida complicated by blindness is a serious problem. Such children are usually placed in schools for the physically handicapped with teachers for the blind helping with their education.

Disorders of hearing

Screening programmes for disorders of hearing are organized by health authorities in Great Britain; the aim is that all children should be tested for hearing between the ages of 9 and 12 months and health visitors (public health nurses) are trained for this purpose. However, there are still many defaulters and children who later develop conductive deafness following repeated aural infections are not detected by this means. Howarth (1967) has emphasized that 80% of deaf children can be predicted by 'at risk' factors, either in the family history, in the pregnancy or at birth, and it is particularly important that these children should be screened. The difficulties in administration of hearing tests at different ages are enumerated by Martin (1972). He points out that the three commonest sources of error in testing young children depend upon intensity, frequency and the variation associated with middle ear involvement. He also notes that the clinical expression of deafness is very rarely obvious and often presents as delay in acquisition of language or severe behaviour disorder, and that frequently deaf children are diagnosed as 'mentally retarded, aphasic, emotionally disturbed or plain naughty'.

The management of auditory handicap is one that calls for highly skilled teamwork involving an otologist with his audiometric team, a paediatrician, teacher of the deaf, and speech therapist (Crabtree, 1972). The child should be introduced to a hearing aid as soon as possible. This cannot be done until pure tone audiometry has been used to measure the degree of deafness as amplification of the whole range of sound may not be helpful. Frequent individual sessions between the child and his mother, the teacher of the deaf, and the speech therapist are essential. At the same time the child should be encouraged to communicate by any means at his disposal (Rutter and Martin, 1972). The intelligent child very often learns to lip-read without being taught and speed in picking up visual cues may often mislead testers in the free field situation. A sign language may be developed and if so this should be explicit. Signing and lip reading do not preclude the development of speech and the improvement of hearing.

Consideration has so far been given to children who have demonstrably impaired hearing at peripheral or cochlear level. A more complex and difficult situation arises when the child's hearing for pure tone is normal, as demonstrated by a normal audiogram, but the child makes no response to speech and does not acquire language. This group of children may be labelled as suffering from perceptual or central deafness and they merge imperceptibly into the group of children with receptive aphasia. Taylor (1964) considered some of the neurological mechanisms involved and it appears probable that this is a heterogenous group consisting of children with specific developmental delay, with specific brain damage sometimes associated with autism or cerebral palsy, or with mental retardation. Treatment lies in communicating by all possible means, including signing, lip-reading, artificial codes and, if helpful, amplified sound. School placement is difficult and must be considered individually. Children with cerebral palsy may attend schools for 'spastics', some may go to schools for the deaf, others to units for autistic or mentally handicapped children.

Disorders of speech and language

Normal development of speech and language requires an adequate input of sensory stimuli, a central ability to perceive, analyse and integrate impressions, and executive motor skill in speech or writing. Education is concerned with all aspects.

Adequate sensory input implies intact visual, auditory and kinaesthetic pathways, and an environment that is reasonably stimulating.

Executive motor skills are impaired in cerebral palsy, when disordered motor patterns may cause dysarthria typical of the spastic, athetoid or ataxic lesion. Motor control may be improved in these children by combined physical and speech therapy (Morley, 1972). Other causes of articulation disorder are less likely to be associated with needs for special education.

Disorders of visual or auditory perception may be associated with delayed language, as may mental retardation, and sometimes the impaired speech in cerebral palsy appears to be associated with perceptual or integrative aspects either in addition to or in place of the executive difficulties.

Inability to integrate the elements of speech and language may produce a receptive or executive dysphasia. This condition may be found either as an isolated condition or in association with cerebral palsy, or in infantile autism when it is an accompaniment of this severe behaviour disorder. Developmental language delay is a condition which usually improves as the child matures but which needs speech therapy.

Recent reviews of the medical aspects of speech and language disorder have been presented by Rutter and Martin (1972) and Rees (1973). The wide implications require that children suffering from these conditions should be assessed and managed by skilled multidisciplinary teams.

The speech of children with hydrocephalus has been shown to be not only hyperverbal as described by Hagberg and Sjorgren (1966) but also inapplicable and bizarre (Swisher and Pinsker, 1971). This clinical expression is well-known but as yet unexplained.

Disorders of perception

These conditions are largely matters for the psychologist to elucidate but there are some connections with specific physical disabilities which need to be remembered. Amongst children suffering from cerebral palsy it is the spastics who are most likely to suffer from spatial perception or visuo-motor disorders (Abercrombie, 1964). Disorders of visual perception have also been noted amongst children with hydrocephalus (Miller and Sethi, 1971) and it is possible that this factor contributes to the idiosyncracies of language in these children. Dare and Gordon (1970) discuss the part played by perceptual disorders in 'clumsy children'. They divide them into those with specific developmental disorder due to problems of either visual perception or motor organization, those with overall mental retardation, and a few with minimal cerebral palsy. It is interesting to note that this type of classification may also be applied to children with disorders of speech and language.

There is thus in this group of children a wide range of perceptual, intellectual and associated disability which offers a fascinating challenge.

'Minimal cerebral dysfunction'

It is by no means certain that this phrase describes a syndrome but its application to certain children is very apt. On clinical examination it is usually possible to elicit a number of signs, such as slight spasticity in the legs, tremor, clumsiness or dysdiadokokinesia in the arms, squint, right/left confusion, or astereognosis combined with psychological deficits in perceptual and psychometric tests. None of these minor difficulties presents a problem in its own right but when joined together the child can be seen to have a formidable disability. the EEG is often abnormal and if so the child may suffer from *petit mal*, minor motor epilepsy or a behaviour disorder. Management, both medical and educational, must be tailored to fit the individual case.

Behaviour disorders

It is perhaps rather stretching the point to consider behaviour disorders as physical disabilities, but as the two are frequently associated this would seem to be the right place for discussion. Serious disorders of behaviour are psychiatric rather than paediatric problems but many moderate conditions can be dealt with by paediatrician, teacher and parents.

Some behaviour disorders stem either from the environment or from an undiagnosed and hence untreated specific handicap. In these children modification of the environment or treatment of the handicap may effect a cure. Examples of the former might be excessive pressure at home or at school, emotional or marital problems or even lack of discipline at home: of the latter untreated deafness, visual handicap, speech disorder, or reaction to phenobarbitone. In other cases the child himself is disturbed and disorientated, and although a change of environment may be beneficial medication may also be necessary. The drug treatment of behaviour disorder is largely empirical. There seems little doubt that knowledgeable use of drugs (Conners, 1971) improves a child's learning ability in certain cases, although this may be due to effects on hyperactivity, depression or epilepsy.

Epilepsy

Some epileptic children can attend normal schools. Their intelligence is normal or above, the onset is usually not until the second decade, and the condition is well-controlled by drugs. Some may never have a fit whilst at school. Concentration and physical exercise are rarely associated with attacks which are more likely to occur on going to sleep, on waking, at periods of excitement, anxiety, boredom or stress. The child's life should be as normal as possible and medical advice should be sought in regard to specific potentially dangerous activities.

The larger group of epileptic children comprises those in whom the epilepsy is a symptom of brain damage, which is often associated with mental retardation, cerebral palsy, blindness or behaviour disorder. Some cases are progressively deteriorating. In these children treatment is difficult as the border-line between uncontrolled fits and oversedation is often very fine. Many drugs may have to be used and sudden infections or minor changes in environment may upset the balance.

Medication of epilepsy must always be continuously and conscientiously controlled. Administration of drugs should never be altered by parent or teacher without medical advice, and any increase of fits or drowsiness should be promptly reported. Many anticonvulsant drugs have side-effects. Phenobarbitone should be viewed with caution; it may be responsible for severe behaviour disorders, on the other hand sudden discontinuance may lead to severe and prolonged epilepsy.

All teachers should be conversant with first-aid treatment for an epileptic fit and should minimize the distress to the other children in the class.

Epilepsy may occur in various forms in addition to the *grand mal* convulsion which is the one most commonly seen. *Petit mal* attacks which occur in the form of short 'absences' can be well-controlled by suitable therapy which has an immediate effect upon the child's ability to concentrate.

Medical skill in the diagnosis and control of epilepsy is an important aspect of special education. The many types and therapeutic approaches are described in more detail by Keith (1963) and Jeavons (1973).

Group III. Children who are educationally backward

The work of Penrose (1963) and Davie *et al.* (1972) emphasizes the bimodal distribution of mental retardation into mild and moderate/severe.

Mild mental retardation in slow-learning children occurs in approximately 2·3% of children and is associated with multifactorial causes. In view of its familial distribution Penrose suggests that the genetic contribution is of greater importance but the impact of social and environmental factors (Davie *et al.*, 1972) appears to be equally cogent. Social factors, which may include low intelligence in the parents, may lead to levels of unemployment and poverty, poor housing and malnutrition. This last factor has been shown by many writers (e.g. Cabak and Najdanvic, 1965; Winick, 1969 and 1970) to cause retarded cerebral development. In addition negligible antenatal care may be associated with increased obstetric hazard and this in turn may be a factor in causing brain damage. When this is followed by inadequate mothering, lack of food, sleep and warmth, an unstimulating environment, increased liability to non-specific infections and lack of acceptance of immunization procedures (Brennan, 1973) it is hardly surprising that these children are unable to make the best of any education provided. The disappointing results of some aspects of the Head Start programme in the United States and of nursery schools in Britain may be associated with these factors. It can be argued that wider spacing of pregnancies and the provision of more help in the home with associated better parenting, feeding, heat and stimulation might be more effective than earlier education. Certainly both aspects need attention; vigorous medical action should be associated with social and educational measures.

Severe mental retardation is invariably due to a physical cause and associated with a variety of pathological conditions. Many of these are determined at or before conception either by inherited genic disorders or chromosomal aberrations (Cowie,

1968). Others are caused by a variety of insults, biochemical, physical, traumatic, vascular or infective, to the developing brain before, during or after birth (Griffiths, 1973a). No cause is known for approximately half of the population of mentally retarded children, but the similarity of their symptoms to diagnosable disorders conditions suggests that eventually a cause will be found for all.

From the medical point of view prevention must be the aim, with wider screening facilities, better health services, and research into causes. It is unlikely that the first case of an autosomal recessive condition or a mutation can be prevented in the foreseeable future but a great deal can be done to detect and prevent occurrence in siblings (Emery, 1973). Early treatment of inborn errors of metabolism often prevents brain damage (Raine, 1972) and prompt detection of visual and auditory handicaps may minimize their effects. The child and his family require continuous medical, educational and social support throughout life.

Early treatment is directed towards socialization, encouraging developmental maturation, if necessary by physiotherapy (Hughes, 1971), and inculcating habits of self-help (Griffiths, 1973d). As the child grows older education must be adapted to his potential, with stress upon his ability to attain maximal independence. Educational procedures may include operant conditioning and behaviour modification techniques although an early start, with help for the family and better community services may later obviate the need for such corrective measures.

CONCLUSION

It is hoped that this brief consideration of such a diversity of subjects emphasizes the wide range of disability which may be encountered in handicapped children, and supports the plea that the needs of each child should be considered individually. Generalization is difficult in both medicine and education, and in dealing with handicapped children it is almost impossible. There can be little doubt that the solution of these children's problems will be simplified if doctors with suitable training and experience can be accepted as essential participants in the child's educational management, and if teachers are able to discuss on equal terms the physical basis of a child's particular disabilities.

CHAPTER 10

Vocational and Social Training

R. I. BROWN

INTRODUCTION

In this chapter it is assumed that very few children can be regarded as totally in-educable, and that all those who have some form of handicap are capable of modifying and adapting their behaviour. This change in behaviour can be facilitated by education procedures.

In the past fifteen years there has been a move away from an academic educational system to a much more socially-orientated training and educational programme (Earl, 1961; Gunzburg, 1960; Haring and Schiefelbusch, 1967; Kolstoe, 1970). Together with this development there has occurred the realization that individuals who are educationally subnormal are subject to considerable developmental changes. They do not always remain retarded and, during certain periods, such as adolescence and young adult life, some may show accelerated cognitive and social growth rates (Clarke and Clarke, 1959). In modern terms the education of the slow learner is seen as preparing the young adolescent and adult for life within a changing society. He must be able to work at a job and make a consistent living throughout his adult life. His work is likely to be semi-skilled or unskilled, although in a number of cases skilled work has been carried out successfully. However, the evidence of workers such as O'Connor and Tizard (1956) and Saenger (1957) points to the fact that the handicapped who succeed are those who have the best and most effective social skills. Therefore, individuals not only need to be taught a specific work skill but also to receive a general vocational training which involves the capacity to transfer skills to a variety of situations. Socially they must learn to arrive on time, take instruction and use language appropriately. An adequate understanding of pay, income tax and budgeting is necessary. Thus, enumeration skills and money concepts of amount and change are important. Home-living skills, such as preparing meals, buying food, keeping a home clean and in good repair, require development, as well as preparation for the appropriate use of leisure time, marriage and family life. It is worth noting that many fail because of lack of appropriate leisure-time skills. For example, excessive drinking may lead to loss of a job or court appearances. The purpose of education for the educationally subnormal young adult, therefore, is to ensure that he is vocationally, socially and educationally trained, and to provide a continuous programme that helps him re-adapt to new situations as they arise.

DEVELOPMENTAL HANDICAP

This chapter is particularly concerned with those children who, by their mid-teens, continue to show problems which necessitate the use of specialized schooling. The majority of these are below average intelligence and many will be regarded as mentally retarded. A number will be severely retarded; their condition resulting in many cases from brain injury or inheritance. Many will come from impoverished industrial environments while others will come from other deprived groups such as the Canadian Indians or, in Britain, certain immigrant groups. In the last two cases the problem may not be so much lack of intelligence as poor adaptation to the prevailing society. The chapter is also relevant to the cerebral-palsied, the deaf and partially sighted, many of whom show learning difficulties. A number of other students, because of lack of motivation and faulty emotional development, may be usefully considered to fall under the heading of the present chapter.

It will be noted that a number of aetiologically distinct groups have been placed together because it can be argued that it is unhelpful to talk in terms of traditional medical classification when we are concerned with education and behaviour. This classification may be of use when carrying out medical diagnosis and treatment. At present it has limited value for training and education, at least among the subnormal, since there is little valid evidence showing differences in behaviour between the various aetiological groups matched for mental age (Clarke and Clarke, 1973a). Eventually such differences may be recognized but it is likely that classification and treatment will become associated with the presenting behaviour and cut across the traditional diagnostic categories (Brison, 1967). There is little reason why, for example, a mongol, a brain-injured person, a cerebral-palsied child and a person from a deprived background who all show similar learning problems should not be treated by similar models, techniques or remedial programmes. Furthermore, we shall find individuals with a similar medical diagnosis requiring very different types of training because they are behaviourally different. Indeed, the sole use of the traditional classification can lead to inappropriate behavioural treatment such as prolonged hospitalization which may eventually lead to secondary mental retardation, including poor cognitive growth, attention and motivation.

In this chapter the term 'developmental handicap' is used for all these conditions since it implies that the problems have occurred during the major periods of growth and have resulted in a deficit requiring habilitative treatment. In addition to the above reasons for a global category of handicaps it can be stated that most conditions are not simple but result from a constellation of interacting symptoms. For example, many persons of low intelligence are also partially deaf, have visual defects, contract physical illnesses, and suffer accidents more easily than others, and conditions of deprivation are common (Mittler, 1970; Douglas and Blomfield,

1958). The cerebral-palsied adult not only suffers from a brain injury to the motor system, but from possible complications of the condition which arise from the ensuing sensory deficit and reduction in stimulation (Stephen and Robertson, 1965). Thus, in most cases, we are dealing with multiple causation.

Obviously certain conditions such as cerebral palsy may require specialized treatment, but the behavioural scientist and the educationalist are particularly concerned with problems of social adaptation and development. Thus we are concerned in all cases with baselines of behaviour and means of changing that behaviour. A general categorization has other advantages. We live in a society where lay bodies have become concerned, along with professional colleagues, in particular types of disability. Thus, there are societies for the autistic child, the cerebral-palsied, the mentally retarded and the dyslexic child, to mention but a few. By dividing concern in this manner the resources available within the community are likewise fragmented and prevent concerted effort being brought to bear on governments, scientific and educational bodies, and the general public. By uniting the approach under one label a more integrated service may be brought about. This does not assume that everybody is the same; rather that similar methods of approach may be of assistance to a much wider range of people than has previously been supposed.

An equally important implication is that the growth of knowledge in the area of handicap argues for a multidisciplinary approach. Services for the handicapped have traditionally been divided between various professional and government establishments; Education, Public Health, hospital services and various governmental departments. Hierarchies of professions have developed accordingly, but the danger of specific professional dominance is also perceived from some of the newer professions who have come to vie with the established hierarchies. The treatment of the handicapped is unlikely to respond well to any rigid hierarchical model. Every handicapped person has a number of problems which require the intervention of a team. A combination of skills amongst a team of people is required whereby the function of the team is highlighted, so that a person is known for his ability in counselling, remedial treatment, handling physical disability or directing a team and so on, and professional labels become submerged.

Moreover, unless each member of the team knows what is going on and is coordinating with his colleagues there is often a breakdown in treatment. It is also true that one rarely treats an individual, but rather an individual within a family context, which in itself increases the range of professional workers involved. Since larger numbers of workers involved in any one particular family can cause confusion and, in effect, the breakdown of the delivery of service, there must be good communication between services and the ability amongst their workers to co-ordinate or hand over their functions to each other. A survey carried out by the author showed thirteen social workers involved with one particular family, while another family in the same street boasted no social workers, despite the fact that there were urgent problems (Brown, 1973b).

A final implication is particularly important for education. Traditionally very little scientific information has been made available to the teacher in the field of special education. Over the past fifteen years a wealth of research has been carried out, particularly in areas such as mental retardation. Units have been set up concerned with the vocational training of these persons. However, despite this work (O'Connor and Tizard, 1956; Clarke and Clarke, 1973b) the findings have not been put into practice on a wide scale. It is difficult for research to bridge the gap between its original discipline within hospital or health setting and the educational environments and vice versa, although attempts to consolidate literature from administratively different fields are helpful (see Loring, 1965). Many research workers are loath to generalize their findings to the practical situation, as conditions may vary and the effects may not be the same. However, this is a poor argument for not making use of available information and assessing the extent to which it can improve the educational training of the handicapped. We can argue further that this same work may have considerable relevance to the education of the normal school child.

An examination of the practical situation will also indicate large areas where research work has not yet been carried out. For example, there is inadequate information concerning the adjustment of handicapped persons who leave school and, as yet, little is known about the incidence of geriatric problems amongst the developmentally handicapped. We have some idea of the prevalence of various forms of handicap and we also know that certain variations occur in relationship to age, the type of area sampled and classification procedures (Kushlick, 1968; Siegal, 1967). Kushlick (1970) is applying population data to the development of community facilities and residences for the severely retarded which, combined with training techniques, offers interesting possibilities.

In many fast-growing urban areas such as the immigrant cities of North America, where there are a large number of young married persons, there probably needs to be more rapid development of preschool and early school services, and of community residences for the handicapped, although the young handicapped will move as a wave through successive age groups as such cities stabilize. Yet it does not appear that many authorities are making use of available population data to pinpoint the need for particular services.

These problems will become extremely relevant as more of the handicapped are given better physical care and a socially-orientated training to assist their habilitation into the community.

ASSESSMENT

This section examines some of the more recent advances and controversies in behavioural assessment. Space is given to discussing the use of intelligence tests and social-educational measures of functioning. It should, however, be recognized that assessment of other factors is important and that a multidisciplinary team approach is necessary. A social history should be obtained which relates, concisely, the individual's past experience to his present performance. A medical history is also relevant. By these means we may isolate some of the weaknesses in the individual's pattern of functioning. This is particularly relevant when dealing with the partially sighted, those with hearing loss and the cerebral-palsied. Physical limitations dramatically affect social and educational performance. Having arrived at some estimate of how an individual may perform it is important to avoid suggesting that the individual is untrainable. Prediction, particularly within the field of handicap, is notoriously poor (Cobb, 1972).

It must be remembered that parents play an important part in the assessment process. The parents, though influenced by their emotional involvement with their child, are often more aware than anyone else of his behavioural assets and deficits and their observations should be actively sought (Mittler, 1970). Many parents will also be providing continued support during and after training so they too will require guidance and support.

A child or adult in need of assessment is usually brought to a clinic, either within a guidance centre, hospital, or school, where he is given a battery of educational and psychological tests. Increasing criticism is being levelled at this type of assessment and testing so far as the developmentally handicapped are concerned, for although the tests may describe the individual on a continuum of performance, they are subject to a variety of errors. They do not necessarily identify the type of difficulties with which we are concerned, nor do they enable us to predict the future outcome effectively. This is not to say that such techniques have no uses. There is obvious research value in them, and in specialized cases they do assist in evaluating a client's functioning level (Brown, 1967). However, some psychologists and educationalists have come to regard them as techniques which classify individuals into one of a variety of pigeon holes, and have limited use in the field of subnormality (Clarke and Clarke, 1973a). These techniques are no longer appropriate when we are concerned with a particular individual's baselines of behaviour and with improvement scores over a wide range of tasks and situations (Brown, 1973a). Evidence has accumulated in recent years showing that subjects, particularly those who are handicapped, become less efficient under unfamiliar conditions such as clinic interviews. Most of us are aware, at a very practical level, of the influence of new and anxiety-provoking situations on our behaviour, but there is some evidence (Brown and Semple, 1970), that those who are handicapped or young are particularly susceptible to such unfamiliarity. In these circumstances performance in educational and psychological tests and during verbal interviews with psychiatrists and social workers is likely to be adversely affected. This argues for the stabilization of an individual in a familiar situation and for seeing him over a period of time while carrying out an assessment. Furthermore, if we wish to determine the type of work an individual can do there is little point in measuring his intelligence or other cognitive abilities, when evidence suggests that the only realistic predictor of such skills is behaviour on a sample of the actual task (O'Connor and Tizard, 1956). There is also evidence from Schubert's (1967) research with the cerebral-palsied that baseline levels of performance may not be as important as immediate improvement on a particular test or skill (see also Clarke and Clarke, 1973a). The type of assessment procedure under discussion here involves realistic tasks and situations that give the individual an opportunity to show the extent to which he can respond to feedback of information and modify his performance. Furthermore, the work of Gunzburg (1968) indicates that appropriate social behaviours are much more relevant to the satisfactory performance of the handicapped individual in society than his performance on personality (see Cromwell, 1967) and intelligence tests or other traditional types of assessment.

There are several methods whereby this type of assessment can be done. Firstly, there are a variety of techniques such as the Gunzburg 'Progress Assessment Charts'. A second method is to simulate work and social situations within school or institute so that a wide range of skills is sampled. These include the ability to get on with an employer, to carry out different skills within a team, to use small tools, work on one's own, to work inside or outside a building, to use transportation and the telephone, and to develop budgeting and a variety of home-living skills including meal preparation and cooking. These all come within the purview of the assessment programme. Of course, this not only means a radical change in assessment, but very decisive changes in the curriculum of the young adult. It implies bringing into the school curriculum a wide range of training skills which have not, as a rule, been represented before, although there are exceptions to this (Tolley, 1967).

Social assessment

There are a variety of techniques for assessing social behaviour. It has already been indicated that this is one of the major areas in which failure can take place. Even very handicapped persons in terms of intelligence may perform effectively in the adult world if social behaviour is acceptable. Over the past few years a variety of scales have been developed such as the Gunzburg Progress Assessment Charts, and the Marlett Adaptive Functioning Index (1971). The Gunzburg P.A.C., of which there are three versions, are intended collectively for use at all age levels. Each chart is divided into four areas: *Self-Help Skills, Communication, Occupation* and *Socialization*. Each quadrant ranges from very simple skills which can be found in the very young normal child to the types of skills that are expected in an industrial community. The Self-Help Skills area covers such activities as feeding and travelling around the neighbourhood, while the Communication area considers the person's ability to follow instructions and express ideas. Included in this are various kinds of mechanical skill in the arithmetic area such as counting and dealing with money. The Socialization area looks at the ability to play and indulge in recreational activities while Occupation deals with simple skills of a mechanical nature, the ability to use tools, and effectiveness in the work situation.

The Adaptive Functioning Index by Marlett is a Canadian test which is divided into three booklets, *Social Educational Test, Residential*, covering home-living skills, and *Vocational*, which involves work and work-related skills. The latter two are check lists and are not dissimilar to the Gunzburg scales. However, unlike the Gunzburg P.A.C., it is possible to obtain objective scores for a proportion of the questions. The Residential booklet is particularly useful in that it covers a variety of activities which are likely to be found in normal home and community social situations. The test is built in such a way that credit levels or tokens can be associated with particular levels of responding. The scheme can also be used for plotting change in behaviour, and as a basis for discussing behaviour problems and changes with the individual student in very concrete terms. It provides the educator with a simple means of estimating the success of any rehabilitation process and also serves as an indicator for revising and expanding habilitative and remedial programmes. The Gunzburg Charts, which were originally developed for the British population, can be used in a similar way but they lend themselves less readily to motivation systems. The advantage of both scales is that baselines of behaviour can be obtained for each individual and gaps within the developmental hierarchy observed. The 'tests' also enable the user to identify gaps in programmes for it often emerges that students are not given opportunities within their home or hospital or school programme for carrying out certain types of behaviour. The Marlett scale is, like the Gunzburg P.A.C., intended for use by supervisors, teachers or parents. It is divided into four levels of functioning; level one, representing basic and immature levels of responding, leading up to level four which suggests that the individual is ready for outside living. Thus a particular trainee may function at quite a high level in one area but not in another. For example, it is often found that an individual is ready for vocational placement whereas his home-living skills are far from adequate and vice versa.

Neither the Gunzburg nor the Marlett scale deals very adequately with problems of sexual adaptation. In most communities sexual behaviour of the handicapped is still regarded as a controversial subject. The trainee who adapts to life outside should be expected to participate in sexual relationships similar to his normal peer group, whether or not he is a slow learner with or without physical handicaps. To what extent particular behaviours are shown depends partly on social, cultural and religious factors as well as on the degree of handicap, and we must help the student to adapt to mores of his particular society. Many trainees have little sexual vocabulary, while others have a vocabulary based on slang or institutional language patterns. It is important that social workers, teachers and others are aware of the language differences and can converse openly and meaningfully with their students. Research in related fields clearly indicates that unfamiliar vocabularies and stress lead to information retention problems (Ley and Spelman, 1965; McLeod, 1972).

Wherever possible sex instruction (e.g. information on contraception) should be given, as well as guidance in making appropriate relationships. If marriage takes place it should not be automatically assumed that the couple can now behave effectively. Continuing advice needs to be readily available to help the couple adjust to marriage and family life. Some of the problems in the area of sexual behaviour are discussed by Rosen (1972).

Cognitive assessment

The advantages and disadvantages of cognitive assessment, particularly as related to the diagnosis of mental retardation, have been argued for a long while. The work of Clarke (1965) demonstrates the dangers of using such techniques as the Binet with the mildly retarded and argues for the use of techniques which employ both visual-perceptual and verbal items. This is important since Bernstein (1958), Wyatt (1965) and others have noted the discrepancy between verbal and non-verbal attainments of adolescents and adults who have below average ability. The above studies suggest that verbal tests, if used alone, are a poor measure of ability and an unreliable predictor of later performance. An individual may have a very wide range of skills in the visual-perceptual area despite low verbal ability. Teachers tend to use language and verbal ability as guides to performance, and may relegate a student of low verbal ability to a future of unskilled work despite very considerable ability in other spheres (Brown, 1973b). Clarke and Clarke (1954), Stein and Susser (1960) and many others have demonstrated the importance of cognitive growth in the adolescent and young adult of below average intelligence and have demonstrated that intelligence is not a constant. Clarke and Clarke (1954) demonstrated rises of intelligence of fifteen or more points in adolescents from adverse home backgrounds. Indeed, about 75% of those from adverse homes, compared with with about 30% of those from less adverse homes, showed increments of amount over a period of six years. Brown (1972) has shown comparable changes, and noted that the individual from the adverse home need not necessarily be moved from his adverse home environment before this growth takes place. This may imply that spontaneous maturational changes occur or that other environmental changes, such as from an educational to a work situation, are important in stimulating accelerated growth. If the latter is the case it can be argued that changes in the school curriculum might accelerate the cognitive change. The adolescent and young adult period appears to represent one that can be capitalized on in terms of providing appropriate learning stimuli (Bloom, 1965) to accelerate growth, particularly in the slow learner from an adverse environment.

One of the obvious uses of intelligence tests is where the individual is underfunctioning in terms of overall performance, but has some areas in which specific abilities are evident (Brown, 1967), or when staff believe the person has greater potential. If intelligence tests are used, they should cover a broad range of abilities (Cattell, 1971 and it would seem wise to associate their use with knowledge of the social background of the student (Clarke and Clarke, 1973b) so that some prediction can be made regarding the likelihood of acceleration in growth rate.

Many of the problems in the severely handicapped adult lie in the area of concept formation (Woodward, 1963). Often the young adult has not reached the point where he can conserve in terms of number and volume, and is functioning below that of a normal seven-year-old. If social development is adequate, and he can come to enumerate accurately without simple perceptual errors, he may function effectively in a simple working environment. Many jobs involve packing and call for an ability to enumerate and to place items in groups. Once again IQ is not a good predictor of whether the individual can function at a particular concept level. The work of Woodward (1962, 1963), points quite clearly to the fact that many of those of relatively high intelligence may be unable to carry out conversation, though some persons of low IQ may be able to do this relatively easily. Therefore, tests involving knowledge of shape, size, numeration and other concepts involved in conversation are necessary. We are not concerned with normative data but merely whether the individual can or cannot carry out these skills. The types of material that are used in the Piaget tests may quite often be inappropriate for adults since they were originally intended for young children. However, the same type of tests can generally be carried out making use of items from industrial settings, such as nails, screws, pieces of wire and transistors. Such assessment results are not, as Clarke and Clarke (1973a) point out, predictors of whether the student will eventually be able to conceptualize at a particular level. They are indicators suggesting the level at which training needs to be directed.

Summary of assessment

Evidence has been produced to suggest that a much broader form of assessment needs to be employed with the handicapped which is multidisciplinary in nature. Practical techniques in familiar situations are necessary and a broad range of testing, including assessment of work, social, home-living and recreational skills is desirable. Assessment of performance on very simple tasks, ranging, for example, from how to open an egg to how to enumerate a group of objects, is highly relevant for the more severely handicapped adolescent. However, educationalists should be concerned not only with the level of performance, but also with the change in performance after training and practice. It should be recognized that an individual, however handicapped initially, may change over time. Much has been said of baseline behaviour, but it is important to recognize that assessment is a continuous process melded to the development of habilitation, and that frequent measures should be taken over time (Brown, 1973a). The ability of the individual to absorb frustration and adapt to unfamiliar environments is also important.

The suggestion that home-living skills need to be assessed indicates an area in which there is a need for curriculum re-evaluation. Of paramount importance is the need to recognize that many of the skills taught to handicapped children in their mid-teens and early adult life could have been taught at a much earlier age. This chapter is not concerned with early childhood, but it is perhaps worth noting that preschool education, advice about programmes to parents and a more realistic practical curriculum which makes use of the concerete aspects of the individual's life during early schooling, are important steps to effective adult behaviour. It should also be borne in mind that many adolescents show gains in ability during their late teens and early twenties so that many of the skills which could not be taught earlier may be able to be taught when this rapid growth occurs. This suggests that there should be a much more continuous educational process for the handicapped that includes social and vocational training.

HABILITATION TECHNIQUES

The education of the handicapped child should be gradually orientated towards training for adulthood. It must be practical, realistic and encompass the main areas of adult life. The individual also needs to be equipped for an adult life which will change over time and therefore the concept of specific training, though relevant, is limited. We must train for transferability of skills. That transfer can take place even in the severely retarded has been clearly demonstrated by Clarke and Cookson (1962) in a series of studies. Habilitation should involve the learning of vocational, social, educational, home-making and leisure time skills. This portion of the chapter is concerned with some learning techniques that have been developed in the field of psychology and are relevant to the training of these skills.

Principles of learning relevant to habilitation

In the fields of educational psychology and mental retardation Gagné (1970) and Clarke and Clarke (1973b) have summarized many of the principles relevant to learning. It is important to note that these techniques apply to all the developmentally handicapped and to every area of training, including social, educational, recreational and vocational skills. Techniques developed in programmed instruction (Haskell, 1966; Platt, 1967), and more recently in the field of computer-assisted instruction with the developmentally handicapped (Hallworth, 1973), have also involved many of these principles.

1. Early learning

Hebb (1949) was one of the first psychologists to draw attention to the difference between early and later learning or transfer. Early learning is original learning and takes place at a slow pace. Stimuli need to be presented many times before learning can be achieved. We know from other studies, for example the work of Sluckin (1964), that once it is achieved early learning tends to be overgeneralized, and the respondent finds it difficult to keep his responses to a particular and relevant situation. Thus, the early learner not only has to learn the responses to particular stimuli, but having learned them, needs to reduce overgeneralization so that he produces them only in the appropriate situation. Most of early learning takes place in the young child, in skills such as walking and talking, but as the child becomes older, so more of his new skills are recombinations of earlier learned material. This later learning we know as transfer. Transfer is more rapid than early learning because the basic elements of the task have already been learnt. However, early learning can occur later in life and in the developmentally handicapped adult may represent a major component in his functioning. Many of the early learning situations have not been mastered by him although frequently we assume this is so. Consequently attention is often directed to the teaching of skills which are beyond that of the slow learner. It is not uncommon for young adults who are of a trainable level of intelligence to show problems at a preconceptual level of development, yet we require them to learn tasks for which this level is a prerequisite. Once again the need for the appropriate kind of assessment is underlined, but assuming the individual has attained a level of functioning from which we can direct teaching or training, the question is, how can we optimize learning?

2. Familiarization of stimulation

Mein and O'Connor (1960) and Mein (1967), in a series of studies on the reading of hospitalized severely subnormal adolescents, indicated that the use of an institutional vocabulary facilitates learning. The use of reading books with a 'regular' vocabulary would not bring about such improvement. They argued that this was due to the fact that the institutionalized severely subnormal was suffering from a language deficit, and that he would be unable to learn unless the language which he received was a meaningful one. In another context Brown (1967) and Brown and Semple (1970) have shown that slow learners are particularly vulnerable to unfamiliar and, therefore, presumably rather meaningless stimulation. Furthermore the unfamiliar is likely to appear unstructured—an aspect of stimulation which seems to debilitate learning. There are two considerations in the context of unfamiliarity.

(i) The Environment. If the environment is unfamiliar, the responses of the trainee are inhibited. It is known that this inhibition influences overt verbalization and motor performance, both of which assist in the learning of new tasks. Thus there is a need in the new learning situation to familiarize the individual with his environment, the persons who are going to train him, and his peer group. Hutt, Hutt and Ounsted (1965) noted that children placed in an unfamiliar environment will wander around a room, touching items and picking them up, before actually directing their attention to specific training materials in the room. They also showed that an adult who is familiar to the child acting as a model can attract that child to the relevant material.

(ii) The Tools and Task. The trainee must be familiar with the tools he is going to use, such as hammers, machines or words. He should be familiarized with the material involved prior to carrying out any formal learning. This may be one very important reason for demonstrating a total task before commencing formal learning.

3. Attention

Many handicapped persons have attention difficulties. Some believe these are particularly common amongst the brain-injured, although increasing evidence suggests they may be equally common among those who come from deprived and institutionalized environments (Brown, 1964); Robinson and Robinson, 1970). Some of the techniques for overcoming attention difficulties were discussed under (2) above. However, a further aspect of this problem, outlined by Zeaman and House (1963), may be the inability of the severely subnormal to sort relevant from irrelevant cues. They suggest that once this difficulty is overcome the learning of the severely subnormal proceeds similarly to that of other subjects. Task difficulty and lack of meaningfulness in the material can produce attention problems, which suggests that the phenomenon described by Zeaman and House is not just a feature of severe retardation, but is related to the problems posed by early learning.

There are a variety of ways in which discrimination can be enhanced. One is to reduce the amount of extraneous stimulation, particularly during the early stages of learning (Brown, 1966a, b). There may also be similar and confusing stimulation within tasks. Examples of this are the sorting of number sixes (6's) from number nines (9's) or b's from d's. Learning may be enhanced by ridding the situation of one of the confusing elements. There are other techniques, such as *Multiple Cue Consistency*, where the relevant characteristic that we wish to discriminate is aligned with other cues which the person already recognizes. A cue fading technique can then be employed as has been done in some of the research of O'Connor and Hermelin (1963). For example, a number six can be presented coloured red and in large size, a number nine can be presented small and black. Colour and size differences are then gradually reduced until the six and nine are equal in terms of these dimensions. Because learning has occurred in small increments effective discrimination can still be carried out.

The use of cubicles to reduce redundant stimulation may be helpful at certain stages, although it should be recognized that normal environmental stimulation must eventually be introduced. There are a number of studies which may also be used at a practical level (see Cruickshank, 1967) although it should be remembered that the techniques are useful, not because a person is brain injured, but because he shows particular behaviour in a given situation regardless of causation.

4. Spaced practice

It is well known that more learning can take place by presenting material for two fifteen-minute periods with a break in between, than by presenting material for a half-hour period. The use of small time units is particularly relevant to the developmentally handicapped. Early learning is fatiguing, particularly in adults who may have physical and psychological difficulties. It is not uncommon to come across handicapped persons who may only be able to concentrate on a task for two minutes at a time although, as they learn, this period can be expanded.

5. Small units

This technique relates to the previous one. Tasks need to be broken down into very small units which can be gradually built into larger ones. It is perhaps important in this procedure, however, to demonstrate the complete task in the first place so that the trainee has some idea of the relevance of the small unit in the context of the total situation. The smallness of the task unit will vary considerably according to circumstance. For example, in one case of an adolescent with spina bifida, it was necessary to break down a three-block bridge-building task into several moves. Finding that he could produce a concatenate series of blocks, it was then necessary to build a parallel set above; in a subsequent move all the blocks were removed except three (i.e. two below and one above), the top one of these was then moved to a middle position and finally the two lower blocks separated. By taking these steps individually the adolescent made no errors, and was able to perform the complete task on subsequent occasions without difficulty.

6. *Language*

It is necessary to consider the language used by the trainee and also the language produced for the trainee by his teacher or parent (see Mittler, 1973). Clarke and Cookson (1962) suggested that overt verbalization by the trainee, in the form of a commentary on the work he is learning, may aid performance. This idea is not dissimilar to the findings of Luria (1961) with much younger children: namely, that language can facilitate appropriate motor activity. It is well known that under pressure normal adults will verbalize aloud, and more recent work suggests that this is quite usual when they carry out tasks which are rather difficult for them (Mittler, 1971). On the other hand, there have been arguments against this process, for example, Bryant (1967) has suggested that verbalization may inhibit the transfer of skills in the severely subnormal. No definitive answer can be given, although the work cited suggests another technique which may be tried with adults who have difficulties in learning. Adults who spontaneously verbalize while learning a new task should not be inhibited by the teacher or supervisor. This often happens in workshops or indeed with younger children in school classes.

More recent work by Brown and Hughson (1972) suggests that the manner in which verbal instruction is given is highly relevant to the learning of tasks. It should be recognized that the developmentally handicapped adolescent may be deprived of language and may not understand all that is being said. This may be exacerbated by sensory defects such as hearing loss. It is possible that the decibel level of information, the speed at which instruction is given, together with the amount of relevant but perhaps superfluous elements of language, all influence his learning. Preliminary experiments suggest that a speed of about 95 words per minute is as much as the severely subnormal can retain in the learning of new tasks, and that increasing the speed by about two-and-a-half times can result in a tenfold decrease in performance. With the subnormal adult this difference is not so marked, although a slower production speed of language would appear to facilitate performance, particularly in early learning. Furthermore, the amount of redundant information seems highly pertinent; that is, the more plain and simple the instructions, the more effective the learning. Subjective evaluations suggest that teachers or trainers who find a person misunderstanding instructions often increase decibel level, speed up instructions and elaborate the language, yet the above results suggest an opposite approach is more effective. These findings are underlined by the study of McLeod (1972) who recorded professional workers interviewing trainees. The results indicate that subnormals experience extreme difficulty in retaining information on interviews as measured by recall thirty minutes later. They remember much more of their own statements in interviews than the counsellor's, but distort information surprisingly little. The shorter (e.g. under twelve minutes) and simpler the interview the greater the degree of retention. The results suggest that repetition of information with the trainee verbalizing the content would also increase the effectiveness of interviews.

Visual demonstration is apparently more effective than auditory instructions in the teaching of the handicapped, at least with very simple vocational type tasks, and therefore, whenever possible, visual components should be introduced. However,

172

many situations must inevitably involve the use of language and the experimental results outlined above would seem relevant.

7. Overlearning

Many studies in psychology have shown that learning is best retained when it is overlearned. In other words, repetition of the task after perfect performance has been attained is to be encouraged. It is tempting to move on to new tasks with the slow learner once adequate performance has been attained, but further practice of the particular task leads to better retention over time. This is important because when a handicapped person transfers to a new environment he is likely to experience stress and fatigue, and overlearning is likely to help offset any decrement in performance which might otherwise occur. This phenomenon of environmental stress is common to everyone, but it is particularly relevant to the handicapped because any lessening of their performance may make them vulnerable in terms of loss of job.

8. Transfer

In order for a person to behave appropriately, it is important that tasks are not just learned, but can also be transferred to other situations. Consequently provision should be made during training for students to transfer their skills to new situations. This applies not only to the task but also to supervisors and peer groups. The individual may learn to function with a person he knows well but break down when placed with an unfamiliar individual. Transfer also relates to overlearning since repetition by itself can become a boring and, therefore, a punishing routine. If the situation can be varied it trains for transfer while at the same time encouraging overlearning and keeping motivation and interest high.

9. Motivation

Low motivation is a major cause of underfunctioning in the slow learner. It is very common in institutionalized persons (Pringle, 1965) although it is found in a variety of other groups and is probably one of the major stumbling blocks in the rehabilitation of the handicapped. It may often be difficult to heighten motivation, nevertheless, whenever the individual shows some interest, incentives and rewards can be given which may enhance learning and performance. Evidence relating to rewards is found in the studies cited by Clarke (1973b). Rewards seem most effective when they are of a concrete nature. We have also seen that work broken down into small units enhances performance, perhaps because the individual experiences an increased success rate. Rewards, when given frequently and over small intervals, are likely to be effective in promoting effective behaviour. Additional reward techniques involve competition, either with the individual's own previous performance, or with other individuals, or between a group of trainees. Verbal praise and facial changes on the part of the supervisor also have an important part to play.

Since reward plays an important part in learning, monetary reward can be used effectively in relation to a wide range of behaviour and not, as is often done in training or sheltered workshops, for work production alone. Levels of social and vocational performance can be associated with rewards such as money, token or other recognized incentives, by means of periodical behaviour counts or by the use of such techniques as the Marlett Adaptive Functioning Index. These techniques offer opportunities for motivating behaviour, although the way they are applied and for how long depends very much on the individual and the scheme under which he is functioning.

10. Teaching of correct behaviour

Skinner (1961) holds that one of the basic tenets of programming is to minimize error in learning, but error is often learnt even when simple motor skills, such as handling a knife and fork, riding a bicycle or using the telephone, are being performed. This means that behaviour then has to be unlearned and because behaviour is modified very slowly in the handicapped, it is extremely important that these errors do not take place in the first instance. It may be tempting to allow an individual to perform a task incorrectly so that he achieves the end goal but, with the exception of extreme circumstances where the individual is physically handicapped, this should not be permitted. The learning of correct behaviour implies a need to measure the baseline of behaviour in the first instance. Training is then divided into small units so that the individual can gradually make increments in performance with a minimal number of errors.

Summary

The relevance of any learning technique, such as spaced practice, for any specific individual cannot be stated. What is important is that the principles or techniques are useful guidelines to the educator. The extent to which they are used and the manner in which they are used will vary in the individual case.

SOCIAL TRAINING

While it is likely that many of those with IQs above 55 can function reasonably well within the community, given adequate training in vocational and social skills, it should be pointed out that there is not a high correlation between vocational success and intelligence level (McKerracher and Orritt, 1972). Some persons of IQs below 55 may function quite effectively (Saenger, 1957). The severely retarded person with acceptable social habits may well be able to make his way successfully in the outside environment. While many will function adequately in sheltered workshops, others may perform well provided they are linked to groups of other trainees within the outside work environment. As any trainee in the group improves over time he can bud-off and function separately within the industrial setting.

Training centres and sheltered workshops for severely retarded adults *should not* be in the same physical area because the functions of these two units are entirely different. One is concerned with developing behaviours for maximum performance whereas the other is carrying out maximum production activity and keeping behaviour at an optimum level. Obviously the two areas overlap but the type of staff, contracts and premises required differ considerably.

Social-educational skills

There are several social and social-educational skills which the adolescent or young adult has to learn if he is to function effectively within the normal environment. Ideally he should learn to read at a ten-to-eleven year level. If he cannot attain this he should, wherever possible, gain a social sight vocabulary (Gunzburg, 1960). In the area of social arithmetic, he will need to learn addition and subtraction. It is hardly necessary for him to be taught the skills of multiplication or division, particularly as he may not understand the concepts involved and may thus forget the process fairly readily later on (Brown and Dyer, 1963). The majority of mathematical skills required in social life, for example, in housekeeping, involve addition and, to a lesser extent, subtraction. Many severely handicapped persons will not be able to carry out these basic addition and subtraction skills by age sixteen and will have difficulty with Piagetian concepts at the concrete operational stage because conservation will not have been attained.

It is often necessary in industry for an individual to count out groups of objects. He may have to classify them into dozens or bag them into lots of twenty. Thus basic enumeration skills are important. Even the very severely retarded can be taught this process provided the situation is concrete and the rules discussed above are applied. Conservation, however, is relevant to a number of other areas. For example, in shopping it is important that the individuals recognize size and shape in relation to weight, amount and cost. Normal adults sometimes confuse size variations in relation to price and yet for the handicapped, who may receive low wages, this type of error may be important in terms of effective economic functioning.

This raises the need for budgeting and training in home-living skills. In some centres lifelike situations are simulated and trainees given an opportunity to buy food, prepare meals, entertain their friends and, in some cases, to function in living apartments, where they are required to carry out all home-living skills under appropriate supervision. Most schools do not interest themselves in this type of training despite the fact that the major reason for failure in adult life appears to be social and not vocational ineptness. There is considerable evidence that failure occurs because the individual is unwilling to tolerate his work conditions, his foreman, or his peers, arrives drunk for work, or shows other social ineptitudes in home behaviour. Charles (1953) showed that the majority of a group of 151 handicapped people leaving opportunity classes in the United States were still functioning adequately after fifteen years. The vast majority were still employed and the most critical comment made was that the incidence of social misdemeanours was above average. The need for social training is underlined by the fact that the majority of trainees from the Vocational and Rehabilitation Research Institute who were successful (i.e. succeeded in the community for six months or more) had experienced a home-skills training programme. Out of approximately one hundred placements, failure, where it occurred, was due to social inadequacy rather than work performance (Brown, 1972b). Many trainees single themselves out as handicapped because of their stance, walk, clothing or verbal behaviour. These points underline the need for social training, the importance of revising the school curriculum and also the need for developing home-living training programmes. The last item should include training for leisure-time skills since, without these, the trainee is likely to become isolated, or become involved in socially inappropriate behaviour. It is important that trainees be treated as adults and not children, and that they receive opportunities and encouragement to behave as their more normal peers; hence the importance of supervisors acting as peer group models rather than substitute parent figures. Leisure training can be developed in a number of ways, for example, by the development of evening clubs for the handicapped or by mixing groups of trainees with the normal population. The latter seems desirable wherever possible, although specialized facilities may be necessary for the severely retarded. Recreation serves a variety of purposes. Apart from developing leisure-time skills, it facilitates improvement in both muscle tone and motivation, both of which are known to be associated with handicap and poor performance. Indeed, a wide variety of physical recreation opportunities should be offered to the handicapped person.

INTEGRATED EDUCATION AND WORK

It would appear that not only does there need to be a thorough revision of the school curriculum but also an extension of the age range of persons considered for special education. It is not suggested that full-time education is necessarily required throughout this range, but that there should be provision for linking vocational and educational training that extends into the person's adult life. He should, for example, be able to attend school, either on a day-release or evening basis, for periods of home-living training while remaining at work for the rest of the time. Furthermore, there is a need to include vocational and social training in the normal school curriculum. This should be introduced as early as possible in the child's life. It is recommended that workshops be set up which are integrated with the school. This has been done in a few programmes, (e.g. Tolley, 1967). Whenever an individual leaves the workshop or school for employment and fails, he should immediately return to the previous environment. This is usually an easy matter when there are good school—parent and child relationships, the majority of young people being willing to return to school and to receive retraining for further jobs. In this way a person is not forced to live idly on welfare, risking the development of poor social and work habits, or losing motivation and even drifting into crime.

PARENTS AND TRAINING

So far there has been little discussion on the role of parents with the young adult. Obviously, the earlier the parents are involved and share in a programme the better (Goldberg and Rooke, 1967). By the time the child has reached young adulthood the uninvolved parents may either feel resentful that nothing has apparently been done or so set in their ways that they have become dependent on having a handicapped person within their household. The author has known several individuals who could have been rehabilitated, but whose parents have insisted that this was not possible and required them to remain at home. Parents can be introduced into a programme in a number of ways. Firstly, they can assist in the social assessment of their child. Secondly, they should be familiar with the programme that is being developed for their child. Thirdly, they can be given support and advice in relation to problems which emerge in the home. Sometimes these are learning problems. In the early phases of training it may be important to discourage the parents from participating in the education of the child. For example, many illiterate adolescents have parents who exhaustively attempt to teach reading every night, thus building up frustration and an emotionally tense relationship between parent and child. In other cases the parent may not understand how to handle social and emotional problems and, with the more severely retarded, have difficulties in encouraging language and appropriate speech. It has been argued that many parents have emotional difficulties in relation to their handicapped child. Some of the work recently carried out at the Vocational and Rehabilitation Research Institute suggests that many parents, when they have an opportunity to deal with concrete problems, find that some of the emotional difficulties disappear. This is consistent with the comments on parent involvement by Mittler (1970). Two other points should be mentioned. Firstly, there are some children and their parents who are so disturbed that counselling involving psychotherapy is necessary. Secondly, if good relationships are formed between parent, child and the school or training centre, adverse conditions can be more easily dealt with when they arise, because the parents and the trainee are likely to turn to the agency for help.

PLACEMENT AND FOLLOW-UP SERVICES

Adequate placement and follow-up services should always be provided. Many governments set up labour exchanges or manpower centres to provide jobs, or to direct persons to jobs within the community. These can be insufficient for the handicapped because the employer may need to know rather more about the prospective handicapped employee, and to be reassured that he has been trained to a level where he can function effectively. The employer may need to discuss any particular physical handicaps which might affect performance. This can be particularly relevant in the initial stages of placement. Many services do not provide adequate coordination between the agencies involved in placement and follow-up. Trainees are passed to agencies and workers whom the trainees have not experienced before. It may be exceedingly difficult to refer and follow-up, or even place, trainees in certain areas (e.g. rural areas) but the effects of unfamiliarity, not only on the trainee but on the part of the social workers and others involved with him, must be borne in mind and, as far as possible, mitigated. Efficient follow-up services need to be arranged with recognition of the fact that many individuals will require placement on more than one occasion. Follow-up generally involves dealing with common human problems, for example, when an individual is sick and cannot go to work, or is unable to get on with room or work mates. If there is a single contact person for home, residence and work situations, many of the social difficulties which arise can be dealt with before failure occurs. Trainees quite often obtain and maintain jobs in competition with supposedly normal peers; they often keep their jobs longer, are said to be more polite and acceptable in terms of behaviour, and deal with their money and leisure time situations more adequately. There need to be well-designed follow-up studies to assess these observations in terms of hard research data, but if these impressions are well-founded, they underline the need for generalizing special education services to a much wider range of the population.

Manual dexterity and social maturity seem to possess the greatest validity in terms of predicting employability. However, as Cobb (1972) points out, the outstanding finding of follow-up studies in the field of mild and severe retardation, which comprises a large proportion of the developmentally handicapped, is the high proportion of adults who succeed regardless of the criteria used. It should be recognized, however, that training may take a number of years. The challenge to educators and behavioural scientists is to accelerate this process, and identify and remediate the sources of failure in those who cannot yet find an acceptable place in the adult community.

References

Abercrombie, M. L. J. (1963), Eye movements, perception and learning, in Smith, V. H. (Ed.), *Visual Disorders and Cerebral Palsy*, Heinemann

Abercrombie, M. L. J. (1964), *Perceptual and Visuo-motor Disorders in Cerebral Palsy*, Heinemann

Albee, G. W. (1970), Let's change our research priorities in retardation, *Journal of special Education*, **4**, (2), 139–48

Alberman, E. D. and Goldstein, H. (1970), The 'at risk' register: a statistical evaluation, *British Journal of preventive and social Medicine*, **24**, 129–35

Allen, K. and Harris, F. (1966), Elimination of a child's excessive scratching by training the mother in reinforcement procedures, *Behaviour Research and Therapy*, **4**, 79–84

Anderson, U. M. (1967), The incidence and significance of high-frequency deafness in children, *American Journal of Disease of Children*, **113**, 560–5

Ashton-Warner, Sylvia (1961), *Teacher*, Simon and Schuster

Ayllon, T., Smith, D. and Rogers, M. (1970), Behavioural management of school phobia, *Journal of Behaviour Therapy and Experimental Psychiatry*, **1**, 125–8

Ayres, A. J. (1968), Effect of sensorimotor activity on perception and learning in neurologically handicapped children. Unpublished report, University of Southern California

Baer, D. M., Wolf, M. M. and Risley, T. R. (1968), Some current dimensions of applied behaviour analysis, *Journal of applied Behaviour Analysis*, **2**, 119–24

Bailey, J. and Mayerson, L. (1969), Vibration as a reinforcer with a profoundly retarded child, *Journal of applied Behaviour Analysis*, **2**, 135–7

Bailey, P. (1973), *They Can Make Music*, Oxford University Press

Bales, R. F. (1950), *Interaction Process Analysis*, Cambridge

Ball, S. and Bogatz, G. (1970), *The First Year of Sesame Street: An Evaluation*, Educational Testing Services, Princeton, New Jersey

Bandura, A. (1969), *Principles of Behaviour Modification*, Holt, Rinehart and Winston

Baratz, S. and Baratz, J. (1970), Early Childhood Intervention: The Social Science Base of Institutional Racism, *Harvard Educational Review*, **40**, 29–50

Barnet, A. B. and Lodge, A. (1967), Diagnosis of hearing loss in infancy by means of electroencephalographic audiometry, *Clinical Proceedings of Children's Hospital*, Washington D.C., **23**, 1–17

Barth, R. (1969), *Open Education; Theory and Philosophy of Education*, Kensington, Australia

Bateman, B. (1967), Visually handicapped children, in Haring, N. and Schiefelbusch, R. L. (Eds.), *Methods in Special Education*, McGraw-Hill

Bateman, B. (1973), Direct Instruction—research implications and classroom applications, in Silverman, H. and O'Bryan, K. (Eds.), *Proceedings of the First Annual Symposium on Learning Problems*, Toronto: O.I.S.E.

Bauman, M. (1954), *Adjustment to blindness*, Harrisburg, Pennsylvania: Pennsylvania State Council for the Blind

Bayley, N. (1965), Comparisons of mental and motor test scores for ages 1 through 15 months by sex, birth order and race, geographical location and education of parents, *Child Development*, **36**, 379–411

180

Becker, J. L. (1963), *A Programmed Guide to Writing Auto-Instructional Programs,* R.C.A.

Becker, W. C. (1973), Applications of behaviour principles in typical classrooms, in Thomson, C. J. (Ed.) *Behaviour Modification in Education,* Seventy-second Yearbook of National Society for Study of Education, University of Chicago Press

Becker, W. C. and Engelman, S. (1973), Summary Analysis of four year data on achievement and teaching progress with 7,000 children in 20 projects, *University of Oregon 'Follow Through Programme' Technical Report,* 73–1

Becker, W. C., Madsen, C. H., Arnold, C. R. and Thomas, D. R. (1967), The contingent use of teacher attention and praise in reducing classroom behaviour problems, *Journal of Special Education,* **1,** 287–307

Bereiter, C. and Englemann, S. (1966), *Teaching the Disadvantaged Child in the Preschool,* Englewood Cliffs: Prentice-Hall

Bereiter, C. and Englemann, S. (1973), Observations on the Use of Direct Instruction with Young Disadvantaged Children, in Spodek, B., *Early Childhood Education,* Englewood Cliffs: Prentice-Hall

Bereiter, C., Hughes, M. and Anderson, V. (1970), *Teachers Guide to the Open Court Kindergarten Program K.,* La Salle: Open Court Publishing Company

Berg, J. M. and Kirman, B. H. (1959), Some aetiological problems in mental deficiency, *British Medical Journal,* **2,** 848–52

Berger, M. (1972), Modifying behaviour at school, *Special Education,* **61,** 18–21

Berger, M. and Yule, W. (1972), *Cross-cultural survey of educational and psychiatric disorders in school children,* Final Report to the Social Sciences Research Council

Bernstein, B. (1958), Some Sociological Determinants of Perception, *British Journal of Sociology,* **92,** 271–6

Bijou, S. W. (1966), Functional analysis of retarded development, in Ellis, N. (Ed.), *International Review of Research in Mental Retardation,* Academic Press

Bijou, S. W. (1973), Behaviour Modification in teaching the retarded child in Thoresen, C. E. (Ed.) *Behaviour Modification in Education,* Seventy-second Yearbook of National Society for the Study of Education, University of Chicago Press

Bijou, S. W., Peterson, R. F., Harris, F. R., Allen, A. K. and Johnson, M. S. (1969), *Methodology for experimental studies of young children in natural settings, Psychological Records,* **19,** 177–210

Birch, H. G., Richardson, S. A., Baird, D., Horobin, G. and Illsley, R. (1970), *Mental subnormality in the community,* Williams and Wilkins

Birnbauer, J. S., Wolf, M. M., Kidder, J. D. and Tague, C. E. (1965), Classroom behaviour of retarded pupils with token reinforcement, *Journal of Experimental Child Psychology,* **2,** 219–35

Bleuler, E. (1910), Vortrag über Ambivalenz, *Zentralblatt für Psycho-analyse,* **1,** 266

Bloom, B. S. (1965), *Stability and Change in Human Characteristics,* Wiley

Blurton-Jones, N. J. (Ed.) (1972), *Ethological Studies of Child Behaviour,* Cambridge University Press

Bobath, B. (1967), The very early treatment of cerebral palsy, *Developmental Medicine and Child Neurology,* **9,** 373–90

Bobath, K. (1966), *The Motor Deficit in Patients with Cerebral Palsy,* Heinemann

Bowlby, J. (1958), Psycho-analysis and child care, in Sutherland, J. D. (Ed.) *Psychoanalysis and contemporary throught,* Hogarth Press

Brazelton, T. B., Robey, J. S. and Collier, G. A. (1969), Infant development in the Zinacantico Indians of Southern Mexico, *Pediatrics,* **44,** 274–90

Brennan, M. E. (1973), Prevention: medico-social aspects, in Griffiths, M. I. (Ed.) *The Young Retarded Child, Medical Aspects of Care,* Edinburgh and London: Churchill Livingstone

Bricker, W. A. (1973), Behaviour modification programmes, in Mittler, P. (Ed.) *Assessment for Learning in the Mentally Handicapped,* Churchill

Bricker, W. A. and Bricker, D. D. (1969), Four operant procedures for establishing auditory stimulus control with low functioning children, *Journal of Mental Deficiency*, **73**, 981

Bricker, W. A. and Bricker, D. D. (1972), The use of programmed language training as a means of differential diagnosis and remediation among severely retarded children. U.S. Office of Education

Bricker, W. A. and Bricker, D. D. (1973), Behaviour Modification Programmes, in Mittler, P. (Ed.) *Assessment for learning in Mentally Handicapped*, Institute of Research in Mental Retardation Symposia No. 5, Edinburgh and London: Churchill Livingstone

Brison, D. W. (1967), Definition, Diagnosis and Classification, in Baumeister, A. A. (Ed.) *Mental Retardation: Appraisal, Education, Rehabilitation*, Chicago: Aldine Publishing Co. Ltd.

British Paediatric Association (1972), *Paediatrics in the '70s* (Nuffield Provincial Hospitals Trust), Oxford University Press

Brown, D. E. (1962), An experiment in mental health consultation, in Irvine, E. E. (Ed.), *Ventures in professional co-operation*, London: Association of Psychiatric and Social Workers

Brown, R. I. (1964), The effects of visual distraction on perception in subjects of subnormal intelligence, *British Journal of Social and Clinical Psychology*, **1**, 20–8

Brown, R. I. (1966a), The effects of varied environmental stimulation on the performance of subnormal children, *Journal of Child Psychology and Psychiatry*, **7**, 251–61

Brown, R. I. (1966b), The effects of extraneous auditory stimulation on learning and performance, *American Journal of Mental Deficiency*, **71**, 2, 283–90

Brown, R. I. (1967), *The Assessment and Education of Slow Learning Children*, University of London Press

Brown, R. I. (1972a), Cognitive changes in the adolescent slow learner, *Journal of Child Psychology and Psychiatry*, **13**, 183–93

Brown, R. I. (1972b), *6th Annual Report of the Vocational and Rehabilitation Research Institute*, Calgary

Brown, R. I. (1973a), Research to Practice in Rehabilitation, *International Seminar Report on Vocational Rehabilitation for the Mentally Retarded*, American Association for Mental Deficiency

Brown, R. I. (1973b), *A Follow-up Study of Slow Learners Leaving School*, Report to Joseph Rowntree Social Service Trust, U.K. (in preparation)

Brown, R. I. and Dyer, L. (1963), Social arithmetic training for the subnormal, *Journal of Mental Subnormality*, **9**, 8–12

Brown, R. I. and Hughson, A. (1972), *Verbal Instruction in the Performance of Non-verbal Tasks*, Report to Human Resources Research Council, Alberta, Canada

Brown, R. I. and Semple, L. (1970), Effects of unfamiliarity on the overt verbalization and perceptual motor behaviour of nursery school children, *British Journal of Educational Psychology*, **40**, 3, 291–8

Bryant, P. E. (1967), Verbal labelling and learning strategies in normal and severely subnormal children, *Quarterly Journal of Experimental Psychology*, **19**, 155–67

Bucher, B. and Lovaas, O. I. (1968), Use of aversive stimulation in behaviour modification, in Jones, M. R. (Ed.) *Miami Symposium on the Prediction of Behaviour: Aversive Stimulation*, Coral Gables, Florida: University of Miami Press

Burden, R. (1969), A truly comprehensive education, *Special Education*, **48**, 11–15

Burrello, L. C., Tracy, M. M. and Schutz, E. W. (1973), Special education as experimental education: a new conceptualization, *Exceptional Children*, **40**, 1–29

Burt, C. (1925), *The Young Delinquent*, University of London Press

Burt, C. (1937), *The Backward Child*, University of London Press

Burt, C. (1950), *The causes and treatment of backwardness*, National Children's Home

Bushell, D. (1973), The Behaviour Analysis Classroom in Spodek, B. (Ed.) *Early Childhood Education*, Englewood Cliffs: Prentice-Hall

Cabak, V. and Najdanvic, R. (1965), Effects of undernutrition in early life on physical and mental development, *Archives of Disease in Childhood*, **40**, 532–4

Calder, J. R. (1970), 'Widening gulf over objectives', *Programmed Learning Bulletin*, No. 1, 42–5

Caldwell, F. M. and Drachman, R. H. (1964), Comparability of three methods of assessing the developmental level of young infants, *Pediatrics*, **34**, 51–7

Campbell, D. T. and Stanley, J. C. (1963), *Experimental and quasi-experimental designs for research*, Rand McNally & Co.

Carillo, L. W. (1964a), *Let's Look*, Chandler Publishing Co.

Carillo, L. W. (1964b), *The Language Experience Approach to the Teaching of Reading*, Paper given at the International Reading Conference, University of London, Institute of Education, London

Carter, C. (1958), A life-table for mongols with the cause of death, *Journal of Mental Deficiency Research*, **2**, 64–74

Cashdan, A. and Pumphrey, P. D. (1969), Some effects of the remedial teaching of reading, *Educational Research*, **11**, 138–42

Caspari, I. (1962), Problems of school consultation, *New Era*, **43**, 78–81

Caspari, I. (1970), *Emotional stability: the contribution of the curriculum towards the emotional stability of the child*, Conference held at Queen Elizabeth Hall, London, June 1970

Castell, J. and Mittler, P. (1965), The intelligence of patients in mental subnormality hospitals: a survey of admissions in 1961, *British Journal of Psychiatry*, **11**, 219–25

Cattell, R. B. (1971), The structure of intelligence in relation to the nature–nurture controversy, in Cancro, R. (Ed.), *Intelligence: Genetic and Environmental Influences*, New York: Grune and Stratton

Chall, J. S. (1970), Learning and not learning to read: current issues and trends, in Young, F. A. and Lindsley, D. B. (Eds.), *Early Experience and Visual Information Professing in Perceptual and Reading Disorders*, Washington D.C.: National Academy of Sciences

Charles, D. C. (1953), Ability and accomplishments of persons earlier judged mentally deficient, *Genetic Psychology Monographs*, **47**, 3–71

Chazan, M. (1962), School phobia, *British Journal of Educational Psychology*, **32**, 209–17

Chazan, M. (1967), The effects of remedial teaching in reading: a review of research, *Remedial Education*, **2**, 4–12

Christopolos, F. and Renz, P. (1969), A critical examination of special education programs, *Journal of Special Education*, **3**, 371–410

Clark, M. M. (1970), *Reading Difficulties in Schools*, Harmondsworth: Penguin Books

Clarke, A. D. B. and Clarke, A. M. (1954), Cognitive changes in the feeble minded, *British Journal of Psychology*, **45**, 173–9

Clarke, A. D. B. and Clarke, A. M. (1959), Recovery from the effects of deprivation, *Acta Psychologica*, **16**, 137–44

Clarke, A. D. B. and Clarke, A. M. (1973), Assessment and prediction in the severely subnormal, in Mittler, P. J. (Ed.), *Psychological Assessment of the Mentally Handicapped*, J. and A. Churchill Ltd., London

Clarke, A. M. and Clarke, A. D. B. (1973a), What are the problems? An evaluation of recent research relating to theory and practice, in *Mental Retardation and Behavioural Research*, London: Churchill-Livingstone

Clarke, A. M. and Clarke, A. D. B. (Eds.), (1973b), *Mental Deficiency: The Changing Outlook*, (3rd Edition), London: Methuen

Clarke, A. D. B. and Cookson, M. (1962), Perceptual-motor transfer in imbeciles: a second series of experiments, *British Journal of Psychology*, **53**, 321–30

Clausen, J. (1967), Mental deficiency—development of a concept, *American Journal of Mental Deficiency*, **71**, 727–45

Clausen, J. Quo Vadia, AAMD (1972), *Journal of Special Education*, **6**, (1), 51–60

183

Cobb, H. V. (1972), *The Forecast of Fulfilment,* Columbia University: Teachers College Press

Cohen, H. J., Molnar, G. E. and Taft, L. T. (1968), The genetic relationship of progressive muscular dystrophy (Duchenne type) and mental retardation, *Developmental Medicine and Child Neurology,* **10,** 754–65

Cohen, H. L. and Filipcjak, J. A. (1971), A new learning environment, San Francisco: Jossey Bass

Cohen, H. L. (1973), Behaviour modification and socially deviant youth, in Thoreson, C. E. (Ed.), *Behaviour Modification in Education,* Seventy Second Yearbook of National Society for the Study of Education, University of Chicago Press

Cohen, J. S. and De Young, H. (1973), The role of litigation in the improvement of programming for the handicapped, in Mann, L. and Sabatino, D. (Eds.), *A First Review of Special Education,* vol. 2, Philadelphia, J.S.E. Press with Buttonwood Farms

Coleman, J. (1964), *Abnormal Psychology and Modern Life,* New York: Scott Foresman

Coleman, J. S. (1966), *Equality of Educational Opportunity,* Washington D.C.: U.S. Government Printing Office

Coleman, J. S. (1968), The concept of equality of educational opportunity, *Harvard Journal Review,* **38** (1), 7–22

Collings, G. D. (1973), Case review: rights of the retarded, *Journal of Special Education,* **7** (1), 27–37

Collins, J. E. (1961), *The effects of Remedial Education,* London: Oliver and Boyd

Conners, C. K. (1971), Drugs in the management of children with learning disabilities, in Tarnopol, L. (Ed.), *Learning Disorders in Children,* Boston: Little, Brown

Connolly, K. J. (1973), Ethological techniques and the direct observation of behaviour, in Mittler, P. (Ed.), *Assessment for Learning in the Mentally Handicapped,* Institute of Research in Mental Retardation Symposia No. 5, Edinburgh and London: Churchill Livingstone

Court, S. D. M. (1971), Child Health in a changing community, *British Medical Journal,* **2,** 125

Cowie, V. (1968), Genetics of mental subnormality, *British Journal of Hospital Medicine,* **1,** 945

Crabtree, N. (1972), Assessment and treatment in hearing impaired children, *Proceedings of Royal Society of Medicine,* **65,** 11

Craig, H. B. and Holland, A. L. (1970), Reinforcement of visual attending in classrooms for deaf children, *Journal of Applied Behaviour Analysis,* **3,** 2, 97–109

Crane, A. R. (1959), An historical and critical account of the accomplishment quotient idea, *British Journal of Educational Psychology,* **29,** 252–9

Cratty, B. J. (1970), *Perceptual and Motor Development in Infants and Children,* Collier-Macmillan

Critchley, M. (1953), *The Parietal Lobes,* London: Arnold

Crome, L. (1960), The brain and mental retardation, *British Medical Journal,* **1,** 897–904

Cromwell, R. L. (1967), Personality evaluation, in Baumeister, A. A. (Ed.), *Mental Retardation: Appraisal, Education, Rehabilitation,* Aldine, Chicago

Cruikshank, W. M. (Ed.) (1966), *The Teacher of Brain Injured Children,* Syracuse University Press, Syracuse

Cruickshank, W. M. (1967), *The Brain Injured Child in Home, School and Community,* Syracuse University Press, Syracuse

Cruickshank, W. M. et al. (1961), *A Teaching Method for Brain-Injured and Hyperactive Children,* (Syracuse University Special Education and Rehabilitation Monograph Series 6), Syracuse University Press, Syracuse

Cruickshank, W. M. and Hallahan, D. P. (1973), *Psychoeducational Foundations of Learning Disabilities,* Prentice-Hall

Dalton, A. J., Rubino, C. A. and Hislop, M. W. (1973), Some effects of token rewards on school achievement of children with Downes Syndrome, *Journal of applied Behavioural Analysis,* **6,** 251–9

Daniels, J. C. and Diack, H. (1956), *Progress in Reading,* Institute of Education, University of Nottingham

Dare, M. T. and Gordon, N. (1970), Clumsy children: a disorder of perception and motor organisation, *Developmental Medicine and Child Neurology,* **12,** 178–85

Davie, R., Butler, N. and Goldstein, H. (1972), *From Birth to Seven,* National Children's Bureau, London: Longmans Green

Davies, I. K. (1971), *The Management of Learning,* McGraw-Hill

Delacato, C. H. (1963), *The Diagnosis and Treatment of Speech and Reading Problems,* Charles C. Thomas

Delacato, C. H. *et al.* (1966), *Neurological Organisation and Reading,* Charles C. Thomas

Denhoff, E. (1964), *Drugs in Cerebral Palsy,* London: Heinemann

Department of Education and Science (1972), *The Education of the Visually Handicapped,* London: H.M.S.O.

Department of Education and Science (1973), *Special Education: a fresh look,* D.E.S. Report of Education No. 77, London: H.M.S.O.

Doll, E. (1962), An historical survey of research and management of mental retardation in the United States, in Trapp, E. P. and Himmelstein, P. (Eds.), *Readings on the Exceptional Child: Research and Theory,* New York: Appleton-Century Crofts

Douglas, J. W. and Blomfield, J. M. (1958), *Children Under Five,* London: Allan & Unwin

Douglas, J. W. D., Ross, J. M. and Simpson, H. R. (1968), *All Our Future,* London: Peter Davies

Drabman, R. S., Spitalnik, R. and O'Leary, K. D. (1973), Teaching self-control to disruptive children, *Journal of Abnormal Psychology,* **82,** 1, 10–16

Dunn, L. M. (1968), Special education for the mildly retarded—is much of it justifiable? *Exceptional Children,* **34,** 5–22

Dunn, L. M., Horton, K. B. and Smith, J. O. (1968), *Peabody Language Development Kits,* American Guidance Service Inc.

Durrell, D. J. (1956), *Improving Reading Instruction,* New York World Book Company

Earl, C. J. C. (1961), *Subnormal Personalities: Their Clinical Investigation and Assessment,* London: Bailliere, Tindall and Cox

Edwards, T. J. (1965), The language experience attack on cultural deprivation, *The Reading Teacher,* **18** (7), 546–51, 556

Elder, H. H. A. (1962), *Diseases of childhood, in Morbidity Statistics from General Practice: vol. 3, Disease in General Practice,* (Studies on Medical and Population Subjects, No. 14), London: H.M.S.O.

Emery, A. E. H. (1973), (Ed.), *Antenatal Diagnosis of Genetic Diseases,* Edinburgh, London: Churchill Livingstone

Evans, E. D. (1971), *Contemporary Influences in Early Childhood Education,* New York: Holt, Rinehart and Winston

Eysenck, H. J. (1953), *Uses and Abuses of Psychology,* Harmondsworth: Penguin Books

Eysenck, H. J. (1960), *Behaviour Therapy and the Neuroses,* London: Pergamon

Finnie, N. R. (1968), *Handling the Young Cerebral Palsied Child at Home,* London: Heinemann

Flanders, N. A. (1970), *Analysing Teaching Behaviour,* Reading, Mass.: Addison-Wesley

Fleming, W. G. (1971), *Schools, Pupils and Teachers,* University of Toronto Press

Forfar, J. O. (1968), At risk registers, *Developmental Medicine and Child Neurology,* **10,** 384–95

Fowles, B. (1973), *A Pilot Study of Verbal Report in Formative Research in Television,* Unpublished doctoral dissertation, Yeshiva University, New York

Francis-Williams, J. (1970), *Children with Specific Learning Difficulties,* Oxford: Pergamon

Francis-Williams, J. and Yule, W. (1967), The Bayley infant scales of mental and motor development, *Developmental Medicine and Child Neurology*, **9**, 391

Frankenburg, W. K. and Dodds, J. B. (1967), The Denver developmental screening test, *Journal of Pediatrics*, **71**, 181–91

Fransella, F. and Gerver, D. (1965), Multiple regression equations for predicting reading age from chronological age and WISC verbal IQ, *British Journal of Educational Psychology*, **35**, 86–9

Franzen, R. H. (1920), The accomplishment quotient, quoted in Crane, A. R. (1959)

Freedman, D. G. (1971), Behavioural assessment in infancy, in Stoeling, G. B. A. and van der Werff Ten Bosch, J. J. (Eds.), *Normal and Abnormal Development of Brain and Behaviour*, Leiden: University Press

Freud, S. (1908), '*Civilised' Sexual Morality and Modern Nervous Illness*, 9, (1959) 177–204 (see below)

Freud, S. (1912), *The Dynamics of Transference*, 12, (1958), 97–108 (see below)

Freud, S. (1926), Inhibitions, symptoms and anxiety, 20, (1959), 77–175: *Standard Edition of the Complete Psychological Works of Sigmund Freud*, London: Hogarth Press

Fries, C. C. (1963), *Linguistics and Reading*, New York: Holt, Rinehart and Winston

Froebel, F. L. (1909), *The Education of Man*, New York: Appleton-Century-Crofts

Frostig, Marianne (1963), *Developmental Test of Visual Perception*, Consulting Psychologists Press, N.F.E.R.

Frostig, M., Horne, D. and Miller, A. (1972), *Pictures and Patterns; and Teachers' Guides to Pictures and Patterns* (Rev. ed.), Chicago: Follett

Frostig, M. and Marlow, P. (1973), *Learning Problems in the Classroom*, Grune and Stratton

Gagné, R. M. (1970), *The Conditions of Learning*, Second Edition, New York: Holt, Rinehart and Winston

Gahagan, D. M. and Gahagan, G. A. (1970), *Talk Reform*, Routledge and Kegan Paul

Gardner, D. E. M. (1966), *Experiment and Tradition in the Primary School*, London: Methuen

Gardner, J. M. (1973), Training the trainers: A review of research on teaching behaviour modification, in Rubin, R. D., Brady, J. P. and Henderson, J. D. (Eds.), *Advances in Behaviour Therapy*, Vol. 4, New York: Academic Press

Gardner, W. I. (1971), *Behaviour Modification in Mental Retardation*, Aldine Atherton

Gesell, A. (1925), *The Mental Growth of the Pre-School Child*, New York: MacMillan

Gesell, A. and Armatruda, C. S. (1947), *Developmental Diagnosis*, New York and London: Hoeber

Gibson, E. J. (1963), Development of perception: Discrimination of depth compared with discrimination of graphic symbols, in Wright, J. and Kagan, J. (1963), *Basic Cognitive Processes in Children*, Cambridge: Harvard University Press

Giles, D. K. and Wolf, M. M. (1966), Toilet training institutionalized severe retardates: On application of operant behaviour modification techniques, *American Journal of Mental Deficiency*, **70**, 766–80

Gilhool, T. K. (1973), Education: An inalienable right, *Exceptional Children*, **39**, 8, 597–610

Glaser, R. (1972), Individuals and learning: The new attitudes, *Educational Researcher*, **1**, 6, 5–13

Glaser, R. (1973), Educational psychology and education, *American Psychologist*, **28**, 557–66

Goldberg, I. J. and Rooke, M. L. (1967), Research and educational practices with mentally deficient children, in Haring, N. G. and Schiefelbusch, R. L. (Eds.), *Methods in Special Education*, New York: McGraw-Hill

Goldstein, K. (1948), *Language and Language Disturbances*, Grune and Stratton

Grantham, E. (1971), Handicapped children in preschool playgroups, *British Medical Journal*, **4**, 346–7

Grantham-McGregor, S. M. and Back, E. H. (1971), *Developmental Medicine and Child Neurology*, **13**, 79

Gray, W. S. (1956), *The Teaching of Reading and Writing*, U.N.E.S.C.O., Paris

Griffiths, M. I. (1962), Assessment—the team approach, *Spastics Quarterly*, **11**, 31–3

Griffiths, M. I. (1973a), *The Young Retarded Child, Medical Aspects of Care*, Edinburgh and London: Churchill Livingstone

Griffiths, M. I. (1973b), Early detection: developmental screening, in Griffiths, M. I. (Ed.), *The Young Retarded Child, Medical Aspects of Care*, Edinburgh and London: Churchill Livingstone

Griffiths, M. I. (1974), The use of C.C.T.V.R. in the assessment of children with handicaps, *Medical and Biological Illustration*, **24**, 28–31

Griffiths, M. I. and Bowie, E. M. (1973), The use of dimethothiazine (Fusaban) in the treatment of childhood cerebral palsy, *Developmental Medicine and Child Neurology*, **15**, 25

Griffiths, M. I. and Smith, V. H. (1963), Squint in relation to cerebral palsy, in Smith, V. H. (Ed.), *Visual Disorders and Cerebral Palsy*, London: Heinemann

Griffiths, R. (1954), *The Abilities of Babies*, London: University of London Press

Gruenberg, E. M. (1964), Epidemiology, in Stevens, H. A. and Heber, R. (Eds.), *Mental Retardation: A Review of Research*, Chicago: University of Chicago Press

Gruenberg, E. M. (1966), Epidemiology of mental illness, *International Journal of Psychiatry*, **2**, 78–134

Guerney, B. F. (Ed.) (1969), *Psychotherapeutic Agents: New Roles for Non-Professionals, Parents and Teachers*, New York: Holt, Rinehart and Winston

Gulliford, R. (1971), *Special Educational Needs*, London: Routledge and Kegan Paul

Gulliford, R. and Widlake, P. (in press), *The Use of Schools Council Materials by Teachers of Disadvantaged Pupils*, Report to Schools Council

Gunzburg, H. C. (1960), *Social Rehabilitation of the Subnormal*, London: Bailliere, Tindall and Cox

Gunzburg, H. C. (1966), *The Progress Assessment Charts*, Third Edition, London: National Association for Mental Health

Gunzburg, H. C. (1968), *Social Competence and Mental Handicap*, Baltimore: Williams and Wilkins Company

Hagberg, B. and Sjorgren, I. (1966), The Chronic brain syndrome of infantile hydrocephalus, *American Journal of Diseases of Children*, **112**, 189–196

Hallworth, H. J. (1973), Symposium on Computer Assisted Instruction, in Primrose, D. A. A. (Ed.), *Proceedings of the 3rd. Congress International Association for the Scientific Study of Mental Retardation*, (in preparation)

Harden, A. and Pampiglione, G. (1970), Neurophysiological approach to disorders of vision, *Lancet*, **1**, 805–9

Harding, G. F. A., Thompson, C. R. S. and Panayatopoulos, C. P. (1969), Evoked response diagnosis in visual field defects, *Proceedings of Electrophysiological Technologists Association*, **16**, 159–63

Haring, N. G. (1968), Behaviour modification and special education. The experimental unit—University of Washington, 4th Annual Engineering Conference, School of Education, U.C.L.A.

Haring, N. and Hauck, M. (1969), Contingency Management Applied to Classroom Remedial Reading and Maths for Disadvantaged Youth, *Department of Institutions Research Report*, 41–5

Haring, N. G. and Phillips, E. L. (1972), *Analysis and Modification of Classroom Behaviour*, Englewood Cliffs: Prentice-Hall

Haring, N. G. and Schiefelbusch, R. L. (1967), *Methods in Special Education*, New York: McGraw-Hill

Haskell, S. (1966), Programmed Instruction and the Mentally Retarded, in Gunzburg, H. C. (Ed.), The Application of Research to the Education and Training of the Severely Subnormal Child, *Monograph Supplement, Journal of Mental Subnormality*, 15–24

Hawkins, R. P., Peterson, R. F., Schweid, E. and Bijou, S. W. (1966), Behaviour therapy in the home, *Journal of experimental Child Psychology*, **4**, 99–107

Head, H. (1926), *Aphasia and kindred disorders of speech*, Cambridge University Press

Hebb, D. O. (1949), *The Organisation of Behaviour*, London: Chapman-Hall

Heber, R. (1961), *A manual on terminology and classification in mental retardation*, American Journal of Mental Deficiency (Monograph Supplement, 2nd Edn)

Heber, R. and Garber, H. (1971), An experiment in prevention of cultural-familial mental retardation, in Primrose, D. A. (Ed.), *Proc. Second Congr. Internat. Assoc. Scientific Stud. Ment. Defic.*, 31–5, Amsterdam: Swets and Zeitlinger

Herbert, G. W. and Wedell, K. (1970), Communication handicaps of children with specific language deficiency. Paper read at the Annual Conference of the British Psychological Society, Southampton, April, 1970

Hersov, L. A. (1960), Refusal to go to school, *Journal of Child Psychology and Psychiatry*, **1**, 137–45

Hewett, J. M. (1965), Teaching speech to an autistic child through operant conditioning, *American Journal of Orthopsychiatry*, **35**, 927–36

Hewett, F. (1968), *The Educationally Disturbed Child in the Classroom*, Boston: Allwyn and Bacon

Hewett, F. M. and Forness, S. R. (1973), *Education of Exceptional Learners*, Boston: Allyn and Bacon

Hilgard, E. H. (1972), The translation of educational research and development into action, *Educational Researcher*, **1**, 18–21

Hindley, C. B. (1965), Stability and change in abilities up to 5 years: Group trends, *Journal of Child Psychology and Psychiatry*, **6**, 85–99

Holt, K. S. (1964), The use of diazepam in childhood cerebral palsy, *Annals of Physical Medicine, Supplement*

Homme, L. E., de Baca, P. C., Devine, J. V., Steinhorst, R. and Rickert, E. J. (1963), Use of the Premack Principle in controlling the behaviour of nursery school children, *Journal of experimental Analysis of Behaviour*, **6**, 544

Howorth, I. E. (1967), The 'at risk' infant, *Lancet*, **2**, 887

Hughes, N. A. S. (1971), Developmental physiotherapy for mentally handicapped babies, *Physiotherapy*, **57**, 399–408

Hutchinson, D. and Clegg, N. C. (1972), Experiment in further education, *Special Education*, **61**, 3, 21–3

Hutt, C., Hutt, S. J. and Ounsted, C. (1965), The Behaviour of Children with and without Upper CNS Lesions, *Behaviour*, **24**, 3–4, 246–68

Ingram, T. T. S. (1963), Report of the Dysphasia Subcommittee of the Scottish Paediatric Society. Unpublished Report

Ingram, T. T. S. (1972), The classification of speech and language disorders in young children, in Rutter, M. and Martin, J. A. M. (Eds.), *The Child with Delayed Speech*, Clinics in Developmental Medicine No. 43. London: Spastics International Medical Publications and William Heinemann

Jacobson, L. I., Kellogg, R. W., Greeson, L. E. and Bernal, G. (1973), Programming the intellectual and conceptual development of retarded children with behavioural techniques, in Rubin, R. D., Brady, J. P. and Henderson, J. D. (Eds.), *Advances on Behaviour Therapy*, Vol. 4, London: Academic Press

Jeavons, P. M. (1973), Special handicaps: Epilepsy, in Griffiths, M. I. (Ed.), *The Young Retarded Child, Medical Aspects of Care*, Edinburgh and London: Churchill Livingstone

Jensen, A. R. (1969), How can we boost IQ and scholastic achievement, *Harvard Educational Review*, Reprint Series No. 2

Jensen, A. R. (1973), *Educability and Group Differences*, London: Methuen

Johnson, C. (1964), *Old-Time Schools and School Books*, New York: Dover Books

Johnson, C. A. and Katz, R. C. (1973), Using parents as change-agents for their children: a review, *Journal of Child Psychology and Psychiatry,* **14,** 181–200

Johnson, D J. and Myklebust, H. (1967), *Learning Disabilities,* Grune and Stratton

Johnson, J. M. (1972), Punishment of Human Behaviour, *American Psychologist,* **27,** 1033–54

Johnson, J. M. (1973), Discrimination training in retardates, in Rubin, R. D., Brady, J. P. and Henderson, J. D. (Eds.), *Advances in Behaviour Therapy,* New York: Academic Press

Jones, C. H. and Leith, G. O. M. (1966), Programming an aspect of reading readiness, *Remedial Education,* **1,** 5–8

Jones, E. (1957), *Sigmund Freud: life and work. V.3, The last phase* (1919–1939), London: Hogarth Press

Joseph, A. and Parfitt, J. (1973), *Playgrounds in an Area of Social Need,* London: National Foundation for Educational Research

Josephson, E. (1968), Social life of blind people, *American Foundation of the Blind,* Research Series, No. 19, 1968

Junkala, John (1972), 'Task Analysis and instructional alternatives', *Academic Therapy,* **8** (1), 33–40

Kamii, C. (1972), A Sketch of the Piaget Derived Preschool Curriculum Developed by the Ypsilanti Early education program, in Braun, S. and Edwards, E. (Eds.), *History and Theory of Early Childhood Education,* Worthington, Ohio: C. A. Jones

Kanfer, F. H. (1973), Behaviour Modification—An Overview, in Thoreson, C. E. (Ed.), *Behaviour Modification in Education,* Seventy-second Yearbook of National Society for the Study of Education, University of Chicago Press

Kanner, L. (1968), The first Kenneth Cameron Memorial Lecture, London: Institute of Psychiatry

Kass, C. E. (1969), Introduction to learning disabilities, *Seminars in Psychiatry,* 240–4

Kazdin, A. E. and Bootzin, R. S. (1973), The token economy: an examination of issues, in Rubin, R. D., Brady, J. P. and Henderson, J. D. (Eds.), *Advances in Behaviour Therapy,* Vol. 4, New York: Academic Press

Kazelin, A. E. (1973), The effect of vicarious reinforcement on attentive behaviour in the classroom, *Journal of applied Behavioural Analysis,* **6,** 71–8

Keith, H. M. (1963), *Convulsive Disorders in Children,* London: Churchill

Kendall, P. H. (1964), The use of muscle relaxants in cerebral palsy. In Denhoff, E. (Ed.), *Drugs in Cerebral Palsy,* London: Heinemann

Keogh, B. K. (1971), A compensatory model for psychoeducational evaluation of children with learning disorders, *Journal of Learning Disabilities,* **4,** 544–8

Keogh, B. K. and Becker, L. D. (1973), Early identification of children with learning disorders: Questions, cautions and guidelines, *Exceptional Children,* **40** (1), 5–11

Keogh, B. K., Becker, L. D., Kukic, M. B. and Kukic, S. J. (1972), *Programs for educationally handicapped and educable mentally retarded pupils: Review and recommendations.* Technical Report SERP 1972-All. Graduate School of Education, University of California, Los Angeles

Keogh, B. K., Cahill, C. W. and MacMillan, D. L. (1972), Perception of interruption by educationally handicapped children. *American Journal of Mental Deficiency,* **77,** 1, 107–8

Kephart, N. C. (1971), *The slow learner in the classroom,* Merrill

Kerschner, J. R. (1968), Doman Delacato's theory of neurological organization applied with retarded children, *Exceptional Children,* **34,** 441–52

King, R. D., Raynes, N. V. and Tizard, J. (1971), *Patterns of residential care,* London: Routledge and Kegan Paul

Kirk, S. A. (1966), *The diagnosis and remediation of psycholinguistic disabilities,* University of Illinois Press, Illinois

Kirk, S. A. and Johnson, O. (1951), *Educating the Retarded Child,* Boston: Houghton Mifflin

Kirk, S. A., McCarthy, J. J. and Kirk, W. D. (1968), *Illinois test of psycholinguistic abilities,* Revised Edition, University of Illinois Press

Klaus, R. A. and Gray, S. W. (1968), The early training project for disadvantaged: A report after five years, *Monographs of the Society for Research in Child Development,* **33,** 4

Klein, M. (1929), Infantile anxiety-situations reflected in a work of art and in the creative impulse. In Klein, M., *Contributions to psycho-analysis,* London: Hogarth Press

Knobloch, H. and Pasamanick, B. (1963), Predicting intellectual potential in infancy, *American Journal of Diseases of Children,* **106,** 43–57

Kolstoe, O. P. (1970), *Teaching Educable Mentally Retarded Children,* New York: Holt, Rinehart and Winston

Komrower, G. M. and McKeith, R. C. (1966), A clinical approach to the problem of the backward child, *Developmental Medicine and Child Neurology,* **8,** 444–55

Krasner, L. and Krasner, M. (1973), Token economies and other planned environments in Thoreson, C. E. (Ed.), *Behaviour Modification in Education,* Seventy-second yearbook of National Society for Study of Education, University Chicago Press

Kravetz, R. J. and Forness, S. R. (1971), The special classroom as a desensitization setting, *Exceptional Children,* **37,** 389–91

Kushlick, A. (1961), Subnormality in Salford, In Susser, M. W. and Kushlick, A., *A report on the mental health services of the City of Salford for the year 1960.* Salford Health Department

Kushlick, A. (1966), A community service for the mentally subnormal, *Social Psychiatry,* **1,** 73–82

Kushlick, A. (1968), Social Problems of Mental Subnormality, in Miller, E. (Ed.), *Foundations of Child Psychiatry,* Oxford: Pergamon Press

Kushlick, A. (1970), Residential Care for the Mentally Subnormal, *Royal Society of Health Journal,* **90,** 5, 254–61

Kuypers, D. S., Becker, W. C. and O'Leary, K. D. (1968), How to make a token system fail, *Exceptional Children,* **35,** 101–9

Laing, A. F. (1968), Compensatory Education for Young Children, in *Compensatory Education: an Introduction,* Swansen: Schools Council Publishing Co.

Lappé, M., Gustafson, J. M. and Roblin, R. (1972), Ethical and social issues in screening for genetic disease, *New England Journal of Medicine,* **286,** 1129–32

Leland, H. (1972), Mental retardation and adaptive behaviour, *The Journal of Special Education,* **6,** 1, 71–79

Lemkau, P., Tietze, C. and Cooper, M. (1943), Mental hygiene problems in an urban district, Fourth paper, *Mental Hygiene,* **27,** 279–95

Levitt, E. E. (1971), Research on psychotherapy with children, in Bergin, A. E. and Garfield, S. L. (Eds.), *Handbook of psychotherapy and behaviour change: An empirical analysis,* New York: John Wiley

Ley, P. and Spelman, M. (1965), Communication in an Outpatient Setting, *British Journal of Social and Clinical Psychology,* **4,** 114–16

London, P. (1972), The end of ideology in behaviour modification, *American Psychologist,* **27,** 913–20

Lorber, J. (1972), Spina bifida cystica. Results of treatment of 270 consecutive cases with criteria for selection for the future. *Archives of Disease in Childhood,* **47,** 854–73

Loring, J. A. (Ed.) (1965), *Teaching the Cerebral Palsied Child,* London: Spastics Society/William Heinemann

Lotter, V. (1966), Epidemiology in autistic conditions in young children, Part I: Prevalence, *Social Psychiatry,* **1,** 124–37

Lovaas, O. I. (1966), A programme for the establishment of speech in psychotic children. In Wing, J. (Ed.), *Early childhood autism,* London: Pergamon Press

190

Lovaas, O. I. and Koegel, R. (1973), Behaviour therapy with autistic children. In Thoreston, C. E. (Ed.), *Behaviour Modification in Education*, Seventy-second Yearbook of National Society for the Study of Education, University of Chicago Press

Lovaas, O. I., Koegel, R., Simmons, J. Q. and Long, T. S. (1973), Some generalization and follow-up measures on autistic children in behaviour therapy, *Journal of Applied Behavioural Analysis*, **6**, 131–66

Lovell, K., Byrne, C. and Richardson, B. (1963), A further study of the educational progress of children who had received remedial education. *British Journal of Educational Psychology*, **33**, 3–9

Lovell, K., Johnson, E. and Platts, D. (1962), A summary of a study of the reading ages of children who had been given remedial teaching, *British Journal of Educational Psychology*, **32**, 66–71

Lovibond, S. H. (1964), *Conditioning and Enuresis*, Oxford: Pergamon Press

Lovitt, T. C., Guppy, T. E. and Blattner, J. E. (1969), The use of free time contingency with Fourth Graders to increase spelling accuracy, *Behavioural Research and Therapy*, **7**, 155–6

Lowenstein, L. F. (1973), The treatment of school phobia, *Journal of the Association of Educational Psychologists*, **3**, 46–9

Luria, A. R. (1961), The Role of Speech in the Regulation of Normal and Abnormal Behaviour, in *Recent Soviet Psychology*, O'Connor, N. (Ed.), London: Pergamon Press

Luria, A. R. (1963), Psychological studies of mental deficiency in the Soviet Union. In Ellis, N. (Ed.), *Handbook of Mental Deficiency*, New York: McGraw-Hill

MacDonald, J. (1973), The Open School: Curriculum Concepts, In Spodek, B., *Early Childhood Education*, Englewood Cliffs: Prentice-Hall

McDill, E. L., McDill, M. S. and Sprehe, J. T. (1969), *Strategies for Success in Compensatory Education: An Appraisal of Evaluation Research*, Baltimore: John Hopkins Press

McGraw, M. D. (1943), *The Neuromuscular Maturation of the Human Infant*, Columbia University Press

Macht, J. (1971), Operant measurement of subjective visual acuity in non-verbal children, *Journal of Applied Behavioural Analysis*, **4**, 1, 23–36

MacKeith, R. C. and Rutter, M. (1972), A note on the prevalence of speech and language disorders. In Rutter, M. and Martin, J. A. M. (Eds.), *The child with delayed speech*. Clinics in Developmental Medicine, No. 43. London: Spastics International Medical Publications and William Heinemann

McKerracher, D. W. and Orritt, C. P. (1972), Prediction of vocational and social skill acquisition in a developmentally handicapped population: A Pilot Study, *American Journal of Mental Deficiency*, **76**, 5, 574–80

McLeod, M. M. (1972), Communication and the Handicapped. Unpublished M.Ed. Thesis, University of Calgary

MacMillan, D. L. (1971), Special education for the mildly retarded: Servant or savant, *Focus on Exceptional Children*, **2**, 1–11

MacMillan, D. L. (1973), Issues and trends in Special Education, *Mental Retardation*, **11**, 3–8

MacMillan, D. L. and Keogh, B. K. (1971), Normal and retarded children's expectancy for failure, *Developmental Psychology*, **4**, 343–8

Madsen, C. H., Becker, W. C. and Thomas, D. R. (1968), Rules, praise and ignoring: elements of elementary classroom control, *Journal of Applied Behavioural Analysis*, **1**, 139–50

Madsen, C. H., Becker, W. C., Thomas, D. R., Koser, L. and Plager, E. (1968), An analysis of the reinforcing function of 'Sit-down' commands, in Barker, R. K. (Ed.), *Readings in Educational Psychology*, Boston: Allyn and Bacon

Madsen, C. H. and Madsen, C. K. (1970), Teaching discipline: behavioural principles towards a positive approach, Boston: Allyn and Bacon

Mahoney, K., Van Wagenen, K. and Meyerson, L. (1971), Toilet training of normal and retarded children, *Journal of Applied Behavioural Analysis*, **43**, 173–81

Marlett, N. J. (1971), *The Adaptive Functioning Index*, The Vocational and Rehabilitation Research Institute: Calgary

Martin, J. A. M. (1972), Hearing loss and hearing behaviour, in Rutter, M. and Martin, J. A. M. (Eds.) *The Child with Delayed Speech*, London: Heinemann

Martinsen, R. A. (1966), Issues in the identification of the gifted, *Exceptional Children*, **33**, 13–16

Meacham, M. C. and Weisen, A. E. (1969), *Changing Classroom Behaviour*, Scranton: Int. Textbook Co.

Mein, R. (1967), Reading with the Severely Subnormal, in Brown, R. I. (Ed.) *The Assessment and Education of Slow Learning Children*, University of London Press

Mein, R. and O'Connor, N. (1960), A Study of the Oral Vocabularies of Severely Subnormal Patients, *Journal of Mental Deficiency Research*, **4**, 130–43

Mercer, J. R. (1971), The meaning of mental retardation, in Koch, R. and Dobson, D. (Eds.), *The Mentally Retarded Child and His Family*, New York: Brunner/Mazel

Miller, D. (1964), Growth to freedom. *The psychological treatment of delinquent youth*, London: Tavistock Publications

Miller, E. and Sethi, L. (1971), The effect of hydrocephalus on perception, *Developmental Medicine and Child Neurology*, **13**, Suppl. 25, 77

Minge, M. R. and Ball, T. S. (1967), Teaching of self-help skills to profoundly retarded patients, *American Journal of Mental Deficiency*, **71**, 864–8

Ministry of Education (1950), *Reading ability: some suggestions for helping the backward*, Pamphlet No. 18, London: H.M.S.O.

Ministry of Education (1955), Report of the Committee on *Maladjusted Children* (The Underwood Report), London: H.M.S.O.

Ministry of Education (1959), *The Handicapped Pupils and Special Schools Regulations 1959* (S.I. no. 365), London: H.M.S.O.

Ministry of Education (1962), *The Health of the School Child 1960–61*, London: H.M.S.O.

Ministry of Education (1963), *Half Our Future*, London: H.M.S.O.

Mittler, P. J. (Ed.) (1970), *The Psychological Assessment of Mental and Physical Handicaps*, London: Methuen

Mittler, P. J. (1971), Practical Applications of Psychological Research, in Primrose, D. A. A. (Ed.) *Proceedings of Second Congress of the International Association for the Scientific Study of Mental Deficiency*, Amsterdam: Swets and Zeitlinger

Mittler, P. J. (1973), Language and Communication, in Clarke, A. M. and Clarke, A. D. B. (Eds.) *Mental Deficiency: The Changing Outlook*, Second Edition, London: Methuen

Moore, J. R. (1973), Comprehensive assessment, in Griffiths, M. I. (Ed.) *The Young Retarded Child: Medical Aspects of Care*, Edinburgh and London: Churchill Livingstone

Morley, M. E. (1972), *The Development and Disorders of Speech in Childhood*, Third Edition, Edinburgh: Churchill Livingstone

Morris, J. (1966), *Standards and Progress in Reading*, Slough, Bucks.: N.F.E.R.

Moseley, D. (1972), The English Colour Code programmed reading course, in Southgate, V. (Ed.) *Literacy at All Levels*, U.K.R.A.: Ward Lock

Myers, P. I. and Hammill, D. D. (1969), *Methods for Learning Disorders*, Wiley

Naidoo, S. (1972), *Specific Dyslexia*, London: Pitman

Neale, M. D. (1958), *Neale Analysis of Reading Ability Manual*, London: Macmillan

Nelligan, G. and Prudham, D. (1969), Norms for four standard developmental milestones by sex, social class and place in family, *Developmental Medicine and Child Neurology*, **11**, 413–22

Nelson, C. M., Worell, J. and Polsgrove, L. (1973), Behaviourally disordered peers as contingency managers, *Behaviour Therapy*, **4**, 270–6

Newland, T. E. (1961), Programs for the superior: Happenstansical or conceptual? *Teachers College Record,* **62,** 513–28

New York State Mental Health Research Unit (1955), *A special census of suspected referred mental retardation, Onondaga County, New York.* Technical Report (cited in Kushlick, 1966)

Nordqvist, V. M. and Waler, R. G. (1973), Naturalistic treatment of an autistic child, *Journal of Applied Behavioural Analysis,* **6,** 79–87

O'Bryan, K. G. (1966), *A Test of Indian Intelligence,* Paper presented to the Alberta Guidance Association, Edmonton

O'Bryan, K. G. (1972), *Indian Cognitive Development: A Study of Children on an Ontario Reservation,* Paper presented to the Learned Societies, Montreal

O'Connor, N. and Hermelin, B. (1963), *Speech and Thought in Severe Subnormality,* London: Pergamon Press

O'Connor, N. and Tizard, J. (1956), *The Social Problem of Mental Deficiency,* London: Pergamon Press

O'Leary, K. D. (1973), Establishing token programmes in schools: issues and problems, in Klein, R. O., Hapkieuricz, W. A. and Roden, A. H. (Eds.), *Behaviour Modification in Educational Settings,* Springfield, Illinois: Thomas

O'Leary, K. D. and Becker, W. C. (1967), Behaviour modification of an adjustment class: a token reinforcement programme, *Exceptional Children,* **9,** 637–42

O'Leary, K. D. and Drabman, R. (1971), Token reinforcement programmes in the classroom: a review, *Psychological Bulletin,* **75,** 379–98

Oppé, T. (1972), Unpublished Working Paper on Risk Registers

Orton, S. T. (1937), *Reading, Writing and Speed Problems in Children,* New York: Norton

Osborne, J. G. (1969), Free time as a reinforcer in the management of classroom behaviour, *Journal of Applied Behavioural Analysis,* **2,** 113–18

Patterson, G. R. (1971), *Families. Applications of Social Learning to Family Life,* Champaign, Illinois: Research Press

Patterson, G. R. (1973), Programming Families of Aggressive Boys, in Thoreson, C. E. (Ed.) *Behaviour Modification in Education,* Seventy-second Yearbook of National Society for Study of Education, Part I, University of Chicago Press

Patterson, G. R. and Gullion, M. E. (1968), *Living with children: new methods for parents and teachers,* Illinois: Research Press

Penrose, L. S. (1963), *The Biology of Mental Defect,* 3rd edn. London: Sidgwick and Jackson

Piaget, J. (1952), *The Origins of Intelligence in Children,* New York: Norton

Piaget, J. (1954), Les Relations entre l'intelligence et L'Affectivité dans le Developpement de l'Enfant, *Bulletin de Psychologie,* **7,** 143–50

Platt, H. *et al.* (1967), *Automization in Vocational Training of the Mentally Retarded,* Devon, Pennsylvania: The Devereux Foundation

Plowden, Lady Bridget (Chairman) (1967), *Children and their Primary Schools: A Report of the Central Advisory Council for Education,* London: H.M.S.O.

Popham, W. J. and Husek, T. R. (1969), Implications of criterion-reinforced measurement, *Journal of Educational Measurement,* **6,** 1, 1–9

Prechtl, H. F. R. (1971), Motor behaviour in relation to brain structure, in Stoeling, B. G. A. and Van der Werff Ten Bosch (Eds.) *Normal and Abnormal Development of the Brain and Behaviour,* Leiden: University Press

Premack, D. (1965), Reinforcement Theory in Levine, D. (Ed.) *Nebraska Symposium on motivation,* Lincoln: University of Nebraska Press

Pringle, K. L. M. (1965), *Deprivation and Education,* London: Longmans, Green

Pringle, M. L. K., Butler, N. and Davie, R. (1966), *11,000 Seven-year-olds,* London: Longmans, Green

Project HUMID (1966), Teaching Beginning Reading to Hearing Impaired Children, using a Visual Method and Teaching Machines, U.S. Dept. of Health, Education and Welfare,

Project No. 1204

Quay, H. C. (1973), Special Education: assumptions, techniques and evaluative criteria, *Exceptional Children*, **40**(3), 165–70

Rabinovitch, R. D., Drewe, A. L., De Jong, R. N., Ingram, W. and Withey, L. (1954), A research approach to reading retardation, *Research Publications of the Association for Research into Nervous and Mental Disease*, **34**, 363–96

Rachman, S. (1971), *The Effects of Psychotherapy*, Oxford: Pergamon

Raine, D. N. (1972), Management of inherited metabolic disease, *British Medical Journal*, **2**, 329–36

Raine, D. N. (1973), Early detection by biochemical screening, in Griffiths, M. I. (Ed.) *The Young Retarded Child. Medical Aspects of Care*, Edinburgh and London: Churchill Livingstone

Rapin, I. and Bergman, M. (1969), Auditory evoked responses in uncertain diagnosis, *Archives of Otolaryngology*, **90**, 71–8

Ravenette, A. T. (1961), Vocabulary level and reading attainment: an empirical approach to the assessment of reading retardation, *British Journal of Educational Psychology*, **31**, 96–103

Rees, H. M. N. (1973), Special handicaps. Disorders of Communication, in Griffiths, M. I. (Ed.) *The Young Retarded Child. Medical Aspects of Care*, Edinburgh and London: Churchill Livingstone

Reid, J. F. (1966), Learning to think about reading, *Educational Research*, **9**, 1, 56–62

Reynell, J. K. (1969), *Test Manual, Reynell, Developmental Language Scales*, Experimental Edition, London: National Foundation for Educational Research

Rigley, L. (1968), The relevance of the Isle of Wight Study, in *Research relevant to the education of children with learning handicaps*, London: The College of Special Education

Risley, T. (1966), The effects and side effects of punishing the autistic behaviours of a deviant child, *Journal of Applied Behavioural Analysis*, **1**, 21–34

Risley, T. and Wolf, M. M. (1967), Establishing functional speech in echolalic children, *Behaviour Research and Therapy*, **5**, 73–88

Robbins, M. P. (1966), The Delacato interpretation of neurological organisation, *Reading Research Quarterly*, **1**, 57–78

Roberts, J. and Baird, J. T. (1972), Behaviour patterns of children in school, *Vital and Health Statistics*, Series 11, No. 113

Robins, L. N. (1966), *Deviant children grown up*, Baltimore: Williams and Wilkins

Robins, L. N. (1970), Follow-up studies investigating childhood disorders, in Hare, E. G. and Wing, J. K. (Eds.) *Psychiatric Epidemiology*, Oxford University Press

Robinson, H. B. and Robinson, N. (1970), Mental Retardation, in Mussen, P. H. (Ed.) *Carmichael's Manual of Child Psychology* (3rd edition), New York: John Wiley

Rogers, M. G. H. (1971), The early recognition of handicapping disorders in childhood, *Developmental Medicine and Child Neurology*, **13**, 88–101

Rosen, M. (1972), Psychosexual Adjustment of the Mentally Handicapped, Paper presented to the *American Association of Mental Deficiency*, Region IX

Rosenthal, R. and Jacobsen, L. (1968), *Pygmalion in the Classroom*, New York: Holt, Rinehart and Winston

Ross, S. L. Jr., De Young, H. C. and Cohen, J. S. (1971), Confrontation: Special Education placement and the law, *Exceptional Children*, **38**, 5–12

Rossmiller, R. A., Hale, J. A. and Frohreich, L. E. (1970), *Educational Programs for Exceptional Children: Resource Configurations and Costs*, National Educational Finance Project Special Study No. 2, Madison, Wisconsin: Department of Educational Administration, University of Wisconsin

Rutter, M. (1965), Classification and categorization in child psychiatry, *Journal of Child Psychology and Psychiatry*, **6**, 71–83

Rutter, M. (1969), The concept of 'dyslexia', in Wolff, P. and MacKeith, R. C. (Eds.) *Plan-*

ning for Better Learning Clinics in Developmental Medicine No. 33, London: Spastics International Medical Publications and Heinemann

Rutter, M. (1970), Psychological development: predictions from infancy, *Journal of Child Psychology and Psychiatry,* **2,** 49

Rutter, M. (Ed.) (1971), *Infantile Autism: Concepts, Characteristics and Treatment,* London: Churchill Livingstone

Rutter, M., Graham, P. and Yule, M. (1970), *A neuropsychiatric study in childhood,* London: Heinemann

Rutter, M., Lebovici, S., Eisenberg, L., Sneznevskij, A. V., Sadoun, R., Brooke, E. and Lin, T-Y. (1969), A tri-axial classification of mental disorders in childhood: an international study, *Journal of Child Psychology and Psychiatry,* **10,** 41–62

Rutter, M. and Martin, J. A. M. (1972), *The Child with Delayed Speech,* London: Heinemann

Rutter, M. and Sussen Wein, F. (1971), A developmental and behavioural approach to the treatment of preschool autistic children. *Journal of Autism and Childhood Schizophrenia,* **1,** 376–97

Rutter, M., Tizard, J. and Whitmore, K. (Eds.) (1970), *Education, Health and Behaviour,* London: Longmans, Green

Rutter, M. and Yule, W. (1973), Specific reading retardation, in Mann, L. and Sabatino, D. (Eds.), *First Review of Special Education,* Philadelphia: J.S.E. with Buttonwood Farms

Saenger, G. (1957), *The Adjustment of Severely Retarded Adults in the Community,* New York: State Health Resources Board

Sailor, W. (1971), Reinforcement and generalization of productive plural allomorphs in two retarded children, *Journal of Applied Behavioural Analysis,* **4,** 4, 305–10

Salzinger, K., Feldman, R., and Portnoy, S. (1970), Training parents of brain injured children in the use of operant conditioning procedures, *Behaviour Therapy,* **1,** 4–32

Schonell, F. J. (1942), *Backwardness in the Basic Subjects,* Edinburgh: Oliver and Boyd

Schonell, F. J. (1945), *The Psychology and Teaching of Reading,* Edinburgh: Oliver and Boyd

Schools Council (1968), *Curriculum Innovation in Practice,* Evans, *Science 5/13,* Macdonald

Schools Council (1970), *Cross'd with Adversity,* Working paper 27, London: Evans/Methuen Educational

Schools Council (1972), *A Study of Nursery Education,* London: Evans/Methuen Educational

Schubert, J. (1967), Effect of training on the performance of the WISC Block Design Subtest, *British Journal of Social and Clinical Psychology,* **7,** 144–9

Scottish Council for Research in Education (1949), *The Trend of Scottish Intelligence,* University of London Press

Scottish Education Department (1964), *Ascertainment of Maladjusted Children,* Report of Working Party, Edinburgh: H.M.S.O.

Scrivens, M. (1973), The philosophy of behaviour modification, in Thoreson, C. E. (Ed.), *Behaviour Modification in Education,* Seventy-second yearbook of National Society for the Study of Education, University of Chicago Press

Shearer, E. (1967), The long-term effects of remedial education, *Educational Research,* **9,** 219–22

Shepherd, M., Oppenheim, B. and Mitchell, S. (1971), *Childhood Behaviour and Mental Health,* University of London Press

Sheridan, M. D. (1960), *The Developmental Progress of Infants and Young Children,* Ministry of Health Report No. 102, London: H.M.S.O.

Sheridan, M. D. (1969), Definitions relating to developmental paediatrics, *Health Trends,* **1,** 4

Siegal, S. S. (1967), *No Child is Ineducable—Special Education Provision and Trends,* Oxford: Pergamon Press

Skinner, B. F. (1957), *Verbal Behaviour*, New York: Appleton-Century-Crofts

Skinner, B. F. (1961), *Cumulative Record: A Selection of Papers*, (Third Edition), New York: Appleton-Century-Crofts

Skinner, B. F. (1968), *The Technology of Teaching*, New York: Appleton-Century-Crofts

Skinner, B. F. (1971), *Beyond Freedom and Dignity*, New York: Alfred A. Knopf

Slade, P. (1954), *Child Drama*, University of London Press

Sloan, H. W., Johnston, M. K. and Harris, F. R. (1968), Remedial procedures for teaching verbal behaviour to speech deficient or defective young children, in Sloan, H. W. and Macaulay, R. (Eds.), *Operant Procedures in Speech and Language Training*, Boston: Houghton Mifflin

Sluckin, W. (1964), *Imprinting and Learning*, London: Methuen

Solomon, R. W. and Wahler, R. G. (1973), Peer reinforcement control of classroom problem behaviour, *Journal of Applied Behavioural Analysis*, **6**, 49–56

Southgate, V. (1972), The importance of structure in beginning reading, in Morris, J. *The First R*, Ward Lock

Spence, J. C., Walton, W. S., Miller, F. J. W. and Court, S. D. M. (1954), *A Thousand Families in Newcastle-upon-Tyne*, Oxford University Press

Spodek, B. (1973), *Early Childhood Education*, Englewood Cliffs, New Jersey: Prentice-Hall

Staats, A. W. (1968), *Learning, Language and Cognition*, New York: Holt, Rinehart and Winston

Staats, A. W. (1970), *Learning, Language and Cognition*, New York: Holt, Rinehart and Winston

Staats, A. W., Brewer, B. A. and Gross, M. C. (1970), Learning and cognitive development: Representative samples, cumulative-hierarchical learning and experimental longitudinal methods, *Monographs of the Society for Research in Child Development*, **35**, (8)

Start, K. B. and Wells, B. K. (1972), *The Trend of Reading Standards*, Slough, Bucks.: N.F.E.R.

Stein, Z. and Susser, M. (1960), Families of dull children, *Journal of Mental Science*, **106**, 1296–319

Stephen, E. and Robertson, J. (1965), Normal Child Development and Handicapped Children, in Howells, J. G. (Ed.), *Modern Perspectives in Child Psychiatry*, Edinburgh: Oliver and Boyd

Stolz, S. B. and Wolf, M. M. (1969), Visually discriminated behaviour in a 'blind' adolescent retardate, *Journal of Applied Behavioural Analysis*, **2**, 1, 65–77

Strauss, A. A. and Kephart, N. C. (1955), *Psychopathology and Education of the Brain Injured Child*, Vol. 2, Grune and Stratton

Strauss, A. A. and Lehtinen, L. E. (1947), *Psychopathology and Education of the Brain Injured Child*, Vol. 1, Grune and Stratton

Surratt, P. R., Ulrich, R. E. and Hawkins, R. P. (1969), An elementary student as a behavioural engineer, *Journal of Applied Behavioural Analysis*, **2**, 85–92

Swisher, L. P. and Pinsker, E. J. (1971), The language characteristics of hyperverbal, hydrocephalic children, *Developmental Medicine and Child Neurology*, **13**, 746–55

Taber, J., Glaser, R. and Schafer, H. H. (1965), *Learning and Programmed Instruction*, Reading, Mass.: Addison-Wesley

Tate, B. G. and Barroff, G. S. (1966), Aversive control of self-injurious behaviour in a psychotic boy, *Behaviour Research and Therapy*, **4**, 281–7

Taylor, I. G. (1964), *Neurological Mechanisms of Hearing and Speech in Children*, Manchester: University Press

Tharpe, R. and Wetzel, R. (1969), *Behaviour Modification in the Natural Environment*, New York: Academic Press

Thorndike, R. L. (1963), *The Concept of Over- and Under-Achievement*, New York Bureau of Publications, Teachers College, Columbia University

Thorndike, R. L. (1968), Review of Rosenthal, R. and Jacobsen, L., Pygmalion in the Classroom, *American Educational Research Journal*, **5**, 708–11

Tizard, J. (1964), *Community Services for the Mentally Handicapped*, Oxford University Press

Tizard, J. (1966a), Epidemiology of mental retardation: a discussion of a paper by E. M. Gruenberg, *International Journal of Psychiatry*, **2**, 131–4

Tizard, J. (1966b), Mental subnormality and child psychiatry, *Journal of Child Psychology and Psychiatry*, **7**, 1–15

Tolley, J. N. (1967), The social education and work placement of educationally subnormal school leavers, in Brown, R. I. (Ed.) *The Assessment and Education of Slow Learning Children*, University of London Press

Tuckey, L., Parfitt, J. and Tuckey, S. (1973), *Handicapped School Leavers*, Slough: N.F.E.R.

Turner, R. K., Young, G. C. and Rachman, S. (1970), Treatment of nocturnal enuresis, *Behaviour Research and Therapy*, **8**, 367–82

Tyerman, M. J. (1968), *Truancy*, University of London Press

Umans, S. (1963), *New Trends in Reading Insttruction*, New York: Columbia University

Underwood, B. J. (1964), Laboratory studies of verbal learning, in *Theories of Learning and Instruction*, Chicago: National Society for the Study of Education

Uzgiris, I. and Hunt, J. (1966), An instrument for assessment infant psychological development. Paper presented at the International Congress of Psychology, Moscow

Vaughn, R. W. (1973), Community, courts and conditions of special education today: Why? *Mental Retardation*, **11**, 43–6

Vernon, M. D. (1957), *Backwardness in Reading: A Study of its Nature and Origin*, Cambridge University Press

Wallin, J. E. (1955), *Education of Mentally Handicapped Children*, New York: Harper and Row

Ward, J. (1970), On the concept of criterion referenced, *British Journal of Education Psychology*, **40**, 314–23

Ward, J. (1971), Modification of children's deviant classroom behaviour, *British Journal of Educational Psychology*, **41**, 304–13

Wasik, B. H. (1970), The application of Premack's generalization on reinforcement to the management of classroom behaviour, *Journal of Experimental Child Psychology*, **10**, 33–43

Watson, L. S. (1968), Applications of behaviour shaping devices to training severely and profoundly retarded children in an institutional setting, *Mental Retardation Abstracts*, **4**, 1–18

Watson, L. S. (1973), *Child Behaviour Modification. A Manual for Teachers, Nurses and Parents*, New York: Pergamon

Wedell, K. (1967), Some implications of perceptual motor impairment in children, *Remedial Education*, **2**, 2

Wedell, K. (1973), *Learning and Perceptuo-Motor Disabilities in Children*, Wiley

Whelan, E. (1973), Developing work skills: a systematic approach, in Mittler, P. (Ed.), *Assessment for Learning in the Mentally Handicapped*, Institute for Research into Mental Retardation Symposia No. 5, Edinburgh and London: Churchill and Livingstone

White, Burton L. (1969), Fundamental Early Environmental Influences on the Development of Competence, Paper presented at Third Western Symposium on Learning, Western State College, Bellingham, Washington, October

White, Burton L. (1971), An Analysis of Excellent Early Educational Practices: Preliminary Report, *Interchange*, **2**, 2, 71–89

Whitlock, C. and Bushell, D. (1967), Some effects of 'Back Up' reinforcers on reading behaviour, *Journal of Experimental Child Psychology*, **5**, 50–7

Whitman, T. I., Zakaras, M. and Chardos, S. (1971), Effects of reinforcement and guidance procedures on instruction following behaviour of severely retarded children, *Journal of Applied Behavioural Analysis*, **4**, 4, 283–90

Williams, P. (1973), Social Skills, in Mittler, P. (Ed.), *Assessment for Learning in the Mentally Handicapped*, Institute for Research into Mental Retardation Symposia No. 5, Edinburgh and London: Churchill Livingstone

Winick, M. (1969), Malnutrition and brain development, *Journal of Pediatrics*, **74**, 667–79

Winick, M. (1970), Biological correlations, *American Journal of Disease of Children*, **120**, 416

Winnicott, D. W. (1971), *Playing and Reality*, London: Tavistock Publications

Winsberg, B. G. (1969), Programmed learning, teaching machines and dyslexia, *American Journal of Orthopsychiatry*, **39**, 418–27

Wolf, M. M., Giles, D. K. and Hall, R. V. (1968), Experiments with token reinforcement in a remedial classroom, *Behaviour Research and Therapy*, **6**, 51–64

Wolf, M. M., Phillips, E. L. and Fixsen, D. L. (1973), The teaching family: a new model for the treatment of deviant child behaviour in the community, in Bijou, S. W. and Ribes-Inesta, E. (Eds.), *Behaviour Modification: Issues and Extensions*, London: Academic Press

Wolpe, J. (1969), The Practice of Behaviour Therapy, New York: Pergamon Press

Wood, B. S. B. (1970), *A Paediatric Vade-mecum*, 7th edition, London: Lloyd-Luke

Woodward, M. (1962), The application of Piaget's theory to the training of the subnormal, *Journal of Mental Subnormality*, **8**, 17–25

Woodward, M. (1963), The application of Piaget's theories to research in mental deficiency, in Ellis, N. R. (Ed.), *Handbook of Mental Deficiency*, New York: McGraw-Hill

Wyatt, F. L. (1965), *A Study of the Relation Between Certain Aspects of Developmental Experience and the Psychometric Test Performance of Mentally Subnormal People*, Unpublished M.Lit. Thesis, University of Bristol

Yeomans, E. (1969), *Education for Initiative and Responsibility*, National Association of Independent Schools

Younghusband, E. *et al.* (1970), *Living with Handicap*, London: National Children's Bureau

Yule, W. (1967), Predicting reading ages on Neale's Analysis of Reading Ability, *British Journal of Educational Psychology*, **37**, 252–5

Yule, W. (1973), Comment on Bricker, W. A. and Bricker, D. D. behaviour modification programmes, in Mittler, P. (Ed.), *Assessment for Learning in the Mentally Handicapped*, Institute for Research into Mental Retardation Symposia No. 5, Edinburgh and London: Churchill Livingstone

Yule, W. (1973a), Differential prognosis of reading backwardness and specific reading retardation, *British Journal of Educational Psychology*, **43**, 244–8

Yule, W. (1973b), Education and enigma, (Educational aspects of Epilepsy), *Special Education*, **62**, 16–18

Zangwill, O. (1960), *Cerebral Dominance and its Relation to Psychological Function*, Henderson Trust

Zeaman, D. and House, B. J. (1963), The role of attention in retardate discrimination learning, in Ellis, N. R. (Ed.), *Handbook of Mental Deficiency*, New York: McGraw-Hill

Zifferblatt, S. M. (1973), Behaviour systems, in Thoreson, C. E. (Ed.), *Behaviour Modification in Education*, Seventy-Second Yearbook of National Council for Study of Education, University of Chicago Press

Zimmerman, E. H., Zimmerman, J. and Russell, C. D. (1969), Differential effects of token reinforcement on instruction following behaviour in retarded students instructed as a group, *Journal of Applied Behavioural Analysis*, **2**, 101–12

Subject Index